Athens

and the Classical Sites

Sevan Nisanyan

Mitchell Beazley

THE AMERICAN EXPRESS ® TRAVEL GUIDES

Published by Mitchell Beazley, an imprint of Reed Consumer Books Ltd, Michelin House, 81 Fulham Road, London SW3 6RB and Auckland, Melbourne, Singapore and Toronto

Edited, designed and produced by Castle House Press, Llantrisant, Mid Glamorgan CF7 8EU, Wales

First published 1992 as *The American Express Pocket Guide to Athens and the Classical Sites*. This edition, revised, updated and expanded, published 1994.

A cataloguing-in-publication record for this book is available from the British Library.

ISBN 1 85732 308 4

The editors thank Neil Hanson, Alex Taylor and Steve Ramsay of Lovell Johns, David Haslam, Anna Holmes and Sylvia Hughes-Williams for their help and co-operation during the preparation of this edition. Special thanks are due to Mr. A. Vafiade, Director, and staff of the Greek National Tourist Organization, London, to Olympic Airways, London, and to the National Archeological Museum, Athens.

FOR THE SERIES:
Series Editor:
David Townsend Jones
Map Editor: David Haslam
Indexer: Hilary Bird
Gazetteer: Anna Holmes
Cover design:
Roger Walton Studio

FOR THIS EDITION:
Edited on desktop by:
Sharon Charity
Art editor:
Eileen Townsend Jones
Illustrators: Jeremy Ford (David Lewis Artists), Illustrated Arts, Sylvia Hughes-Williams, Rodney Paull.
Cover photo: Tony Stone Worldwide/George Grigoriou

FOR MITCHELL BEAZLEY:
Art Director: Andrew Sutterby
Production: Katy Sawyer
Publisher: Sarah Bennison

PRODUCTION CREDITS:
Maps by Lovell Johns, Oxford, England
Typeset in Garamond and News Gothic
Desktop layout in Corel Ventura Publisher
Reproduction by M & E Reproductions, Great Baddow, Essex, England
Linotronic output by Tradespools Limited, Frome, England
Printed and bound in Great Britain by Clays Ltd, St Ives plc

Contents

Culture, history and background

Athens

Where to stay

Eating and drinking

Nightlife and entertainment

Shopping

Recreation

The outskirts of Athens

The Classical sites

Practical information

Maps

How to use this book

Few guidelines are needed to understand how this book works:

- For the general organization of the book, see CONTENTS on the pages preceding this one.
- Wherever appropriate, chapters and sections are arranged alphabetically, with headings appearing in **CAPITALS.**
- Often these headings are followed by location and practical information printed in *italics.*
- As you turn the pages, you will find subject headers, similar to those used in telephone directories, printed in CAPITALS in the top corner of each page.
- If you still cannot find what you need, check in the comprehensive and exhaustively cross-referenced INDEX at the back of the book.
- Following the index, a LIST OF STREET NAMES provides map references for all streets, squares etc. mentioned in the book that fall within the area covered by the main Athens maps (color maps **1a**, **1** and **2** at the back of the book).

CROSS-REFERENCES
These are printed in SMALL CAPITALS, referring you to other sections or alphabetical entries in the book. Care has been taken to ensure that such cross-references are self-explanatory. Often, page references are also given, although their excessive use would be intrusive and ugly.

FLOORS
We use the European convention in this book: "ground floor" means the floor at ground level (called by Americans the "first floor").

AUTHOR'S ACKNOWLEDGMENTS
Sevan Nisanyan would like to express his indebtedness to George Kalogeropoulos, Alkis Kourkoulas and Melina Zirini for their invaluable advice and criticism, and to Mr. Euripides Jordanides of American Express, Athens, for his kind support, which has made the research for this book very much less toilsome than it would otherwise have been.

Key to symbols

☎	Telephone		➤	Restaurant
Fx	Facsimile (fax)		▦	Air conditioning
★	Recommended sight		♿	Facilities for disabled
☆	Worth a visit			people
i	Tourist information		AE	American Express
➤	Parking		⊙	MasterCard/Eurocard
⬛	Classical site		VISA	Visa
⛪	Byzantine church/monastery		▢	TV in each room
⛨	Fortress/castle		✿	Garden
⬛	Traditional architecture		⛱	Beach
⊡	Free entrance		∿	Swimming pool
⬛	Entrance fee payable		⚲	Tennis
⬳	Good view		♪	Live music/dancing
⬱	Hotel		▲	Camping

PRICE CATEGORIES

▭	Cheap	▥	Expensive
▥	Inexpensive	▨	Very expensive
▨	Moderately priced		

Our price categories for hotels and restaurants are explained in the WHERE TO STAY and EATING AND DRINKING chapters.

About the author

Sevan Nisanyan was born in Istanbul and educated at Yale (philosophy) and Columbia (politics). His exploits have included stints as the boss of a large computer firm, adventurer in the Andes and the Caucasus, political prisoner, nightclub manager and gentleman farmer. His previous publications have included *Insight Guide Istanbul* and, in this series, *American Express Vienna & Budapest* and *American Express Prague*. He currently lives in Sirince, an ancient village in the Aegean hills of Turkey.

A message from the editors

Months of concentrated work were dedicated to making this edition accurate and up to date when it went to press. But time and change are forever the enemies, and between editions we are very much assisted when you, the readers, write to tell us about any changes you discover.

Please keep on writing — but please also be aware that we have no control over restaurants, or whatever, that take it into their heads, after we publish, to move, or change their telephone number, or, even worse, close down. Our authors and editors aim to exclude trendy ephemera and to recommend places that give every indication of being stable and durable. Their judgment is rarely wrong. Changes in telephone numbers are something else. We apologize for the world's telephone authorities, who seem to change their numbers like you and I change shirts.

My serious point is that we are striving to change the series to the very distinctive tastes and requirements of our discerning international readership, which is why your feedback is so valuable. I particularly want to thank all of you who wrote while we were preparing this edition. Time prevents our responding to most such letters, but they are all welcomed and frequently contribute to the process of preparing the next edition.

Please write to me at **Mitchell Beazley**, an imprint of Reed Illustrated Books, Michelin House, 81 Fulham Road, London SW3 6RB; or, in the US, c/o American Express Travel Guides, **Prentice Hall Travel**, 15 Columbus Circle, New York, NY 10023.

David Townsend Jones, Series Editor, American Express Travel Guides

Athens

and the Classical Sites

Cradle of civilization

It is the lure of history that brings many travelers to the Greek capital. It was in Athens, the city of Themistocles, Pericles, Herodotus, Phidias, Socrates, Sophocles, Plato, Aristotle and Demosthenes, that ancient Greek civilization reached its maturity. It was here that it laid down the brilliant milestones that were to be the basis of Western civilization.

Athenian democracy was the first great experiment of free citizens coming together to debate, organize and defend a free society. Athenian philosophy was man's great attempt to face the universe with an open and curious mind, free from the prejudices of faith and the constraints of tradition. Athenian theater and Athenian sculpture were two splendid endeavors to express the timeless, the immortal and the divine. Athenian architecture was a never-equaled exercise in the discovery of beauty in pure forms and natural proportions.

Other visitors come for the magic of Greece itself, to which Athens constitutes the near-obligatory gateway. Greece is a land of uncompromising sunshine and all-pervading sea; of villages and towns that bask in the easy security of a lifestyle perfected over the ages; of people who seem to have an instinctive grasp of what is, and what is not, worth worrying about in life.

An astonishing geography dissects Greece into a thousand little worlds that are at once intimate, unique and splendid. Its culture blends the civility of Europe with the spontaneous charm of the poorer lands. For four out of five visitors, Athens forms the first and last stop on a journey in this most fascinating of countries.

THE MODERN METROPOLIS

The city itself may disappoint those who come to it with inflated expectations. Modern Athens is a young city: the somewhat smug capital of a small Balkan republic, in which the yellowed skeletons of old monuments stand out, like shipwrecks from a dead and forgotten past, in an expanse of modern apartment blocks. Athens can claim to have been the birthplace of Western civilization, but its history is blank for the millennium-and-a-half before its rebirth, as the capital of modern Greece, in 1834, and has been somewhat provincial ever since.

As a result, the city is a far cry from the decadent complexity of Rome or Istanbul, the other great metropolises of the old Mediterranean world. Athens lacks those barnacles of urban growth that make the great historic cities of the world so fascinating to explore and so difficult to exhaust.

It has no intractable slums and few impenetrable pockets of luxury; no hidden neighborhoods that resist the city like stubborn organisms; no obscure alleys burying unknown monuments; no cultural minorities of any size; no mafias worthy of the name.

The Parthenon is magnificent, but it stands alone, with almost no other monument to compare to it in size or beauty. Athens has a wealth of archeological treasures of Classical antiquity, but the city's collections of more recent art would make a small Italian country town laugh. The music is lively: but, at least until the opening of the new Megarón Mousikís

11

Athenon (Concert Hall) in 1991, it scarcely ventured beyond the *bouzouki* and the drunken *zeibékiko* of noisy taverns.

Nor is Athens a particularly beautiful city. There is no river or seacoast to lend its skyline breadth and coherence. The avenues are narrow and clogged, the public architecture mostly undistinguished. On clear days there is wonder in the sight of the Acropolis against the violet evening sky, or the bold thrust of the Lykavitos and the Imitos in the sharp-edged Mediterranean sun. But the wonder is too often hidden from view by the nefarious *nefós* — the pollution-induced smog that enwraps the city in winter — or the numbing summer haze.

Yet millions flock to Athens each year from around the world, and a great majority of them — like this author — learn to love this mildly disappointing, slightly provincial city. This book is intended to help the first-time visitor to Athens, as well as the aficionado, along with that learning process.

THE CLASSICAL SITES

In addition to Athens and its immediate vicinity, this book covers the great sites of Classical archeology (Delphi, Olympia, Epidaurus, Corinth) and many lesser localities situated within a 200-kilometer (125-mile) radius of Athens. The area covered corresponds to the southern part of mainland Greece, including all of the Peloponnese as well as Attica, Boeotia and Phocis. We also cover the Greek islands that lie within little more than an hour by sea from Athens.

Future ages will wonder at us,
as the present age wonders at us now.
(Pericles)

A note on Greek spelling

The transliteration of **modern Greek** defies systematization: despite repeated efforts and countless amendments by the Greek authorities, no uniform rule has taken root. So, public signs within a few feet of each other can proclaim Syntagma, Sintagma or Sindagma as the central square of Athens. Nauplia, Nauplion, Navplion, Nafplion and Nafplio all refer to one place.

Most of the confusion arises from the romanization of the following letters or letter combinations (for a fuller table, and a brief introduction to the language, see GREEK IN A NUTSHELL, pages 189–95).

Greek letter	name	Romanization
H	(eta)	*i* or *e*
K	(kappa)	*k* or *c*
Ψ	(ipsilon)	*y* or *i*
Φ	(phi)	*f* or *ph*
Ξ	(chi)	*h* or *ch*
AI	(alpha-iota)	*e* or *ai*
neuter ending		*-o* or *-on*

We have usually opted for the first of each pair of alternatives above, except where we feel a word is too entrenched in another spelling to try to make it fit a mold — thus Lykavitos (not Lycavitos or Likavitos), but Acropolis (not Akropolis).

In the case of sites and personal names of Antiquity we have used the more familiar **Classical Greek** form, followed, where appropriate, by the modern Greek form in parentheses — thus Eleusis (Elefsína), Theseum (Thísion).

The transliteration of Classical Greek is problematic in its turn: traditional English usage calls for Latinized forms (Delphi, Parnassus, Mycenae), and that is the rule we have largely followed here, although a purist might well insist on strict transliteration (Delphoi, Parnassos, Mykenai).

To complicate things further, official Greek usage until 1976 favored the *katharevousa,* a classicizing form of speech that differs from common (demotic) Greek especially in word endings (Athíne, Piréefs and Hálkis rather than Athína, Piréas and Hálkida). Pre- and post-1976 forms still coexist happily on road signs and maps, but *katharevousa* makes no appearance in this guide.

Culture, history and background

Landmarks in Greek history

EARLIEST TIMES

5000–3000BC: Neolithic settlements on the mainland, especially in Thessaly. **3200–2000BC**: Cycladic culture flourishes in the Aegean islands. "Pelasgian" fortified towns built on the mainland. **2200–1800?BC**: Greek language is introduced by invading Indo-European tribes from the N. **2000–1375BC**: Minoan "Palace" civilization in Crete (Middle and Late Minoan period); high point between **1700BC** and **1450BC**.

1600–1200BC: High point of Mycenaean civilization. Royal palaces in Mycenae, Tiryns, Pylos. **c.1220BC**: The Trojan War: coalition of Mycenaean princes attacks Troy in Asia Minor.

1200–700BC: Greek Dark Ages. Invading tribes from the N (Dorians) destroy Mycenaean culture. **c.1000BC**: Greeks colonize the west coast of Asia Minor (Ionia).

ARCHAIC AND CLASSICAL ATHENS

Before 1200?BC: The legendary king, Theseus, unites the clans of Attica under Athenian leadership. **680–640BC**: Landowning nobles eliminate kingship; two *archons* (chief magistrates) are elected annually. Earliest written record: Cylon, a winner of the foot-race at Olympia, attempts a coup d'etat.

621BC: Draco reforms Athenian law, establishing a criminal code to discourage private revenge and setting "draconian" penalties. **594–593BC**: Solon appointed *archon*. He reforms social and economic laws, broadens Athenian citizenship, establishes coinage, standardizes weights and measures, and sets up the Council of 400.

560s–527BC: Peisistratus, an enlightened tyrant, seizes power and rules with popular support. He initiates major building projects, codifies Homeric poems and introduces the cult of Dionysus. Athens becomes an important city under Peisistratus. **530s BC**: Temple of Apollo at Delphi built by aristocratic enemies of Peisistratus (the Alcmaeonids).

527–510BC: Dictatorial rule of Hippias and Hipparchus, sons of Peisistratus. **508–500BC**: Reforms of Cleisthenes inaugurate Athenian democracy. City and Attica divided into 10 *demes* (clans), each electing 50 representatives to the Council of 500. Ostracism: any citizen can be exiled for 10 years by popular vote.

490BC: First Persian War. Athenians and Plataeans defeat Persians at Marathon. **480s BC**: Themistocles, the leader of the democratic party, dominates Athens. Policy of naval build-up pursued; port of Piraeus is established and fortified.

480–479BC: Second Persian War. Vast Persian army under Xerxes breaks Greek defenses at Thermopylae, occupies Athens and destroys the Acropolis. The Persian navy is defeated at Salamis, and the Persian army finally defeated at Plataea. The Athenian navy expels the Persians from Asia Minor. **477BC**: Cimon exploits Athenian naval supremacy to create the League of Delos, an alliance of most Aegean city-states. Members pay tribute to a common fund controlled by Athens. Attempts to secede from the League are suppressed forcibly by Athens.

462–429BC: Pericles, leader of the democratic party, dominant in Athens. The city reaches a peak of political power and cultural brilliance. **460–451BC**: First war against Sparta. Sparta resists the expansion of Athenian hegemony over the mainland. **c.450BC**: Start of massive rebuilding program on the Acropolis, lying ruined since the Persian invasion. Construction of the Parthenon. Classic age of Doric temple architecture.

431–404BC: Peloponnesian War between Athens and Sparta. The war ruins Greece and exhausts Athens economically. **429BC**: Death of Pericles in a plague epidemic. **415–413BC**: Sicilian expedition of Alcibiades ends in disaster. **405–404BC**: Athenian navy wiped out by Spartans at Aegospotami. Athens capitulates. The League of Delos dissolved. Regime of terror (30 Tyrants) in Athens under Spartan aegis.

403BC: Moderate democracy restored by Thrasyboulos. **399BC**: Socrates put to death on charges of corrupting youth. **371–362BC**: Thebes, led by Epaminondas, breaks the ascendancy of Sparta after a series of battles (Leuctra, Mantinea). Theban success allows Athens to recoup some of its earlier losses.

368–357BC: Second League of Delos, a narrower and weaker alliance than the first. It collapses when Athenians are lured away by Philip II of Macedon. **359–336BC**: Rise of Philip, a brilliant diplomatist and general, as the dominant force in Greek politics. Demosthenes, in famous speeches (known as Philippics), urges Athenians to lead Greece against Macedonian ascendancy.

338BC: Battle of Chaeronia establishes Philip's mastery over Greece. City-states remain autonomous, but Macedonian military presence leaves little room for independent policy. **334–323BC**: Alexander, son of Philip, conquers Asia Minor, Syria, Egypt, Mesopotamia, Persia and northern India. Rapid Hellenization of the Eastern Mediterranean world.

322BC: Final Athenian revolt against Macedon ends in failure. Demosthenes commits suicide.

HELLENISTIC AND ROMAN GREECE

323–281BC: Alexander's generals fight over the spoils of his empire. Antigonus Gonatas emerges victorious in Macedon and Greece; suppresses revolts by various alliances of Greek cities. **279BC**: Gauls (Celts) invade Greece, but turn back at Delphi.

199BC: Philip V of Macedon defeated by Romans at Cynoscephalae (N of Lamia). Roman consul Flaminius announces the liberation of Greece at the Isthmian Games in 196. Rome becomes the arbiter of Greek affairs.

146BC: Romans destroy Corinth and suppress the Achaean League, an alliance of Peloponnesian states. Greece subjected to the Roman province of Macedonia (afterwards the separate province of Achaea in the s, with Corinth as capital). Athens and other loyal Roman allies remain nominally independent.

88–86BC: Athens sides with Mithridates against Rome; defeated and plundered by Sulla. **60s–31BC**: Greece suffers heavily in the civil wars of republican Rome. Strabo describes it as a ravaged and depopulated land, with many ancient cities reduced to ruins. Athens remains alive and important because of its philosophical schools. Cicero, Caesar, Antonius and Augustus visit it as tourists.

AD54: St Paul preaches in Athens and Corinth. Dionysius the Areopagite becomes the first Athenian convert to Christianity. **66–67**: Nero spends a year traveling in Greece, amassing a vast collection of ancient Greek art. He participates in the Olympic, Pythian and Isthmian Games, winning in 1,808 categories.

117–180: Period of revival under the Antonine dynasty. Hadrian (117–138) promotes ancient Greek culture, rebuilds temples and reactivates ancient games. Herodes Atticus, a wealthy Athenian, endows public buildings throughout Greece in the reign of Antoninus Pius (138–161). Marcus Aurelius (161–180) reorganizes Athenian schools into a university. **c.170**: Pausanias visits Greece and writes the earliest known traveler's guide to its antiquities.

BYZANTINES, FRANKS, VENETIANS

331: Constantine transfers the capital of the Roman Empire to Byzantium, renamed Constantinople. Major works of art carried off to the city. Christianity becomes state religion. Steep decline in all provinces including Greece.

391: Edict of Theodosius: all pagan temples closed down and oracular activities prohibited, and Olympic Games discontinued after 1,000 years.

395: Goths under Alaric invade Greece and sack Eleusis. **529**: Edict of Justinian: the Athenian schools, final bastions of paganism, dismantled. Parthenon becomes a church. Athens sinks thereafter into historic insignificance. **c.580**: Slavs invade Greece and sack Athens.

747: Great plague depopulates Greece. Slavs settle in the Peloponnese. Greek language and Christianity disappear throughout Greece, except in some fortified towns. **c.860**: Byzantine attempts to convert Slavs to Christianity. Earliest monasteries in Greece.

c.1020: Reassertion of Byzantine authority in Greece. **1054**: Final schism between Rome and the Byzantine Orthodox church.

1204: The Fourth Crusade captures Constantinople and expels Byzantine emperors (until 1261). European knights acquire feudal domains in southern Greece. Principality of Achaea in the Peloponnese (Geoffroi de Villehardouin), with 12 subordinate duchies. Duchy of Athens and Thebes (Othon de la Roche, Guy de Brienne). Parthenon becomes a Roman Catholic cathedral.

1311–86: Athens captured by Catalan mercenaries, becoming the property of the kingdom of Aragón. **1386–1456**: Athens acquired by the

Florentine banking family of Acciaiuoli (**1386**), who subsequently come under Venetian protection. Attica resettled by Albanians. **1349–1460**: The Peloponnese recaptured by the Byzantines, who set up a semi-independent government (despotate) based in Mistra.

TURKISH RULE

1456–60: Ottoman Sultan Mehmed II captures Athens and various Italian, Frankish and Greek possessions in southern Greece. Greeks allowed communal autonomy under the rule of the Orthodox church, headed by the Patriarch of Constantinople.

1499, 1540: Last Venetian strongholds on the Greek mainland fall to the Turks. **c.1600**: 25 percent of Greece's population estimated to be Muslim (Turkish or Albanian). In Athens the Acropolis houses Muslim and Jewish quarters, while Greeks live downhill. Parthenon becomes a mosque, with the addition of a minaret.

1687: Venetians under Morosini capture the Peloponnese. Athens is besieged without success; Parthenon is heavily damaged by Venetian shelling. **1715**: Turks reoccupy the Peloponnese. **1764–66**: Society of the Dilettanti undertakes the earliest European archeological expedition to Greece. **1799–1815**: Napoleonic wars awaken British interest in Greece, both as strategic asset and as travel destination. **1801–03**: Lord Elgin purchases the Parthenon friezes, which are later placed in the British Museum.

MODERN GREECE

1821: Germanos, Bishop of Patras, raises the flag of Greek revolt in Kalavryta on March 25. Athens is captured and Turkish inhabitants massacred in **1822**. Philhellenic sentiment in Europe: Lord Byron joins the Greek war of independence.

1825–27: Ottoman counterattack mounted under Ibrahim Pasha, commander of a private Egyptian army. Greek revolt effectively crushed with the capture of Missolonghi and Athens. **1827**: Britain, France and Russia intervene on behalf of the Greeks. Turkish navy destroyed at Navarino.

1830: The London Protocol declares Greece (comprising southern Greece and the Cyclades) a sovereign monarchy. Prince Otto of Bavaria appointed king in **1832**, with Nafplio as his capital. **1834**: Athens, a town of 5,000, becomes the capital of Greece. European architects begin to rebuild the city.

1863: Otto overthrown in a revolt. Prince George of Denmark appointed king after Allied intervention. **1881**: Thessaly granted to Greece by European powers. **1897–1949**: Greece experiences "six major wars, four foreign invasions, two civil wars, all manner of coups d'etat and pronunciamentos, several revolts, three serious revolutions and a succession of economic catastrophes" (Harold Nicolson).

1912–13: Greece obtains Macedonia and Epirus in the Balkan wars. **1915**: *Dichasmos* (discord) between royalists and followers of Venizelos divides Greek politics for a generation. **1919–22**: West coast of Turkey granted to Greece by the victors of World War I. Greek invasion of Asia

Minor results in disastrous defeat by the Turks. The Treaty of Lausanne repatriates nearly all Greek inhabitants of Turkey (1.5 million) to Greece, causing huge social problems.

1924–35: King George II deposed by republicans; returns 11 years later after a monarchist referendum. **1940**: Italy, under Mussolini, invades Greece. One-word reply of General Metaxas to the Italian ultimatum of October 28: *óhi* (no). **1941**: Germany invades Greece after Italian failure. **1944**: Britain, aided by local partisans, forces German army to retreat in October. First civil war in Athens between partisans and British-supported government forces.

1946–49: Truman Doctrine places Greece under US protection. Second civil war, with vicious fighting between communist-led partisans and US-supported government forces. The wounds of the civil war fester until the 1980s. **1951–63**: Conservative governments under A. Papagos and Constantine Karamanlis. **1963–65**: Center-left government of George Papandreou unleashes political chaos.

1967: Military coup of Colonel Papadopoulos. King Constantine II goes into exile. **1973**: Student uprising at the Athens Polytechnic forces Papadopoulos out. New junta under General Gizikis. **1974**: Coup and Turkish intervention in Cyprus. Military regime collapses; Karamanlis returns from exile and is elected prime minister (1974–81). Monarchy abolished by referendum.

1981: Greece admitted to the EC. **1981–89**: Pan-Hellenic Socialist Alliance (PASOK) government under Andreas Papandreou. Economic crisis and allegations of corruption bring PASOK down. **1990**: Constantine Mitsotakis, leader of center-right Nea Demokratia, comes to power after three inconclusive elections. Karamanlis elected President. **1992–3**: Macedonian dispute (see page 30) affects Greece's relations with its EC partners. **1993**: General election narrowly won by PASOK. Return of Papandreou to the Prime Ministry causes further strains in Greece's ties with the West.

The ages of Greek culture

CYCLADIC AND EARLY BRONZE AGES *(3200-2000BC)*

The discoveries of James Theodore Bent in 1883–84 revealed the first traces of this hitherto unsuspected civilization, which flourished on the Aegean islands of Paros, Naxos, Melos, Delos, Amorgos and others. Its most characteristic products were graceful **marble idols**, ranging from tiny to life-sized. The best collections are to be found at the Goulandris Foundation's Cycladic Art Museum and at the National Archeological Museum in Athens, and at the British Museum in London. A pre-Hellenic language, thought to have contributed some of the non-Greek sounds (such as the -nth in Corinth) in Greek place names, was in use during this period.

Cycladic
marble idol

Traces of **walled settlements** dating back to the early Bronze-Age period have been discovered in a number of places on the mainland of Greece (for example, within the Athenian Acropolis). The ancient Greeks knew these early inhabitants under the general name of "Pelasgians." Their masonry, which made much use of heavy, irregular stone blocks, was attributed to the Cyclopes, the one-eyed monsters of legend.

MINOAN *(2000-1375BC)*

The excavations of Sir Arthur Evans (after 1900) brought to light the civilization of the legendary King Minos of Crete. The **frescoes** that were discovered at Knossos and the other Cretan royal palaces revealed an elegant, pleasure-loving and sophisticated society.

More recently, discoveries have showed the presence or influence of Minoan culture at numerous places around the southern Aegean, and particularly on the island of Santorini, at the peak period before 1500BC.

The Minoan civilization employed the "Linear A" script, which has yet to be deciphered, although its language is unknown. The great era of Minoan palace-building lost its momentum after the volcanic eruption of the island of Santorini around 1500BC, and the palaces were subjugated by Mycenaean invaders from the mainland of Greece a century later.

Minoan **fresco**: *Prince of the Lilies*

All important works of Minoan art and architecture are kept in Crete, excepting the Santorini frescoes, which are housed in the National Archeological Museum in Athens.

MYCENAEAN *(1600-1200BC)*

The earliest truly "Greek" civilization has been named after the royal stronghold of Mycenae, where, in 1874–76, the archeologist Heinrich Schliemann discovered its first, and so far most important, material remains. The Greeks of Classical Antiquity knew of this period as the Heroic Age, the vaguely remembered history of which formed the basis of the Homeric legends.

The foundation myths of the various royal dynasties of the Heroic Age suggest a complicated pattern of cultural give-and-take. Thus, a Phoenician (Kadmos) founded Thebes, an Egyptian (Danaos) started the royal dynasty of Argos, some Cretans founded Delphi, and a Lydian (Pelops) fathered most late-Mycenaean rulers of the Peloponnese.

Architecture: The major surviving examples of Mycenaean architecture are the royal palaces of Mycenae, Tiryns and Pylos, of which the first two are heavily fortified. The *megaron,* a royal hall consisting of a rectangular throne room, an open vestibule in front and two columns supporting the porch, formed the basis of Greek temple architecture in subsequent ages.

Art: By far the most important collection of Mycenaean art is at the National Archeological Museum of Athens, and includes golden deathmasks, bronze ornamented weapons, bronze and gold cups and jewelry. Their "barbaric" quality contrasts with the graceful elegance of Minoan art.

Writing: A script known as "Linear B" was adapted from a Cretan original in around 1400BC and used for inventories and official transactions. This has now been fully deciphered as an early form of Greek, thanks to a large collection of tablets discovered at Pylos. Examples can be seen in many museums.

"GEOMETRIC" *(1200-700BC)*

A series of ill-understood events destroyed Mycenaean civilization c.1200BC. The warlike Dorians from the N invaded the Peloponnese, whose earlier inhabitants (called "Achaeans" and "Ionians") either migrated or were enslaved. Knowledge of stone architecture and writing disappeared for more than 500 years. Toward the end of this period, Homer compiled the oral traditions about the Heroic Age into the epics of the *Iliad* and the *Odyssey*.

The only tangible relics of this dark era are **ceramic pots** (illustrated left), generally decorated with simple geometric patterns. Some splendid specimens are at the National Archeological Museum of Athens.

ARCHAIC *(700-480BC)*

Urban culture revived rapidly in the 7thC, at first on the w coast of Asia Minor (Miletus, Ephesus, Samos), then on the mainland itself. Old aristocracies were replaced by the so-called tyrants, popular leaders who came to power by coup d'etat. Greek colonies were planted around the Mediterranean world, notably in Italy and on the Black Sea coast. The **Greek alphabet** was adapted from the Phoenician script. The disciplines of philosophy (Thales, Heraclitus), mathematics (Pythagoras, Euclid), historiography (Hecataeus) and lyric poetry (Sappho) flourished.

Architecture: The earliest Greek temples built of stone came into existence around 550. Temples on the Greek mainland adopted the **Doric Order**, while those in Asia (including the Eastern Aegean islands) developed the **Ionic**. (See explanation of the Classical Orders on page 24.)

Traces of these early structures are prominent beneath or near most temples of later date, but few survived the following century, and with the exception of the Temple of Hera in Olympia and Corinth's largely ruined Temple of Apollo, none survives today.

Sculpture: Sculpture moved quickly from the depiction of gods in human form to depicting men of godly bearing. The most common types of statue are those known as **kouros** (young man) and **kore** (young woman), characterized by a stiff hieratic pose and a strange, distant smile. Some magnificent examples of these are to be found in the archeological museums of Athens, Delphi, Piraeus and Thebes. (See illustration of **Anavysos kouros** on page 71.)

Pottery: Some of the finest art of the Archaic period was executed on clay vases, a field in which Athens emerged at around 550BC as the undisputed leader. In the earlier part of this period, potters employed the **black figure** technique, in which figures were painted onto the clay in black glaze and the detail was added by incision.

By the year 500, Athenian artists had perfected the **red figure** style, in which unpainted figures stood out against a black background and were detailed by brush. Examples of both black- and red-figure ceramics abound

Detail from Athenian **black figure vase**, c.540BC, by Exekias

in the National Archeological Museum of Athens and a number of local museums throughout the country.

CLASSICAL *(480-330BC)*

Broadly used, the term "Classical" can be taken as covering the whole of pagan antiquity, from the early Archaic age to the downfall of Rome more than 1,000 years later. More narrowly, it refers to the 150-year period after the Persian Wars, or even its middle part (450–404) alone, into which all of the greatest achievements of Greek art, architecture and literature were crowded.

Athens was the dominant political power of Greece in the early part of this epoch, followed by Sparta (404–371) and Thebes (371–362). The country collapsed into chaos in the 4thC as a result of protracted wars.

Culture: In 472, the City of Athens voted to stage Aeschylus' tragedy *The Persians* for the annual festival of Dionysus. Just eight years earlier, Athens had narrowly won a bitter defensive war against the Persians in which the playwright himself had been wounded. The tragedy, however, presented the war entirely from the viewpoint of the Persian king, and dwelled in extraordinary human detail upon the fears and agonies of his female relatives. The underlying message may have been one of boasting, but this particular way of expressing triumph is unique in world history. Pericles himself expressed the Athenian ideal in his funeral oration for the victims of the Peloponnesian War:

"We are lovers of the beautiful, yet simple in our tastes, and we cultivate the mind without loss of manliness . . . .

We regard a man who takes no interest in public affairs, not as a harmless, but as a useless character. The great impediment to action is, in our opinion, not discussion, but the want of that knowledge which is gained by discussion preparatory to action . . . .

While our government is a democracy, the claim of excellence is also recognized; and when a citizen is in any way distinguished, he is preferred to the public service. There is no exclusiveness in our public life, and in our private intercourse we are not suspicious of one another, nor angry with our neighbor if he does what he likes . . . .

And we have not forgotten to provide for our spirits many relaxations from toil; we have regular games and sacrifices throughout the year; our homes are beautiful and elegant; and the delight which we daily feel in these things helps to banish gloom."

Architecture: The Greek **temple** reached its zenith during a wave of building activity toward the middle of the 5thC. Many Archaic temples that lay in ruins after the Persian War were rebuilt on a more ambitious scale. The **Temple of Zeus** at Olympia, completed in 456, was the first great work of the period. At the **Parthenon** of Athens, completed in 438, the architects Ictinus and Callicrates achieved a level of refinement rarely equaled since.

The Greek temple was intended only to accommodate the image of the deity, while public worship took place at an altar that was placed outdoors. The emphasis in temple architecture was therefore on the external aspect.

With a few exceptions, such as the Ionic **Erechtheum** of Athens (pictured on page 50), temples on the mainland were built in the Doric Order, ideally suited to a severe and monumental style (see the Classical Orders, page 24). Most major temples consisted of an inner sanctum (*naos* or *cella)* with halls in front and back *(pronaos* and *opisthodomos),* surrounded by a single row of columns *(peristyle)* with six on the short side. Arches being unknown, the roof was held up by wooden beams, which have disappeared in all instances. The reconstruction of the Doric **Temple of Aphaia**, below, is a good illustration of these basic features of temple architecture.

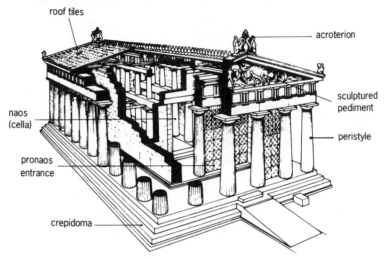

Temple of Aphaia, Aegina: cutaway reconstruction

The **agora**, which was the hub of public life in cities, was adorned with **stoas** (porticoes), colonnaded vestibules intended equally for commerce and for socialization.

The custom of building open-air **theaters** in stone appeared toward the middle of the 4thC. The fully preserved **theater of Epidaurus** dates from this period, as does the stone reconstruction of Athens' **Dionysus Theater**. Theaters were built to accommodate the entire adult male population of cities, and were designed for maximum acoustic effect. They were used for public assemblies and parades as well as dramatic performances.

Sculpture: The expression of human beauty in marble, bronze and ivory reached a level of extraordinary eloquence in the works of Phidias and Polyclitus. The severe nobility of these sculptors of the Periclean age was replaced by the gentler, more individual style of Praxiteles and Scopas in the following century.

With the possible exception of the *Hermes* of Praxiteles (illustrated on page 158), none of the masterpieces of the great sculptors have survived in the original. The excellence of such anonymous works as the Trident-hurling *Poseidon* and the *Anacythera Youth* (both at Athens' Archeological Museum) and the *Delphi Charioteer* (at Delphi) only hint at the quality of the far more famous works that have been lost.

The Classical Orders

Ancient Greek buildings made use of columns and beams. Three column styles evolved, known today as **the Classical Orders**. The earliest, the **Doric Order** (6thC BC), developed on the Greek mainland; the **Ionic Order** (4thC BC) was found in Asia Minor. Doric columns were powerful-looking, usually with 20 sharp-edged flutings. Sculptured metopes (rectangular panels) and triglyphs (projections) on the frieze of the column evolved from timber antecedents. Ionic columns typically had 24 flutes separated by fillets, and volute or "scroll" capitals.

The brief ascendancy of Corinth in the 3rdC BC led to the development of the elaborate **Corinthian Order**, popular in the Hellenistic and Roman periods. Stylized acanthus leaves embellished the capitals, while the entablature was undistinguishable from that of the Ionic Order, almost always with a frieze.

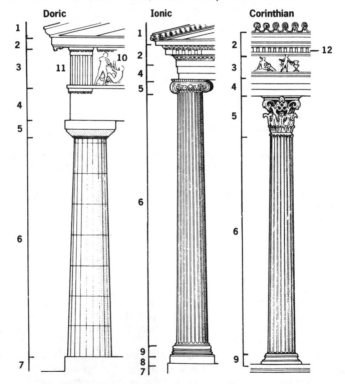

KEY: 1 Pediment **2** Cornice **3** Frieze **4** Architrave (**2, 3** and **4** form entablature) **5** Capital **6** Shaft of column **7** Crepidoma **8** Plinth **9** Base **10** Metope **11** Triglyph **12** Dentils

Surprising for the modern eye, accustomed to the bare marble surfaces of Classical sculpture, was the fact that both free-standing statues and reliefs were originally painted in full color. Some traces of paint are still visible, for example, on temple friezes at the Acropolis Museum.

Painting: Free painting developed into an important branch of art in the 5thC, and the paintings of Polygnotus at the Pinakotheke of the Athens Acropolis, of Paeonius at the "Painted" Stoa of the Athens Agora, and of Polyclitus at the Heraeum of Argos drew admiring visitors. None of these works survives. Pottery painting, on the other hand, no longer attracted great talents as in the Archaic age, and generally declined in quality.

Literature: The traditional "goat songs" *(tragoidia)* of the Dionysian festival were developed into an art form by Aeschylus (524–456) in the 470s. In the austere and aristocratic drama of Sophocles (496–406) and the psychological realism of Euripides (480–406), ancient tragedy reached its high point. Aristophanes (446–388) lampooned contemporary Athenian manners in his comedies.

Philosophy: The Ionian traditions of philosophy were carried to Athens in the mid-5thC by Anaxagoras, who taught both Pericles and Socrates. Socrates (died 399) influenced a whole generation of Athenians by his relentless questioning of fundamental values.

Plato (427–347) and Aristotle (384–322) founded in the next century two rival schools of philosophy that defined the opposing poles of Western thought until the modern age.

HELLENISTIC *(330-30BC)*

The Hellenistic Age, which was a period of great economic and artistic vitality elsewhere in the Eastern Mediterranean, found Greece exhausted by war and emigration. Cities were depopulated, and many ceased to exist. Thebes (336) and Corinth (146) were ruined, the cities of Arcadia and Messenia were deserted, and only two minor towns continued to exist in Boeotia. Works of art left from this era are accordingly few in Greece and of no great significance.

Architecture: The **Corinthian Order** became the most popular form of temple architecture during the Roman era, although surviving examples are rare in Greece.

Similarly, the brilliant reinterpretation of the Ionic Order, introduced by Hermogenes in Asia Minor in the 3rdC, found no echo in Greece.

Sculpture: In the transition from Classical to Hellenistic, Lysippus carried the work of Praxiteles one step further with his precise realism, light touch and technical virtuosity. The compositional mastery of the bronze *Horse with Child Rider* at the Athens Archeological Museum is typical of the period. In the 3rdC, Pergamum in Asia Minor captured the leadership in this field with its entirely new school of sculpture.

Philosophy: Philosophy was one field in which Athens maintained its lead through the Hellenistic era. Two new philosophical schools, Stoicism (founded by Zeno, 336–263) and Epicurianism (founded by Epicurus, 342–271), emerged in Athens. Both turned away from public issues to emphasize the private fulfillment of the individual.

ROMAN *(146BC-AD395)*

The early centuries of Roman rule only perpetuated the barrenness of the Hellenistic period. While the 2ndC AD witnessed an era of widespread revival under the Antonine emperors, Greece never really recovered a position among the richest and most advanced provinces of the Roman empire.

Culture: The Antonine revival was consciously antiquarian in spirit, in the sense of a renewed interest in the past glories of the Classical age. Hadrian rebuilt temples in the style of 400 years earlier. Pausanias, with his enthusiasm for ancient traditions and historic monuments, was a typical author of his age. The philosophical schools of Athens clung to the traditions formulated in the 4thC BC.

Architecture: The major technical advance of the Roman era was the **arch**, which formed a prominent feature in all types of public building. New and characteristic architectural forms included the public bath, the aqueduct, the monumental fountain *(nymphaeum)* and the triumphal arch. Roman-period theaters added elaborate stage-building with arched entryways.

The new types of temple architecture that were emerging in Italy, Syria and Asia Minor found no echo in Greece, where the only significant temple to be erected in the Roman period was that of the Olympian Zeus in Athens.

Sculpture: In the field of realistic portraiture, Roman-age sculptors developed a level of mastery rarely equaled in any other era. High demand for the portraits of emperors, governors and wealthy citizens created a type of commodity art with generally superb standards of workmanship but hardly any outstanding names.

BYZANTINE *(330-1460)*

Under the Byzantine Empire the center of Greek culture shifted definitively to Constantinople (Istanbul), while Greece itself entered an era of unmitigated disaster. What remained of its cultural vitality was sapped when pagan cults and temples were outlawed by Theodosius in 391 and by the closing of the Athenian schools in 529. A succession of barbarian invasions devastated the land. By the 9thC, Slavic tribes predominated and the Greek language and Christian religion disappeared from the countryside.

Monasteries played an important role in recivilizing Greece after the return of Byzantine authority in the 11thC. Democratic in structure and popular in background, they had an immense influence among the common folk, often voicing the people's sentiments as against the court.

Court culture experienced a period of late flourish in the 14th–15thC, when close contacts with the Latin West, especially the Italian city republics (Venice, Genoa), produced a mutual cross-fertilization. In Greece this was reflected most of all in the southern Peloponnese, which was ruled in 1349–1460 by a feudal Byzantine principality (Despotate of Morea) based at Mistra.

Architecture: Early Byzantine churches (4th–6thC) were built in the form known as *basilica,* which consisted of an oblong hall with a semicircular recess (apse) in the E wall and two parallel rows of interior pillars supporting the roof. No church from this period survives in southern Greece except in the form of barely recognizable traces.

In the Middle (9th–12thC) and Late (13th–15thC) Byzantine periods, the **cross-in-square** construction became the standard. Churches consisted of a cross-shaped hall with a dome usually surmounted on a cylindrical drum, preceded by an entrance hall *(narthex)* and occasionally an outer hall *(exonarthex);* the sanctuary *(bema)* was separated from the nave by a solid curtain decorated with icons *(iconostasis)*.

Classic examples in Greece are the monastery churches of Daphni and Osios Loukas. Later churches generally opted for five domes instead of one, and experimented with increasingly complex compositions.

Painting: Church painting followed a rigidly conventional scheme with regard to both subject and disposition within the church. Each saint and each biblical scene had its precisely defined pictorial conventions. The banning of church images in the iconoclastic period (8th–10thC) had the effect of further consolidating Orthodox sentiment about the immutability of the holy pictures. Mosaic was generally abandoned after the 11thC in favor of the cheaper fresco.

An artistic revolution got under way toward the end of the 14thC, which had its main centers at Crete, Constantinople and Mistra. The best Byzantine artists developed a boldness of expression and a wealth of color that was reminiscent of the early masters of the Italian Renaissance. The ultimate outcome of this trend was El Greco, who was born Kyriakos Theotokopoulos in Crete. Excellent examples of late Byzantine painting can be seen at Mistra, as well as at the Byzantine and Benaki Museums of Athens.

"FRANKISH" AND VENETIAN *(1204-1715)*

The Byzantine Empire was temporarily overthrown in 1204 by the armies of the Fourth Crusade. Within a few years Greece was taken over by an assorted pack of European knights: Geoffroi de Villehardouin, a Burgundian nobleman, conquered the Peloponnese; Othon de la Roche, another Burgundian, took Attica and Boeotia, while three Veronese gentlemen shared Euboea.

There was a French barony at Salona, near Delphi, and an Italian marquisate near Thermopylae. The Catalans, the Genoese, and even some Flemings entered the fray later on, and feudal domains changed hands with astonishing celerity and inconsequence.

By the late 14thC the Republic of Venice emerged as the only Western power to own well-entrenched strongholds in mainland Greece. These were lost to the Turks piecemeal between 1456 and 1540, partly recovered in 1687 and lost again in 1715.

Architecture: The "Frankish" legacy in Greece consists of scores of **castles**, particularly common in the Peloponnese. All are in various degrees of ruin, although they command magnificent views. The best preserved are at Mistra and Clairmont (Hlemoutsi, near Kyllini).

Venetian fortifications are usually **citadels**, either enclosing a town or capable of accommodating its inhabitants during a siege. The finest examples are the strongholds of Methoni and Koroni. Nafplio preserves a wide range of Venetian civil architecture.

Venetian **citadel**

More indirectly, the Byzantine "Renaissance" shown in the architecture of **Mistra** displays strong Frankish and Italian influences, both in the feudal foundations on which it rested and the Westernizing forms of art that its court favored.

TURKISH *(1456-1828)*

Toward the end of the Byzantine era, the common people, the church and the provincial nobles of Greece had for a variety of reasons come to prefer "the turban of the Turk to the miter of a cardinal." The court, which alone pursued a pro-Western policy, was repudiated. The Turks allowed the Greeks broad communal autonomy under the Orthodox church. Monasteries kept their domains and privileges.

Peasants were taxed more equitably than under their Frankish or Byzantine feudal masters; the most enterprising of them generally converted to Islam. Any hint of private power or privilege, however, was ruthlessly stamped out by an all-encompassing bureaucratic state. What little remains of the Turkish era reflects this background.

Religious art: After the Italian-influenced vivacity of the 15thC, Greek church art froze into a rigid conservatism. Painting was reduced to a series of ever-cruder reproductions of Byzantine originals; the term **post-Byzantine** is used to describe this trend. Only naive folk painters such as Georgios Markos, who painted churches in Attica in the 18thC, showed any originality, perhaps because of their ignorance of the models.

Architecture: The only noteworthy examples of Greek civil architecture are in the islands, which enjoyed a certain administrative autonomy and became relatively rich through trade. The pirate villages of Mani are another original case of architectural activity that grew beyond the dead hand of the *pax turcica.* Turkish relics consist of purely functional, small-scale public works, such as mosques, public baths, fountains, poorhouses and schools; a great many of these were destroyed during or after the War of Independence.

Turkish fortresses were generally reconstructions or improvements of earlier strongholds. In a few cases such as Karababa (Halkida) and the fortresses of Rio and Antirio, one can observe new forms introduced by the needs of artillery warfare (squat, sloping walls, projecting bastions).

MODERN (1821-)

The War of Independence: From the 1770s, Russia adopted a policy that aimed to weaken the Ottoman Empire and set up an Orthodox power in Constantinople. Meanwhile, leading Greek intellectuals, influenced by the ideals of the French Revolution, contemplated a revival of ancient Greece.

The collapse of Turkish authority in the 18thC left Greece in the hands of Albanian lords and roving bands of brigands called *klephts*. Attempts by the reforming Sultan Mahmud II to reassert Turkish rule precipitated a general rebellion in 1821 in which *klepht* leaders (Kolokotronis, Mavromichalis) and the pirate fleets of various Aegean islands (Hydra, Psara) played a prominent role.

After initial successes the uprising was mired down in internecine fighting. The intervention of Britain and France in 1827, which saved the rebellion, was motivated by considerations of grand strategy as much as philhellenic sentiment. Western powers determined the status of the new country by the London Protocol of 1830, imposed a Bavarian prince as king in 1832, and directed the foreign (and occasionally domestic) affairs of the kingdom through the end of the 19thC.

Culture: The clash between traditional "folk" culture and the Classical ideal imposed by Europeans and Western-educated elites runs through many aspects of modern Greece.

The *katharevousa,* an artificial dialect based on Classical Greek and incomprehensible to the uneducated, was devised shortly before independence to "raise" the cultural level of the Greeks, and stayed in use as the state's official language until 1976. On a similar level, most place names were changed by fiat to conform with Classical precedent, while the popular names died hard among uneducated folk.

A further factor was that a large segment of the population did not speak Greek as its native tongue: speakers of Albanian, Vlach, Turkish and various Slav languages formed perhaps a majority until the turn of this century.

The Neoclassical architecture of Greece was developed by Europeans, and European court architects built nearly every building of note in 19thC Athens. Similarly, the straight-line plan of the capital and scores of other rebuilt cities was the work of Westerners, and contrasted with the maze-like structure of traditional Greek towns.

The choice of Athens as capital was itself a European imposition, while the devoutly Christian Greeks themselves set their sights upon Constantinople, at least until 1922. In this homeland of European civilization, and, since 1981, member of the European Union, the term "Europe" still refers in popular parlance to the lands west of the Adriatic.

An uneasy symbol of the resurgence of Greek culture is the row over the "Elgin marbles," the Parthenon friezes transported for safe keeping in the 19thC and still residing in London's British Museum. To date, the demands of Greece (with one of the world's finest archeological museums to its credit) for the return of its property have fallen on deaf ears.

Literature: Greece has produced several of the most brilliant poets of the 20thC. Two of them, George Seferis (1900–71) and Odysseus

Elytis (1911–) were crowned with the Nobel prize; two others, whom, many would consider superior, Constantine Kavafis (1863–1933) and Yannis Ritsos (1909–90), were not. The internationally well-known novelist Nikos Kazantsakis (1885–1957) seems to suffer from an excess of folksiness and mush.

Politics: Two great crises stand in the background of contemporary Greek politics: the prolonged quarrel *(dichasmos)* between the liberal-republican followers of Prime Minister Eleftherios Venizelos, on the one hand, and conservatives supporting the king, on the other, in 1915–35, and the bloody civil war against communist partisans in 1944–49. Conservatives were victorious in both instances.

In the 1970s, Andreas Papandreou rallied remnants of the old Venizelist guard under the new, "socialist" banner of PASOK. He reconciled many former communists by offering them a belated amnesty and access to jobs in the early years of his government (1981–89). PASOK's attempt to break the stranglehold of the conservatives on Greek politics enjoyed wide early support, but the party fell victim to the dangers of partisanship, nepotism and corruption inherent in that task. Many critics alleged that Greece had fallen behind the rest of the world in the economic and technological evolution of the 1980s.

The conservative government of Prime Minister Mitsotakis (1989–93) also failed to solve the economic problems facing Greece. Octogenarian and politically weak, Papandreou returned to power in 1993 following a narrow election victory.

❖   The ex-Yugoslav republic of Macedonia has recently become an unusually touchy topic for Greek public opinion. Many Greeks regard Macedonia — the name as well as, perhaps, the country — as an inseparable part of the Greek national heritage.

The Greek government, in defiance of the views of its EU partners, refuses to recognize independent Macedonia under this name, preferring to call the country "Skopje" (from the name of its capital city). The 16-pointed *Star of Vergina,* a symbol of Macedonia, has become the subject of an emotionally-charged dispute.

Inhabited largely by Slavic-speakers, the region of Macedonia was divided almost equally between Greece and Serbia after the Balkan War of 1912. The southern half (with capital Thessaloniki) is now fully integrated into the Greek nation. Nevertheless, Greece accuses the north of harboring annexationist designs over the Hellenized south.

Greek mythology

Ancient Greek gods had local origins and were bound up with specific local myths. Some of these traditions can be traced with reasonable certainty to pre-Greek beliefs and rituals; others seem to hint at some half-remembered prehistoric events. Some of the more popular gods combine several distinct strands of legend. Thus Apollo has separate Cretan, Lycian and Phrygian antecedents, among others.

Later attempts to weave such incompatible histories into a coherent biography often result in utter confusion. Thus, Apollo and Artemis are supposed to be twins, yet they have separate birthplaces, and several other places claim the honor of nurturing one or the other when they were small. Hence the sometimes elaborate myths to explain how they got from one place to another.

Each tribe, town and locality had its own particular deity: Athens worshiped Athena, Argos was devoted to Hera, Ephesus was sacred to Artemis . . . . It never occurred to the Greeks to suppose that their own gods were unique or that their neighbors worshiped false notions, so they simply took note of the multiplicity of gods, occasionally importing some alien deity when he or she had proven his/her efficacy in some way.

They also noted the similarities between the personalities of various gods, and assimilated them under a single name. Thus what appears to have been two distinct goddesses worshiped in Samos and Argos were *both* identified as Hera; or the Anatolian Mother Goddess, usually translated as Artemis, occasionally also got mixed up with Demeter or Leto. (St Paul, incidentally, was worshiped as Hermes when he showed up in Lycaonia to preach the gospel.)

At times alien gods were adopted through family ties: Eros, a god of love worshiped only in the Boeotian town of Thespiae, was said to be a son of Aphrodite, the more common goddess of love.

In this way the Greek Pantheon was consolidated into a set of 12 major divinities, who (with the exception of Hades) were said to reside in the nebulous region of Mt. Olympus, presiding over innumerable godlets. There were some 30 mountains that claimed this name in Antiquity, and it seems possible that the word simply meant "mountain" in some pre-Greek language. The Olympian system was shaken in the late Archaic period when the cult of a new god, Dionysus, arriving from Lydia in Asia Minor, spread through Greece like wildfire.

Inclusiveness, however, had its limits. The pre-Olympian generation or generations of gods (Uranos, Gaea, Cronos and the Titans) were said to have been defeated and overthrown by the current gods. These were almost certainly the divinities of the Early Bronze Age or Neolithic peoples of Greece. However, a sanctuary dedicated to Gaea was scrupulously maintained at Delphi long after Apollo had usurped her reign there by murdering her son; and Cronos was still remembered at Olympia, although he had been knocked out in a wrestling match and banished by his son Zeus.

Originally each god was a full-blown personality with a life story, habits, character traits and anecdotes. Earlier yet, at least some of them were probably depicted as animals: Apollo was a dolphin or a wolf, or even a mouse; Artemis was a bear or a stag; Poseidon was a horse.

Later on, when they were definitively humanized, their earlier attributes still clung to them in the form of their "sacred animals." Thus Artemis was always shown with a stag, while her priestesses adopted the name of she-bears; Athena often brandished a snake; and Poseidon rarely went anywhere without his horse. The association of the gods with abstract notions ("god of music," "goddess of love," etc.) appears to have been a late development. The Roman age went further still, reducing them to poetic allegories: Aphrodite now became a mere personification of Love; Apollo was said to be Light itself.

Apollo

The god of light, youth and music was also the god of mice, lizards, wolves and pestilence, and the bringer of sudden death. He was born on the island of Delos, yet his cult was imported to Greece from Minoan Crete. His mother Leto was the goddess of the Lycians in Asia Minor, and he himself acquired his musical education in Phrygia, which was also in Asia Minor. His twin sister Artemis was a predominantly Asiatic divinity.

Apollo was venerated by the Greeks above all as the god of soothsaying, and Delphi, one of his two holiest sanctuaries (the other was Delos), was honored as the home of the most respected oracle of the ancient world. He was also famous for ravishing lone nymphs and beautiful mortals in faraway places. Daphne saved herself from his pursuit by turning into a laurel tree (on a hillside near Athens, or perhaps near Antioch in Syria), so he cherished the laurel bough; his lover Hyacinth he killed in a sporting accident (at Amyclae near Sparta), so the flower bearing the youth's name was sacred to him.

On Mts. Helicon and Parnassus Apollo was seen playing the zither to the singing and dancing of the Muses; and in Phrygia he flayed the Satyr Marsyas alive after beating him in a flute-playing contest.

Artemis

Artemis, the virgin goddess of the wilderness, came into the Greek world from Ephesus in Asia Minor, where in earlier times she had been worshiped as the Phrygian–Lydian Kubaba (Cybele). (The original Cybele was in fact a meteorite that was idolized at Pessinus in Phrygia. She was later carried off to Rome.) The Cretans also had their Lady of the Wild Beasts, who was certainly related to the Artemis worshiped at Brauron, in Attica.

Artemis spent most of her time hunting in the wilderness with her nymphs. She took a ruthless line with any men who dared to approach her and with those of her nymphs who showed a weakness for men. The hunter Orion was slain and hurled into the skies for his over-familiarity; Actaeon was turned into a stag and then devoured by dogs for looking upon the goddess as she bathed; Kallisto the nymph was made a she-bear for yielding to Zeus. The Ephesian Artemis was depicted with a necklace of severed testicles.

For all her relentless virginity, Artemis was also revered by Greeks as the goddess of childbirth. Her dual character may have influenced the Christian cult of the Virgin Mary, which also had its origins in Ephesus.

Athena

Athena was the patron goddess of the Athenians, whose favor she won by giving them the olive tree. She was born by parthenogenesis, fully grown and armed, from the head of Zeus, who had swallowed up her mother Metis. Her principal attributes were chastity, wisdom and prowess in war.

Her wisdom was practical: she taught Danaos to build the first double-prowed ship; she invented the weaving-loom and the double flute. She led the Athenians in war, and was often depicted with helmet and shield (Athena Promachos). Her holiest sanctuary was the Parthenon on the Athenian Acropolis, where her cult had been established in time immemorial by the Phoenician snake-kings Cecrops and Erechtheus, and where her ancient sacred image in olive wood was kept.

Demeter

The eldest sister of Zeus was perhaps the only pre-Hellenic deity of Greece to survive into Greek religion. She rarely visited Olympus, preferring to wander instead on Earth, whose productiveness she ensured. The death and rebirth of her daughter Persephone was celebrated in the Mysteries of the Eleusinian cult (see page 104).

The primitive Arcadian tribes worshiped an unnamed horse-goddess known as Despoina (Lady), a daughter who was born when Demeter was raped by a stallion. During her interminable wanderings the goddess cut a sorry barefoot figure in rags, reviled and banished by tyrannical kings. This may suggest a time when her cult was suppressed by ruling princes and perhaps carried on in secret.

Dionysus

According to one account, the god of wine and orgies was a native of Lydia in Asia Minor, where he acquired the surname Bacchus. Others said he was the son of Zeus from Semele, a daughter of King Kadmos of Thebes, who was struck dead when the Father of the Gods revealed himself to her in his divine aspect. Zeus then implanted the unborn Dionysus in his thigh, and in due course gave birth to him. The baby Dionysus was spirited away by Hermes, and had to be kept hidden to save him from Hera's wrath.

The cult of Dionysus took Greece by storm in the 7th–6thC BC. His devotees, who were all female and took the name of Maenads, fell into trances and engaged in unspeakable acts during the Bacchic rites they performed in the open countryside. Pentheus, who was once foolish enough to peek in, was ripped apart limb by limb by the demented revelers, who included his own mother.

Various kings who tried to ban the worship of Dionysus met particularly gruesome ends. The Athenian tyrant Peisistratus domesticated the phenomenon by instituting a milder form of the Dionysian rites in the city. Attic drama grew in the 5thC out of the wild performances of the Athenian Dionysia.

Hephaestus

The god of volcanoes and metalsmiths was lame and ugly, so much so that Hera hurled him in disgust down into the sea after she had given birth to him. The spot where he hit the Aegean was marked by the island of Lemnos, where a volcano was still active in Antiquity, and he was saved by the Sintians, an archaic Lemnian tribe.

Later he returned to Olympus, and even married Aphrodite for a short period. According to some accounts he was the father of Erichthonius, one of the half-snake founding kings of Athens. His temple in Athens was built in the market district of the ironsmiths.

Hera

The wife of Zeus was the goddess of the Argives, the dominant tribe of the Mycenaean Greeks. One myth placed her birth at the Stymphalian Lake, near Nemea in the Peloponnese, others at the islands of Euboea or Samos. Her legends almost exclusively concerned her tantrums over Zeus's various loves and her merciless vendettas against their offspring.

She pestered Io with a horsefly so that she had to run as far as Egypt; she led Semele, the hapless mother of Dionysus, to her death by tricking her into asking Zeus to reveal his divine light (it fried her instantly). Leto was driven into destitution for bearing Apollo and Artemis, Zeus's children; Heracles, another illegitimate son of the Father of Gods, was cheated out of his kingdom at Tiryns and made to waste his life in senseless labors.

Yet Hera was also the protectress of the Greeks in the Trojan War: it was at her temple near Argos that Agamemnon was chosen as the leader of that expedition.

Hermes

Hermes was born from the union of Zeus with a nymph in the mountains of Arcadia, and his most famous exploit involved stealing Apollo's cattle from the vicinity of the river Alpheios, an activity in which the wild pastoral nomads of Arcadia, too, often engaged. He was employed as the messenger of the gods; in a similar capacity, he guided the souls of the dead to the nether world (Hermes Psychopompos).

In earliest times he appears to have been worshiped in the form of milestones set upon roadsides. Even in some later representations, he is shown as a stone stele with a human head and penis.

Zeus

The "Father of Gods" was in fact the brother of five (Demeter, Hades, Hera, Hestia, Poseidon) and father of six (Apollo, Ares, Artemis, Athena, Hephaestus, Hermes) Olympians. When his father Cronos took to gulping down his offspring, Zeus was saved by serving the wicked father a stone concealed in a crib. He was spirited away to Mt. Ida in Crete, where he was raised by nymphs, returning to topple Cronos in a wrestling match and forcing him to regurgitate his swallowed children.

Zeus was probably the chief deity of the Indo-European races that invaded Greece in the early 2nd millennium BC, although his association with Crete suggests a parallel Minoan origin. He was the god of heavens and thunderstorms, honored on the peaks of high mountains.

Since most Greek cities claimed him as the ancestor of their founder, royal dynasty or local nymph, he had to be cast as an amazing womanizer; hence his scores of escapades, which were a source of permanent friction with his wife Hera. His chief sanctuary was at Olympia, venerated by all Greeks regardless of the rivalries of tribe or city.

Other deities

Poseidon, the god of the seas, and **Hades**, the god of the underworld, had nearly equal status with Zeus their brother, and there are indications that, in an earlier mythology, the three brothers formed the three constitutive elements of the universe. Hades was worshiped near mysterious holes and foul-smelling caves in the ground, while Poseidon was one of the most popular deities of the seagoing cities of Greece.

Aphrodite was born from the sea foam off the coast of Cyprus. She had a complex personality that involved not only her usual role as the goddess of love, but also an all-encompassing spirit that held the world together. Occasionally, she was even a goddess of war, or of war-madness. Her priestesses served her by prostituting themselves.

Ares, the warrior god, was short on brains but astonishingly good-looking. He had temples in all parts of Greece, although none of great importance.

Hestia was a shadowy spirit who protected the hearth of each house; each city had a perpetually burning flame that was devoted to her cult.

Athens (Athína)

Capital of the Greek Republic

Municipal area	414 square kilometers (160 square miles)
Population	More than 4 million
☎ code	01
Airport	Elinikon, 11 kilometers (7 miles) from city center

Mythology
and history

Athens was the first great metropolis of the ancient world. Although its period of greatness lasted less than 150 years (c.480–338BC), the city was seen and emulated as a model of urban civilization for some 800 years afterwards, until the downfall of pagan antiquity. The most important traditions of Western political democracy, philosophy and drama were born in this city.

During the long centuries of Byzantine, "Frankish" and Turkish rule, Athens declined to the status of an insignificant town. It was rebuilt virtually from the ground after 1834, when it was adopted as the capital of newly independent Greece.

Present-day Athens is a modern city with a small 19th century core. The ruins of ancient monuments lie scattered in almost every corner of the town.

LEGENDS

Athena, the goddess of wisdom, and **Poseidon**, the god of the sea, contended for the patronage of the city. Poseidon struck his trident and caused a spring to flow from the Acropolis; Athena made an olive tree grow, a source of peace and prosperity. The latter was deemed the more valuable gift, so Athena was adopted as the chief divinity of Athens. Her sacred symbols (the olive tree and the owl) were the symbols of the city.

The founder of the Athenian royal line was the Phoenician **Cecrops** (Kekrops), who was born of the earth and was said to be half man and half snake. One of his descendants, **Erechtheus** (who is sometimes confused with Erichthonius, also a serpent-king), introduced the worship of Athena and founded the Panathenaea, the most important religious festival of the Athenians.

Many generations later, **Theseus** put an end to Cretan supremacy by killing the Minotaur, a fiery bull-man who was kept in the famous Labyrinth of the palace of King Minos. He married Ariadne, the daughter of the Cretan king, united the communities *(demes)* of Attica under Athenian leadership, and subjugated the hitherto independent cities of Eleusis and Megara.

In the course of the Dorian invasions of the Dark Age, a wave of Achaean–Ionian refugees from the Peloponnese flocked to Athens. Their leader, **Codrus** (Kodros), married into the Athenian nobility, became king and defeated the Dorians. His sons established the Ionian colonies of western Asia Minor.

HISTORY

Recent research has found signs of Neolithic and early-Helladic ("Pelasgian") settlement on the Acropolis going back to c.5000BC. A Mycenaean royal palace existed on the Acropolis (c.1500–1200BC), although there is no indication that Athens was an important place in this period. It must have acquired some importance as a refugee stronghold around 1200–1000BC, during the Dark Age. It was only under the tyranny of Peisistratus (c.561–527BC), however, that it began to achieve a leadership position among Greek city-states.

The economic base of Athenian prosperity was originally the export of pottery, the marble of Mt. Pentelicon (Pendeli), the honey of Mt. Hymettus (Imitos) and olive oil. In the 5thC BC Athens became the leading naval and commercial power of the Eastern Mediterranean. In Hellenistic and Roman times it survived as an academic and intellectual center and a meeting point of students from all over the ancient world. Its academic institutions were weakened by the advent of Christianity, and were destroyed by the Edict of Justinian in AD529.

Despite mild bouts of resurgence in the early 11thC, under Frankish feudalism (13th–14thC) and the early part of Turkish rule (16th–17thC), Athens was never more than a sleepy town until the beginning of the modern era. The decision to revive it, in 1834, was mostly sentimental, as several Greek towns such as Nafplio, Livadia, Halkida and the port of Syros were at the time better developed than Athens.

Between 1834 and the end of the 19thC a bevy of European architects planned, built and embellished a small, oligarchic city in Athens. Many public buildings were erected in the Neoclassical, or "Othonian" style (from King Otto, 1832–62), a mixture of idealized Greek motifs and Italian *palazzo* architecture.

In 1922, the population of the city more than doubled with the arrival of a huge wave of refugees from Turkey. The newcomers settled mostly in the southern suburbs and Piraeus, which quickly became engulfed within the city. They brought with them their own music, nightlife, food and culture, which were generally regarded as more sophisticated than those of the natives.

To this day the two communities retain their separate identities, with the two major soccer teams of the capital, Panathinaikós and AEK, drawing upon the loyalties of "old" Athenians and Anatolians, respectively. Politically, "natives" have generally been associated with conservative parties, while "refugees" have formed the strongest base of support for liberal-republicans and the left.

Before the wounds of 1922 could fully be healed, the city was hit by a second wave of refugees fleeing the civil wars of 1944–49. The 1960s, in turn, saw the start of rapid industrialization, which drew in an average of 100,000 immigrants a year. The population of Greater Athens surpassed 1 million in the early 1960s, 3 million around 1980, and 4 million at the end of the 1980s.

A majority of Athenians today keep strong ties with the village and region of their origin. Many have family ties and very often property "at home," take their vacations there, and tend to socialize in the capital with compatriots from the same region. The widespread habit of going home for census and elections suggests that the official figures may underestimate the city's real population.

Sudden growth, combined with the refusal of most inhabitants to identify strongly with the city, has created serious urban problems, which over-politicized governments have been inadequately equipped to solve. Construction has gone on in a haphazard manner, with minimal planning and little regard for public spaces. Car traffic is among the worst of any major European city, and air pollution frequently exceeds the limits set by international health agencies.

It must be mentioned, however, that Athens does not have any slums (either of the inner-city variety as in Anglo-Saxon countries, or suburban ones as in the Third World), and hardly any neighborhoods that display conspicuous poverty. A strong middle-class flavor pervades the city. It owes much to the traditional aptitude of the Greeks for small commerce, as well as to the continued existence of solid networks of family and community carried over from the countryside.

Exploring Athens

Athens on foot

Nearly all points of interest in Athens are concentrated in a compact central area that can easily be explored on foot.

The **Acropolis**, the **National Archeological Museum** and **Plaka**, the older part of town with its narrow streets and lively evening crowds, form the main highlights of a visit. Various ancient ruins are scattered in and near Plaka, but virtually all of its narrow lanes and secluded little squares are worth exploring in their own right.

Choose an evening for your exploration if you enjoy the carnival crowds, the music, the shop-browsing and the taverna-hopping; or go in the morning, when Plaka wears a deceptively tame and sleepy face. **Lykavitos Hill** offers a splendid bird's-eye view of the whole city.

The **Benaki** and **Cycladic (Goulandris) Museums**, the historic **First Cemetery**, the **flea market** at Monastiraki and the **meat and produce markets** on Athinas St. are all sights that are worth including on an extended itinerary. In the outskirts of the city, the Byzantine monasteries of **Daphni** and **Kesariani**, and the harbor of **Mikrolimano** in Piraeus, full of popular fish tavernas, justify an excursion.

Three special activities recommend themselves on **Sunday mornings**: Greek Orthodox mass at any church, notably at the Metrópolis (Athens' cathedral); changing of the *Evzones* guard at the Parliament (Syntagma Sq.); and the full-scale flea market at Monastiraki.

The following itinerary covers the area around one of Athens's two key points of interest, the ACROPOLIS.

A WALKING TOUR OF ATHENS

Allow 6 hours (at least). See map on following page and color maps 1 & 2.

Start at Syntagma Square. Follow the crowded and chaotic Filelinon until after the AGIOS NIKODIMOS Russian church, and turn right on Kydathineon, a pedestrian street that forms one of Plaka's main arteries. Visit the MUSEUM OF GREEK FOLK ART at #6. Turn left (s) on Adrianou, the second of Plaka's central axes, which leads to two tiny squares centered around the Byzantine church of **Agia Ekaterini** and the 4thC BC **Lysicrates Monument**.

Continue to the fenced edge of the ACROPOLIS, and begin to follow it clockwise along Thrassilou and then Dion. Areopagitou. Visit the **Odeon of Herodes Atticus** and other monuments on the s slope of the hill, then wind your way up to the entrance of the main archeological area on top.

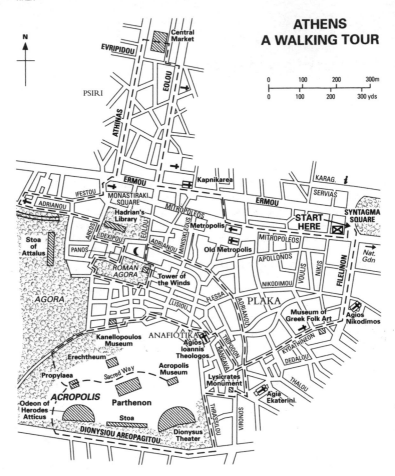

ATHENS
A WALKING TOUR

Devote a couple of hours, at least, to the **Propylaea**, the **Erechtheum**, the **Parthenon** and the **Acropolis Museum**.

Continue your clockwise tour of the hill, making a brief visit to the KANELLOPOULOS MUSEUM or stopping for lunch in one of the neighborhood's superbly panoramic tavernas. Enter the maze of the **Anafiotika**, a real village in the midst of the city, emerging near the Byzantine church of **Agios Ioannis Theologos**. Turn right along either Rangava or Tripodon, which lead back to Kydathineon, not far from where you left it.

Now turn onto Adrianou in the opposite direction (N), and follow it as far as it goes. Turn left on Eolou where Adrianou breaks off, noting the **Tower of the Winds** (Aerides) and the **Bazaar Mosque**, and circling the excavated area that constitutes a part of the **Roman Agora**.

Go N along Panos, turn left on Dexipou, right on Areos, past the mighty colonnade of **Hadrian's Library**, and left again on Adrianou, which emerges here unexpectedly: to your left you will see the vast, dusty desert of the Athenian AGORA. Enter it, if you wish, to see the THESEUM and the **Stoa of Attalus**. Continue left toward the KERAMIKOS excavation if you have a more than passing interest in archeology; otherwise, you should go around the little church near the entrance of the Agora, to reach the flea-market street of **Ifestou**. Turn right, and soon you are in **Monastiraki Square**, the heart of the Athenian "bazaar."

The dowdy hubbub of the bazaar is delightful to some and repulsive to others. If it is not to your taste, hurry back to Syntagma along Ermou. Otherwise, follow Athinas as far as the wonderful **Central Market** of meat and fish. Return s along Eolou, and then turn left on Ermou to meet the incongruous sight of the medieval church of KAPNIKAREA, sunk in the middle of a busy commercial square. Turn right on the next cross-street, which takes you to the **Metrópolis** (cathedral) of Athens and the adjoining, far more attractive, OLD METRÓPOLIS. Continue on Mitropoleos to arrive back at the starting point of your walk on Syntagma Square.

For most people, this will be a good place to end the day's exertions. If you are tired, there is no better place to regroup than the splendid **National Garden** (just off the map on page 42), with entrances both to the right of Parliament (on Amalias) and behind it (on Vassilissis Sofias).

If time and stamina permit, a sally into the more exclusive quarter is an ideal way of escaping the noise, fumes and commotion of plebeian Athens. Map **2**, at the back of the book, will help you to follow this route.

Follow Vassilissis Sofias as far as the BENAKI MUSEUM, which holds a fascinating collection of post-Classical Greek, Byzantine and oriental art. Turn left on Koumbari, which leads immediately to **Kolonaki Square**, the epicenter of fashionable Athens. A series of parallel streets, each smarter than the one before, rise from here stepwise toward the flank of MOUNT LYKAVITOS.

Take Haritos and Souidias as far as the stately edifice of the **American School of Classical Studies**; return via Dinokratous or Kleomenous to Ploutarchou, a cross-street whose upper reaches turn into a flower-banked stairway. At its top is the base station of the **Lykavitos funicular**. Take it to the summit, where a breathtaking panorama and a café-restaurant beckon.

ONE-DAY SIGHTSEEING PROGRAM

For those forced to compress their sightseeing into one day, the following suggested itinerary will give the most of Athens that is possible in the short time you have available.

- Start early in the morning with an overview of the city from the Lykavitos (1 hour).
- Walk to the Archeological Museum for a *very* quick visit ($1\frac{1}{2}$ hours).
- Stroll through Omonia and Athinas St. markets to the Monastiraki flea market (2 hours).
- Visit the Agora (45 minutes) or proceed directly to the Acropolis (2 hours).
- Walk down to Plaka via the district of Anafiotika, join the strolling evening crowds, and choose your favorite taverna for dinner.

Sights and places of interest

Introduction

The principal sights of Athens are listed in this chapter under four headings: **Ancient Athens**, **Byzantine churches**, **Modern Athens** and **Museums in Athens**. Some entries deal with an individual building or monument. Others cover an area or a cluster of sights — such as the ancient monuments of PLAKA, or AREOPAGUS, PNYX AND PHILOPAPPUS, the three hills w of the Acropolis — which in our opinion are more easily toured, understood and described as an ensemble.

If you don't immediately find what you are looking for, consult the INDEX at the end of the book.

HOW TO USE THIS A TO Z SECTION
- The alphabetical listings use English or Greek names according to common English-language usage.
- **Bold type** generally indicates major points of interest.
- Cross-references to other entries or to other sections of the book are printed in SMALL CAPITALS.
- The ★ symbol identifies the most important sights.
- The ☆ symbol identifies others that are definitely worth a visit.
- The 🏛 symbol indicates buildings of considerable architectural interest.
- The 🏠 symbol is used to indicate good examples of traditional architecture.
- The ◁€ symbol is used to indicate places from which the view is especially panoramic or picturesque.
- Places of special interest for children (✿) are also indicated.
- For guided tours, look for the 𝄓 symbol: details follow this symbol where appropriate.
- **For a full explanation of all the symbols used in this book, see page 7.**

Ancient Athens

The city from about the time of Themistocles (early 5thC BC) to that of Hadrian (2ndC AD) formed an irregular elongated circle, with the Acropolis set at the middle, and edges that corresponded to the following current features: north at Eleftherias Square, Sophokleous Street and Klafthmonos Square, east at Filelinon Street and Amalias Avenue, south along a line drawn from Philopappou to the beginning of Syngrou Avenue, and east enclosing the Pnyx and Philopappus hill but excluding Keramikos.

The Emperor Hadrian extended the city to include today's Syntagma Square and National and Zápio Gardens. Most traces of ancient Athens lie within these boundaries.

The Classical monuments that remain relatively intact today are the buildings of the **Acropolis**, the **temples of Hephaestus ("Theseum")** **and Olympian Zeus**, and the **Odeon of Herodes Atticus**. A visit to the **Agora** and some of the various minor edifices that are scattered through **Plaka** can be combined with a tour of PLAKA AND MONASTIRAKI (see pages 62–63 and A WALKING TOUR OF ATHENS, pages 41–43).

Ancient Athens: A to Z

ACROPOLIS (Akrópolis) ▥ ★ ◁€
Entrance on w end, accessible from Dionysiou Areopagitou or Plaka. Map 1E3
▨ *Open Mon–Fri 8am–6.30pm; Sat–Sun 8.30am–3pm. Post office, bank and refreshment stand at entrance.*

The Acropolis ("high town") is a steep limestone hill rising 156m (502 feet) above the Athenian plain. In prehistoric times it was the site of a fortified town and a Mycenaean royal palace. As late as the 6thC BC, Peisistratus ruled Athens from a stronghold on this summit. As urban life took a firm hold on the plain, however, the hill became a sacred enclosure containing only temples and other ceremonial buildings. These Archaic buildings were destroyed by the Persians during the Second Persian War (480BC).

In the mid-5thC BC, Pericles initiated a vast building program on the Acropolis that was expressly designed to embody the highest achievements of Greek art and to confirm the pre-eminence of Athens among Greek cities. All the major monuments preserved or restored today (the **Parthenon**, the **Erechtheum**, the **Propylaea** and the **Temple of Athena Nike**, illustrated on page 47) date from that grandiose effort. The **Erechtheum** (illustrated on page 50), the last to be finished, was completed in 395BC.

In medieval and Turkish times the Acropolis reverted to its earlier role as a military stronghold. Under Turkish rule, it housed both a garrison and a Turkish residential quarter. The garrison, curiously, held on for four years after Greek independence, before eventually surrendering to Bavarian troops after Athens had been inaugurated as the capital.

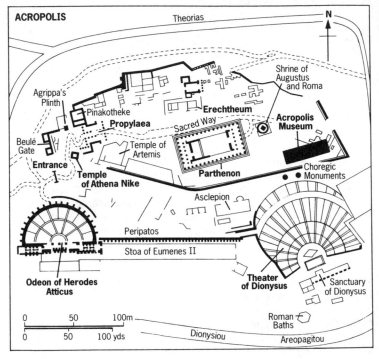

All post-Classical buildings on the hill were cleared by archeologists in the following century (in part at Schliemann's private initiative and expense), and efforts were made to restore the site to its Periclean appearance. The Acropolis monuments were constructed in Pentelic marble, which takes on a rich yellowish hue over the course of the centuries. In recent years air pollution and acid rain have caused an alarming deterioration of the marble surfaces.

Various projects are now under way to protect the monuments against further damage, and certain limitations apply to the movement of visitors (of which there are more than 5 million each year) within the precincts.

Beulé Gate

The historic entrance to the Acropolis was through a monumental Roman gate (3rdC AD) named after French archeologist Charles-Ernest Beulé, who discovered it embedded in a Turkish wall in 1853. The core of the supporting wall of the **Temple of Athena Nike**, on the right, is from the Mycenaean period (13thC BC).

A massive pedestal on the left, the so-called **Agrippa's Plinth**, bore various statues at different points of its career, including one of Antony and Cleopatra during the brief period in which the couple held sway in the East (36–31BC). It was eventually occupied by a monument of Vipsanius Agrippa, son-in-law and commander of Augustus (30BC–AD14).

Propylaea

This magnificent gateway to the sacred precinct, which Pericles intended should "crown the citadel of the gods with a radiant diadem," was executed by the architect Mnesicles in 437–432BC. It consists of three wings. The **central hall** has two porticoes on its front and back sides, each supported by six massive Doric columns, with a vestibule between them lined with more slender Ionic columns. Neither the gilded marble ceiling nor the five monumental gates has survived.

The **N wing**, dubbed the **Pinakotheke**, was decorated by a series of paintings by Polygnotus, which were counted among the greatest masterpieces of ancient art; like all of Classical Greek painting, they have been lost without trace (note the wall-sockets that once held the panels). The **S wing** consists of a front only, and appears to have been left unfinished at the outbreak of the Peloponnesian War.

The Propylaea was used as the residence, in turn, of the Byzantine bishop, the Frankish and Italian dukes, and the Turkish aga of Athens. The Acciaiuoli dukes expanded it into a Florentine *palazzo* and added a tower, which was demolished in 1875. An accidental explosion in 1476, Venetian shelling in 1687, and fighting during the Turkish siege of 1827 caused much damage.

Temple of Athena Nike

Interior not open to visitors.

This charming shrine in the Ionic order was dedicated to Athena Victorious. Pausanias relates the story that it was built for the goddess Nike (Victory), who was normally depicted with wings, but that the Athenians clipped her wings so she would not fly away. The story is false, but the name *Nike Apteros* (Wingless Victory) has stuck.

The heavily damaged **frieze** running around the exterior of the cella depicts an assembly of the gods (E), and the Athenian wars against the Persians and their allies. Those on the E and S sides are originals, the other two sides being copies of the British Museum statues removed by Lord Elgin in the 19thC.

The temple was built in 425BC. The Turkish forces dismantled it to make space for a gun emplacement in the Venetian siege of 1687. The original pieces were carefully put together in 1842, and then taken apart and reconstructed again after repairs in 1940.

Inside the Acropolis

Past the Propylaea, the ruins of several monuments lie scattered over the plateau. These include the **Temple of Artemis Brauronia**, the bear-goddess who was served by little girls; the foundations of the Archaic **Temple of Athena**, built in 529BC and destroyed by the Persians, and the fragments of a **Shrine of Augustus and Roma**.

Pausanias describes more than 40 of the statues he saw within the enclosure of the Acropolis. The most prominent of these works was the bronze **Athena Promachos** (Combatant), a masterpiece by Phidias. The statue was 9m (30 feet) in height and stood facing the Propylaea; a few meager remains of its base are still in place today. The statue was carried off to Constantinople at some late point and perished in riots during the 4th Crusade.

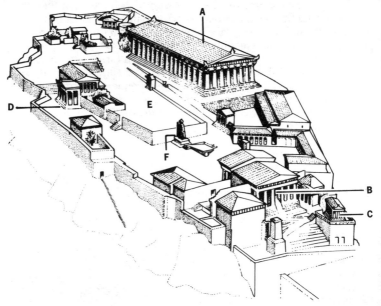

ACROPOLIS, at end of Classical era: **A** Parthenon **B** Propylaea **C** Temple of Athena Nike **D** Erechtheum **E** Site of Old Temple of Athena **F** Statue of Athena Promachos

Parthenon

The Temple of the Parthenos (Virgin Athena) is generally considered to be the greatest masterpiece of ancient architecture. It is a peripteral temple in the Doric Order measuring 69.5 x 30.8m (228 x 101 feet) at the base, with a peristyle of 8 x 17 columns each measuring 10.4m (34 feet) in height.

The architects of the Parthenon were Ictinus and Callicrates, who started work in 447; the temple was dedicated in 438 and the sculpture finished in 432. Phidias created the majestic gold-and-ivory cult **statue of the goddess**, and directed the execution of the matchless **friezes** of the pediments, the metopes and the outer wall of the cella.

The Parthenon was converted into the church of Agia Sophia in the reign of Justinian; a belfry was added and the interior was painted with frescoes. The Latins took it over in 1204 as the Roman Catholic cathedral of St Mary of Athens. The Turks then converted it into a mosque, replacing the belfry with a minaret.

During the Venetian siege of 1687 the mosque was used as an ammunition depot. On September 26, a shell fired by the Venetians hit it, causing a huge explosion that blew apart the naos and demolished 14 of the columns. During the 6-month Venetian occupation that followed, Captain General Francesco Morosini (who was later to become Doge of Venice, 1688–94) made a clumsy attempt to remove the sculptures of the w pediment, destroying them in the process.

In 1801 Lord Thomas Elgin, the British ambassador at Constantinople, secured official permission to remove the remaining friezes. He acquired a 75m (246-foot) section of the Panathenaic frieze (see page 29), the surviving pieces of the E pediment, and 15 of the best-preserved metopes (out of the original 92, of which 57 remained in existence).

No less than 37 ships and 500 workmen were employed for the task; the expense eventually bankrupted Elgin and forced him to sell his loot (the **Elgin Marbles**) to the British Museum. It may be noted in passing that admiration for the marbles was not universal: Byron railed at Elgin and colleagues —

> "Waste useless thousands on their Phidian freaks,
> Misshapen monuments and maimed antiques."

ARCHITECTURE: The Parthenon represents the culmination of more than 100 years of development of the Doric temple, where increasingly more refined solutions were sought for problems of proportion and spatial harmony. The size, form and spacing of the columns, their relationship with the superstructure, and the dimensions of the cella were subject to intense study and experimentation.

Nearly every one of the apparently simple lines of the temple hides geometric complexities. Thus, each of the columns has a slight curvature; the distance between columns decreases on each side toward the edges; corner columns are thicker than the rest; the pavement of the interior rises imperceptibly toward the center. Each of these refinements is designed to enhance the majesty of the overall effect.

The **naos** is unique in containing two halls instead of the customary one, squeezing the front and back vestibules into narrow porticoes. The larger hall (cella) housed the goddess; the smaller one was the *parthenon* (virgin's apartment) proper, and contained the state treasury of Athens.

At the beginning of the Peloponnesian Wars, Athens shocked the civilized world by transferring here the allied treasury of the League of Delos. Traces of a Turkish **minaret** are visible at the corner of the *opisthodomos* (w vestibule).

SCULPTURE: The outer face of the naos was decorated on all four sides with a continuous **frieze** of a total length of 160m (525 feet), which depicted the Panathenaic procession, the dazzling festival that took place in Athens every four years on the feast of Athena. The frieze contained no fewer than 400 human and 200 animal figures. Of this, the w section remains more or less intact; a few slabs are housed in the ACROPOLIS MUSEUM, and much of the rest is in the British Museum.

The 41 **metopes** that remain in place are mostly disfigured beyond recognition. They picture, in serial form, the Trojan War (N), the battle of the gods and giants (E), the battle of the Centaurs and Lapiths (S), and the battle of the Athenians against the Amazons (W).

The **E pediment** represented the birth of Athena, in full armor, from the head of Zeus: what remains of it is in London, while existing fragments of the **w pediment**, depicting the contest of Athena and Poseidon over the city of Athens, are displayed in the ACROPOLIS MUSEUM.

Phidias' great chryselephantine statue of **Athena Parthenos**, 12m (39 feet) high and renowned for the extraordinarily intricate detailing of her dress and shield, has disappeared without trace. An antique copy of poor quality can be seen in the NATIONAL ARCHEOLOGICAL MUSEUM (Hall 20).

Erechtheum

The unusual shape of this Ionic temple resulted from the need to incorporate some of the holiest shrines of prehistoric Athens. The Periclean plan to build an entirely new temple was thwarted and delayed until 406 or 395, when it was opposed by the priests and the people.

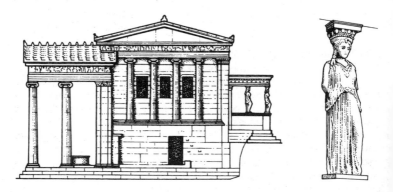

The Ionic **Erechtheum**, with **Caryatid** from the s portico.

It was on this spot that the contest between Athena and Poseidon was believed to have taken place (see page 38): the "marks" left by Poseidon's trident are still shown, and an olive tree has been planted where Athena's sacred tree used to grow in Antiquity. Also here were the tomb of Cecrops and the shrine of Erechtheus, the serpent-kings of the founding myths.

The Erechtheum also housed the olive-wood statue of Athena Polias, the oldest and holiest icon of ancient Athens, which had dropped from the sky in the reign of Cecrops. Every four years this was decked out in new garments and displayed to the populace at the end of the Panathenaic procession.

In the famous s portico of the Erechtheum, six **Caryatids** replace the usual Ionic columns. Of the originals of these statues of young women, one was removed to London by Elgin, and five have been taken to the ACROPOLIS MUSEUM to prevent further deterioration due to exposure. The ones seen in place are copies.

Acropolis Museum

☎ *32.10.219* ✉ *Open Mon 12.30–6.30pm; Tues–Fri 8am–2.30pm; Sat–Sun 8.30am–2.30pm.*

The museum contains statues and fragments discovered in the Acropolis. Individually memorable pieces are few, but the collection as a whole is unique in presenting a comprehensive picture of Athenian sculpture from its Archaic origins through mature Classicism.

A large part of the exhibit consists of frieze fragments from earlier temples on the Acropolis and a series of *korai* (Archaic statues of young women with a characteristic smile), which were presented as votive gifts to Athena. Destroyed by the Persians, these were carefully buried after 480BC and were discovered during excavations in the 1880s. Many bear traces of paint; like all ancient sculpture, they originally stood in vivid color. A huge fragment of a *Bull Attacked by Lions,* apparently from the pediment of the Peisistratid Temple of Athena, is particularly impressive.

The admirable band of the **Parthenon frieze** displayed here *(Hall 8)* was blown off and buried in debris in the 1687 explosion, thus escaping the attentions of Elgin.

ACROPOLIS, THE SOUTH SLOPE ▥ ★

Map 1E2–3.

The imposing **walls** that girdle the Acropolis were erected in the years following the Persian Wars under the guidance of Cimon. Sections of the prehistoric "Pelasgian" wall can be seen behind the s wing of the Propylaea and along the s platform of the Parthenon.

At the foot of the s slope of the Acropolis are the **Theater of Dionysus** and the **Odeon of Herodes Atticus**, separated by the scant ruins of the **Asclepeion** and the **Stoa of Eumenes**. The Asclepeion was a medical center and shrine dedicated to Asclepius, the god of medicine (compare EPIDAURUS, page 136). The Stoa was erected for the convenience of the theater-goers as a gift of Eumenes II, the king of Pergamum (197–158BC), who, like his son Attalus, was a prolific benefactor of Greek cities (see under AGORA, page 53).

Theater of Dionysus

☎ *32.24.625* ✉ *Open Mon–Fri 9am–1pm. Closed Sat, Sun.*

Now in ruins except for some 15 of its bottom rows, this was the principal public stage of ancient Athens; here the plays of Aeschylus, Sophocles, Euripides and Aristophanes had their first performance. In the Classical era the theater consisted of wooden seats and a makeshift stage. A stone structure was first constructed toward the end of the period in 342–326BC, and remained in use for about 750 years.

On the first row, 67 thrones (many of which are still in place) were reserved for the priests of Dionysus and other dignitaries; on the stage stood an altar of Dionysus (now disappeared), where libations were made before each performance.

> ❖ The cult of Dionysus, a relatively late development in Greek religion, was brought to Athens by Peisistratus as a populist alternative to the aristocratic/conservative cults of Athena and Apollo. The annual festival of the Great Dionysia was celebrated with competing choruses and masked satyrs performing *tragoedia* (goat songs) and *comoedia* (ribald songs). Aeschylus was first to develop these primitive shows into a refined art form after 480BC. During the 5thC, the state commissioned a cycle of three tragedies and one comedy for performance each year at the Dionysia.

In addition to drama, the theater was used for annual cockfights, meetings of the assembly (after the 4thC), the presentation of foreign ambassadors and various parades. In Roman times, gladiator fights and wild animal shows became equally popular. The Romans sealed the bottom part of the theater, which was then filled with water for mock naval battles *(naumachia)*.

At the top edge of the theater is the marble **Monument of Thrasyllus**, commemorating a chorus-master of 319BC. The E edge of the theater abuts a platform with the scant foundations of the **Odeon of Pericles**, built entirely from the masts of Persian ships captured at the Battle of Salamis.

Odeon of Herodes Atticus
Closed to the public except during performances.
The best-preserved Roman-period structure in Athens was funded privately by the wealthy patrician Herodes Atticus in the year AD160. The semicircular shape and heavy facade with arched portals are typically Roman. The auditorium, seating 5,000, has been restored and is used for performances during the Athens Festival.

> ❖ Herodes Atticus is the subject of a brilliant passage in Gibbon. "The family of Herod, at least after it had been favored by fortune, was lineally descended from Cimon and Miltiades, Theseus and Cecrops, Aeacus and Jupiter. But the posterity of so many gods and heroes was fallen into the most abject state. His grandfather had suffered by the hands of justice, and Julius Atticus, his father, must have ended his life in poverty and contempt, had he not discovered an immense treasure buried under an old house . . . . Herod became a celebrated orator according to the useless rhetoric of that age; his life was spent in a philosophic retirement at Athens, perpetually surrounded by sophists, who acknowledged, without reluctance, the superiority of a rich and generous rival . . . The most splendid ornaments bestowed on the Temple of Neptune in the Isthmus, a theater at Corinth, a stadium at Delphi, a bath at Thermopylae, and an aqueduct at Canusium in Italy, were insufficient to exhaust his treasures, and many inscriptions of the cities of Greece and Asia gratefully style Herodes Atticus their patron and benefactor."

AGORA ▥

☎ *32.10.185. Map 1D2* ☒ *Open Tues–Sun 8.30am–3pm. Closed Mon.*

The Agora was the center of public life in ancient Athens. In this broad open space, built upon irregularly with temples, colonnades and public edifices, marketers sold their wares, public councils did business, sophists and politicians held forth, and citizens received the latest news.

The area has been excavated since 1931 by American archeologists, who removed about a third of the old town of Athens (more than 350 houses) to reveal a vast field of broken rubbish. Of the three standing edifices within the precincts, one is a late Byzantine church (AGII APOSTOLI, described on page 58), one, the Stoa of Attalus, is a recent reconstruction, and the third, the Temple of Hephaestus or "Theseum," is not strictly speaking a part of the Agora.

The **Stoa of Attalus** was one of several sumptuous colonnaded galleries *(stoae)* that framed the Agora on all sides and were used for promenades and for the retail trade. It was named for Attalus II, Hellenistic king of Pergamum (159–138BC), who pursued his family's longstanding policy of buying the allegiance of Greek cities by lavish gifts. A copy of the original stoa was rebuilt in 1953–56, in part through a generous donation of the Rockefeller family, and is now used as a **museum** to exhibit finds made during the excavations.

The most memorable items on display are the potteries, among others a splendid **calyx** (wide-brimmed urn) by Exekias (c.530BC), the greatest master of the "black figure" style (an example of his work is shown on page 21). The emphasis of the collection, however, is on the nuts and bolts of ancient daily life: a chamber-pot, a marvelously complex election machine, jury cards. Notable also are some of the 1,200 **pot shards** *(ostraca)* that archeologists discovered at the SW corner of the Agora, inscribed in a clumsy hand with such names as Themistocles, Cimon, Pericles, Alcibiades and Demosthenes.

❖ The practice of *ostracism* was one of the more intriguing features of Athenian democracy. Each year in winter the Assembly was asked to submit the names of citizens it wanted to see banished from Athens. Votes were dropped in on shards of broken pottery, and anyone who received 6,000 of these had to go into exile for 10 years under pain of death in case of noncompliance. The practice was instituted by Cleisthenes after the fall of the Peisistratids to bar "for ever" the emergence of another tyrant. Ironically, Cleisthenes himself was one of the first to be ostracized.

In the field of excavations vague traces can be seen of the **Tholos**, a circular structure where the 50 permanent councilors selected from the Council of 500 met and dined at public expense; the **Metroon**, a temple of the mother of gods; the sanctuary of **Apollo Patroos**; and two other **stoae**. The starting point for measuring all distances from Athens, the **Altar of the Twelve Gods**, of which the great *Ara Pacis Augustae* of Rome is said to have been a copy, is now only a few dusty stones.

The excavations have now been extended to the N side of the railroad, where the strip between Adrianou and Ermou is slated for demolition. Here archeologists discovered in 1980 the foundations of the famous **Painted Stoa** *(Stoa Poikile),* where the philosopher Zeno used to hold court and from which his disciples took the name of Stoics. Pausanias describes the paintings of the stoa in great detail.

Theseum (Thísio) 𝐦 ☆

The Doric **Temple of Hephaestus**, which has been misnamed Theseum since the Middle Ages because of a series of friezes on the E facade depicting the exploits of Theseus, is the best-preserved temple of the ancient Greek world and deserves a visit on that account.

Built in the Periclean era, it was dedicated to the god of volcanoes and metalsmiths and apparently stood near a market district populated by iron, copper and brass stores, perhaps like the present Ifestou (Hephaestus) St.

The temple was converted into the church of Agios Georgios in early Byzantine times and remained in Christian religious use until 1834. The barrel-vaulting of the naos dates back to the 5th or 6thC AD; it was allowed to remain when the other post-Classical accretions were removed by archeologists. Buried underneath the marble floor of the temple are a number of tombs dating from the 9th through the 19thC, including those of several Englishmen.

> ❖ Theseus was born of the royal family of Troezen. After defeating the bully Periphetes of the bronze club, the robber "Pine-Bender" Sinis, the wild sow of Crommyon, the man-eating sea turtle of the Isthmus and the wrestler-king of Eleusis, he came to Athens and obtained its kingship against the machinations of the witch Medea. He freed Athens from the Cretan yoke by killing the bull-man Minotaur in the Labyrinth of the palace of King Minos with the help of Ariadne, the king's daughter, although he later abandoned her on the island of Naxos.
>
> After subjugating all of Attica, Theseus took part in the wars against the Centaurs in Thessaly and the Amazons on the Black Sea coast. His last wife Phaedra fell in love with Hippolytus, a son of his from an Amazon concubine, and committed suicide when he rejected her advances.

AGORA, ROMAN   See PLAKA, ANCIENT MONUMENTS, page 56.

AREOPAGUS, PNYX AND PHILOPAPPUS 𝐦 ◁≶
Map 1E2–3.

The three hills W of the Acropolis are rich in Classical associations, even if they have few actual sights. The **Areopagus** (Hill of Ares) gave its name to a council of nobles that was instituted probably by Draco (7thC BC) as a high tribunal for judging murder cases. Later it acted as a sort of senate.

❖ St Paul preached upon the Areopagus without much success (Acts 17.16–34). St Dionysus the Areopagite, perhaps a member of the council, was converted and became the first Bishop of Athens. An immensely influential treatise concerning the celestial hierarchies that appeared in Syria in the 6thC was fraudulently attributed to him. In the 9thC the legend grew that the saint (in French, St Denis) had traveled to France and founded the Parisian church.

The peak of the **Hill of the Nymphs** (Lófos Nimfón) is occupied by an **Observatory** built in 1846 from the funds of the Austrian–Greek banker Baron Sina. A short way below this is the **Pnyx** (Pníka), a large semicircular platform that was the meeting place of the popular assembly in the heyday of Athenian democracy. It is now used as an auditorium for the Acropolis light-and-sound show.

❖ Athenian democracy in its extreme form flourished from Cleisthenes' reforms (c.508BC) to the coup of the 30 Tyrants (404BC). Nearly all political decisions in this period were referred to the assembly *(ecclesia)* of all adult Athenian citizens, which also elected all public officials and military and naval officers for one-year terms. The quorum for meetings was 5,000, and since people were paid for attending, the assembly became dominated by the poorest class of citizens. The system had many critics in Athens, including Socrates, and was generally loathed elsewhere in Greece.

The Philopappus Hill (Lófos Filopappoú), which was known in Antiquity as the Hill of the Muses, is crowned by the **Philopappus Monument** (◀≲), the tomb and memorial (built AD114–116) of a Syrian prince from the royal family of Commagene who lived in exile at Athens. The NW face of the hill is pockmarked with caves, which appear to have been used as dwellings and tombs in different periods. One of them is said, without much evidence, to be the **"Prison of Socrates"** where the philosopher drank his cup of hemlock.

❖ Execution for political crimes was extremely rare in ancient Athens. The condemnation of Socrates in 399BC came shortly after the fall of the terror regime of the "30 Tyrants" in which several of the philosopher's closest associates had played leading roles, although he himself had stayed aloof. Socrates refused to defend himself at the trial or to make the routine plea for the commutation of his sentence to 10 years' exile.

KERAMIKOS ▥

Ermou 148 ☎ *34.63.552. Map 1D2* ▨ *Open Tues–Sun 8.30am–3pm. Closed Mon.*

An unattractive area of railroad tracks and dilapidated workshops beyond the Agora hides the cemetery of ancient Athens, one of the most evocative archeological sites in the city. The name Keramikos refers to the pottery workshops that existed here in archaic times. They lay immediately outside the city walls, near the principal gate (Dipylon) where the ceremonial road (Hiera Odos) to Eleusis and the highways to Corinth and Delphi entered the city.

A large number of funeral stelae (tombstones), sarcophagi (stone caskets) and *naiskoi* (miniature temples) lie scattered along the **Street of Tombs**, although the most important pieces have been removed to the NATIONAL ARCHEOLOGICAL MUSEUM and replaced with copies. A small **museum** exists in the excavation area.

About 1km ($\frac{1}{2}$ mile) NW of Keramikos, at Platonos and Palamidiou *(map 1 B1)*, another excavation has revealed the site of **Plato's Academy**, although almost nothing remains to be seen on the spot. The road between Keramikos and the Academy was dotted with the tombs and the memorials of all the greatest Athenians; these have since been replaced by repair shops and run-down apartments. Farther N, behind the train station, is the hill of **Kolonos**, immortalized as the setting of Sophocles' *Oedipus at Colonus*.

❖   The Academy was a sacred olive grove in the outskirts of Athens. Plato taught at the gymnasium here, unlike his mentor Socrates who had preferred the bustle of the Agora, and was buried nearby. His successors maintained the Platonic School at the Academy for more than 900 years.

LYSICRATES MONUMENT   See PLAKA, ANCIENT MONUMENTS, page 57.

PLAKA, ANCIENT MONUMENTS ▥
Map 1D3–E3. See also PLAKA AND MONASTIRAKI, pages 62–63.
Several minor but relatively well-preserved Classical monuments stand in various parts of Plaka and blend nicely with the surrounding old-town architecture.

The **Library of Hadrian** was described by Pausanias as a building with a "hundred columns of Phrygian marble, and pavilions with gilded roof-work and alabaster, decorated with statues and paintings." The inner courtyard measured 90 x 30m (300 x 100 feet) and had a large water basin at its center. An imposing facade crowned with Corinthian capitals survives along Areos St., s of Monastiraki Sq.

Behind the library lies the large excavated area of the **Roman Agora** *(☎32.45.220 ▨ open Tues–Sun 8.30am–3pm, closed Mon)*. Unlike the Greek original, this was a single architectural complex consisting of a vast rectangular court surrounded by colonnades. It was founded as a gift of Julius Caesar and Augustus, although construction was only completed under Trajan (AD98–117).

Adjoining the Roman market is the **Tower of the Winds (Aerides)**, an octagonal structure of white marble that was built in the early Roman period as a public water-clock, compass and weather-vane. Each of its sides faces one of the cardinal or half points of the compass, and is decorated with symbols of the respective winds. The inside was a reservoir that filled with water at a precise rate and thus allowed people to measure time.

Under the Ottomans the tower was used as a *tekke*, a house of meditation of the Bektashi dervishes. Across the street are the ornamental gate of a destroyed Turkish *medrese* (religious school), dated 1720/21, and the derelict 15thC **Fethiye Mosque** (Conqueror's Mosque).

The **Choregic Monument of Lysicrates**, a circular structure supported by Corinthian columns, graces a pleasant little square near the other end of Plaka. This was one of the countless similar memorials erected along the Street of the Tripods (Tripodon) in honor of winners of the choral competitions at the Great Dionysia, and commemorates the winner of 334BC, a man who was otherwise unknown.

A Capuchin convent that existed here from 1669 to 1827 once incorporated the monument, which was put to use as a little library. Byron, who stayed at the convent during his first visit to Athens in 1809–10, is said to have composed parts of *Childe Harold's Pilgrimage* in it.

TEMPLE OF OLYMPIAN ZEUS AND HADRIAN'S ARCH ☎

☎ *92.26.330. Map 1E3* ▨ *Open Tues–Sun 8.30am–3pm. Closed Mon.*

A group of tall Corinthian pillars survive from this vast temple, which was started in Hellenistic times (2ndC BC) but completed by Hadrian some 300 years later. The statue of the god, dedicated by Hadrian, was, according to Pausanias, larger than any in the world except the Rhodian and Roman colossi; in addition, the Athenians erected a grandiose statue of the emperor himself beside the temple. In the Middle Ages a stylite hermit lived on top of one of the pillars; his shack remained in place until after independence.

The **Arch of Hadrian** is located a short distance from the temple. It separated the ancient city of Athens from the additional district that was walled in by Hadrian, covering roughly today's Syntagma Sq. and the parks. On either side of the gate one reads the inscriptions, "This is Athens, the old city of Theseus," and, "This is Athens, the city of Hadrian and not of Theseus."

❖ Hadrian was one of the most brilliant and active of Roman emperors (reigned AD117–135). He studied as a youth in Athens, developing an enthusiasm for things Greek that earned him the nickname "Graeculus." He came back twice during his reign, once (AD125) to take part in the Eleusinian Mysteries, and a second time (AD128–9) to inaugurate the various monuments built in his name. Hadrian's excessive sexual appetite for men was the subject of comment. His beloved Antinous, an Anatolian youth, was deified after his death, with statues, temples, cities and a constellation named after him.

THESEUM   See AGORA, page 54.

Byzantine churches

Almost all of the dozen Byzantine churches in Athens date from the early 11thC and owe their origins to the Christian restoration that followed the campaigns of Emperor Basil II "the Bulgar-slayer" in the Balkans. Only the **"Old Metrópolis,"** arguably the most graceful of all, belongs in its present form to the late 12thC.

The churches are of minuscule proportions and do not claim any great architectural distinction. Although they have been in more or less continuous use as churches, none has retained frescoes or other interior ornamentation of historic value. Nevertheless, they form quaint oases of peace and quiet that many visitors will cherish amid the frantic rush of modern Athens. (See under OUTSKIRTS OF ATHENS for the DAPHNI and KESARIANI monasteries, on pages 102–3 and 105 respectively.)

AGII APÓSTOLI (Holy Apostles)
Agion Apostolon. Map 1D2.
Located within the excavation area of the AGORA, the church was spared when this part of the old town was razed by the American archeologists. In the 1950s it was stripped of later accretions and restored to its original form of c.1020; the four incorporated Classical columns were replaced by copies, and a number of post-Byzantine frescoes from the demolished church of Ag. Spyridon were transferred here at that time.

AGIOS NIKODÍMOS
Filelinon. Map 2E4.
The largest medieval structure in Athens was founded in 1031 as part of a monastery that survived until 1701. The building was restored with the addition of a belfry by Czar Alexander II in the 1850s, and is now used as the Russian Orthodox church of Athens.

AGII THEODÓRI
Klafthmonos Sq. Map 1D3.
Founded in 1049, this church was completely rebuilt in alternating courses of stone and brick during the following century. The belfry and the interior decoration date from the 19thC.

KAPNIKAREA
Ermou. Map 1D3.
Despite its doubtful attribution to Empress Irene, an Athenian who became the first woman to reign alone in the Byzantine Empire, in 797–803, the church is almost certainly an 11thC work. The porch and N chapel were added in the 13thC. The contrast between the graceful ensemble and the surrounding business district is striking.

❖ A historian calls Irene "scheming and duplicitous, consumed by a devouring ambition and an insatiable lust for power." After the death of her husband Leo IV, she became regent on behalf of her son Constantine VI whom she subsequently blinded and murdered. Charlemagne tried, unsuccessfully, to marry her.

OLD METRÓPOLIS
Mitropoleos Sq. Map 1D3.
Properly Panagía Gorgoepikoos or Agios Eleftherios, this charming little church is entirely constructed of architectural fragments of Classical and early medieval origin. It was used as the Orthodox episcopal seat of Athens when the bishops were ousted from the Parthenon, first by the Franks, then by the Turks.

The adjoining "new" **Metrópolis** (cathedral), a work of large-scale kitsch, was built in 1840–55 as the archiepiscopal church of Athens. A rather impressive **Orthodox mass** (✩) is celebrated here on Sundays with the participation of the archbishop and a substantial crowd of priests and acolytes.

❖ The Metropolitan Archbishop of Athens is the head of the autocephalous Greek church, which formally severed its ties with the Oecumenical Patriarch of Constantinople in 1864. A number of Greek prelates, however, are still subject to the Patriarch, although his authority in their case is "temporarily" relegated to the Archbishop of Athens. The Archbishop of Crete and the monasteries of Mt. Athos have independent status.

OTHER BYZANTINE CHURCHES IN ATHENS
These include **Ag. Nikoláos Rangavás**, **Ag. Ioánnis Theólogos**, **Ag. Anárgyri**, **Ag. Ekateríni** and **Metamórphosis (Sotiráki)** in Plaka; the **Theotokos (Pantánassa)**, which gives its name to **Monastiraki** ("little monastery") square; the nearby **Ag. Ioánnis stin Kolóna**, built around a Roman column believed to have the power of curing fevers; **Ag. Asomaton** at Keramikos; and the chapel of **Panagía Chrysospiliótissa** above the Dionysus theater, the only one still bearing traces of Byzantine wall painting.

There are also several small churches dating from the Turkish period, some replacing or reproducing earlier Byzantine edifices. Notable among these is the church of **Ag. Simeon** in the Anafiotika district, renowned for its miracle-working icon of *Our Lady of the Reeds*.

Modern Athens

Plaka is the heart of tourist Athens, Syntagma the center of government and business, Omonia the lower-class underbelly and Kolonaki the upper-class diadem. A vast city of residential and industrial suburbs spreads around them for miles in every direction, unknown and unvisited by foreigners.

FIRST CEMETERY (Próto Nekrotáfio) ☆
Map 2F4. Open daily 7.30am–5pm ☎ 92.36.118.

This cemetery, containing the tombs of nearly every prominent Greek of the 19th and early 20th centuries, is of the greatest interest both from a historic and artistic point of view. A visit may constitute one of the more satisfying surprises of a tour of Athens.

Many of the tombs are built in the shape either of elaborate Greek temples or Byzantine churches. All are of yellowish Pentelic marble, dazzling against the profusion of palm trees and dark cypresses; they lie thickly together on the irregular terrain, creating a spectacle of monumental pomp. Many contain statues of excellent quality, presenting a parade of bearded statesmen, operetta generals, dreamy-eyed poets, stern matrons and innocent damsels in the flower of youth.

Prominent monuments commemorate prime ministers (Chalcocondylis, Deligiorgis, Koumoundouros, Rallis, two each of Trikoupis, Voulgaris and Zaimis), founding fathers (Kolokotronis, Mavromichalis), dictators (Metaxas), and plutocrats (Averoff, Benaki, Pesmazoglou, Siniosoglou, Syngros, Tositsa, Zarifi). One of the finest tombs, shaped as the portico of a Doric temple (high on the left near the entrance), belongs to Heinrich Schliemann (1822–90).

> ❖ Born in Mecklenburg, Schliemann joined the California gold rush, made a fortune as a St Petersburg merchant during the Crimean War, and devoted the rest of his life to Homeric archeology. In 1873–74 he discovered Troy, confounding 2,000 years of skepticism by proving the reality of the Trojan legend. In 1874–76, he unearthed at Mycenae the first tangible artifacts of the Bronze Age ("Mycenaean") civilization of Greece. He was married to a very young Greek woman, and lived in grand style at the Iliou Melathron, "the Palace of Ilium," on Stadiou St.

KOLONAKI AND MOUNT LYKAVITOS
Map 2D4–5.

The district of Kolonaki, ascending from **Kolonaki Sq**. to the western and southern flanks of Mt. Lykavitos, is the most fashionable residential quarter of central Athens. Many of the city's better restaurants, designer boutiques, art galleries and fine furniture stores are to be found here.

Also located here are the British and French Schools of Archeology, the German Archeological Institute and the American School of Classical

Studies, prestigious institutions that have played a crucial role in shaping the cultural identity of Greece in the past century and a half.

❖ The institutes are supported by the governments and academic institutions of their respective countries. Major archeological achievements include Knossos and Mycenae for the British, Delphi for the French, Olympia for the Germans, and the Athenian Agora and Corinth for the Americans. Apart from their narrowly academic significance, the activities of the schools have been instrumental in transforming the image of Greece from a backward Oriental country into a reincarnation of ancient Greece.

Stepped streets lead up to the higher reaches of Kolonaki, above the cloud of polluted air that often envelops the city; the area at the foot of the **Lykavitos funicular** has a rarefied atmosphere and some of the most exclusive residential streets of Athens.

The peak of the **Lykavitos** (★ ◀ξ) (ancient Mt. Lycabettus, 277m/909 feet), reached either by funicular or footpath, offers a magnificent panorama covering all of Greater Athens, surrounded by the theater of Mts. Parnitha (N), Pendeli (NE) and Imitos (E). The Acropolis is seen against the background of the sea, and on clear days the view extends beyond the craggy masses of Salamis and Aegina to the Peloponnesian mountains. A taverna and a pleasant 19thC church stand at the top.

OMONIA AND VICINITY
Around map 1C3.

Omonia Square (*Homonoia* = Concord) is the center of commercial Athens, with a vast and chaotic mass of shops, offices, discount stores, travel agencies and *souvlaki* stands spreading along each of the eight thoroughfares that intersect here. At night the area tends to be livelier than Syntagma, particularly around the various questionable bars and all-night restaurants that dot the back streets in the vicinity.

For many decades Omonia has attracted visitors from the Greek countryside, just as the Acropolis and Plaka draw foreign tourists — a role that is bound to erode as increasing prosperity minimizes the economic and cultural differences between Athens and the provinces.

Museum and Exarhia

Walking N of Omonia one passes Kaningos Sq., lying in close proximity to Gladstonos and Tsorts Sts.

❖ British Prime Ministers George Canning, William Ewart Gladstone and David Lloyd George played crucial roles in the creation of modern Greece. Canning was instrumental in rallying English support for the War of Independence, Gladstone elevated philhellenism to the level of a moral crusade, and Lloyd George coaxed the Greeks into the ill-fated Anatolian adventure. Philhellenism was one of the cornerstones of the foreign policy of the Liberal Party in the 19thC, and the last Liberal-led government of Britain, that of Lloyd George, was brought to an end by the Greek debacle in 1922.

Farther on is the **Athens Polytechnic**, remembered above all for the student uprising of 1973 that brought down the colonels' junta. The NATIONAL ARCHEOLOGICAL MUSEUM (see pages 69–71) is located next door. Student disturbances at the polytechnic developed into a city-wide revolt on November 13, 1973. Tanks were deployed against the demonstrators, and at least 13 students were killed on the cast-iron gates facing the avenue. On November 25, Colonel Papadopoulos was ousted by a hard-line military faction, but that survived for only a little more than eight months.

To the NE of Omonia lies the district of **Exarhia** *(map2 C4)*, the center of Athenian student life and a hub of "alternative" political and cultural activities. Some of the best cafés in town, as well as the best venues in which to hear the less cliché-ridden forms of Greek music, are to be found in this quarter.

The market district

Running s of Omonia toward Monastiraki, the market street of **Athinas** presents Athens at its most "Oriental." **Kotziá Sq.** (now Ethnikis Andistaseos) has only the facades of elegant old buildings to remind one that this was the center of Athenian high life in the 19thC.

The area is now devoted mainly to the food and grocery trade, although there are also specific parts and side streets that specialize in everything from inexpensive clothes to kitchen utensils, garden implements, gold jewelry, and spices. Old-style grocery stores carry fabulous quantities of cheese, dried codfish, olives, coffee, spiced meats, wild herbs and dried fruit in sacks and barrels; they emit the satisfying smell of a well-stocked cellar.

Of greatest interest to the stout-of-heart is the **Central Market** (★) of meat and fish, a giant cast-iron structure housing several hundred butchers' and fishermen's stalls in separate sections. The stench is strong, sheep's heads roll around freely, but the lively commotion and the sheer scope of the market are worth experiencing.

Noticeable among the marketers is a considerable proportion of Gypsies. Like other Balkan countries, Greece has a substantial Gypsy population. Many speak the Gypsy language (Romany), and lead a seminomadic life as artisans, tradesmen and entertainers.

PLAKA AND MONASTIRAKI 🚌 🏛 🛥 ★

Map 1D3–E3. See also pages 56–57 for PLAKA, ANCIENT MONUMENTS and pages 41–43 for A WALKING TOUR OF ATHENS.

These districts together with the now bulldozed area of the ancient Agora formed the town of Athens as it existed at the time of independence. The narrow, irregular pattern of the streets goes back to pre-independence days; most of the buildings are pleasant, relatively modest 19thC houses or their modern successors.

Thanks exclusively to the tourist industry, Plaka, which had declined into a poor and derelict quarter by the mid-20thC, has been revived in recent decades, and now bustles with lively shops and outdoor tavernas catering to more than 5 million visitors a year. Most of the streets have been closed to vehicle traffic, creating a good setting for strolling at leisure in a small-town atmosphere dotted with traces of Classical, medieval, Turkish and Neoclassical architecture.

❖　　The word *Plaka* appears to derive from *pliaka,* the Albanian for "old." The Christian population of Athens and Attica at the time of independence consisted mainly of Albanians, a fact that modern Greek nationalism still finds uncomfortable to deal with. Albanian was spoken widely until late last century.

Adrianou, lined with souvenir stores, and **Kydathineon**, which is densely populated with outdoor tavernas, form the principal axes of Plaka. Some charming little squares are found around the TOWER OF THE WINDS, the church of Metamorphosis and the LYSICRATES MONUMENT. A number of surprisingly peaceful streets abound in the upper reaches of Plaka at the edge of the Acropolis, in the area called **Rizokastro**, or "Castle's Foot."

No walking tour should miss the district of **Anafiotika** (☆ ☎ ◁≣), settled by immigrants from the island of Anafi, who created a veritable corner of the Cyclades in the heart of the city with its whitewashed houses, corridor-like streets and tiny gardens.

Monastiraki Sq. derives its name from the "little monastery" of Pantánassa that formerly existed here, of which only an ungainly church of (dubious) Byzantine origin survives. The square was the hub of the bazaar district of Turkish Athens, and is dominated by the **Bazaar Mosque** (also known as Mustafa Aga Mosque or Sidriváni). Dedicated in 1759/60, the mosque, minus its minaret, was used from independence until 1918 as a precinct jail, and now houses the ceramics collection of the MUSEUM OF GREEK FOLK ART. The spirit of the bazaar survives on **Pandrossou**, and especially on **Ifestou St**., where a lively flea market is held on Sundays and most other days.

A covered bazaar indeed existed at the site of **Hadrian's Library**, taking in the now excavated area bound by Areos, Pandrossou and Eolou. The middle part of Adrianou (now excavated) ran through it. When the bazaar burned down in 1885, archeologists prevailed upon the government to clear the site so that they could dig for the foundations of Hadrian's Library.

SYNTAGMA AND VICINITY
*Around map **2D4**.*

Syntagma (Constitution) Square is the heart of modern Athens. The **Parliament** dominates the square from a height in the E. Several of Athens' principal hotels, airline companies and the head offices of Greece's major banks occupy the other three sides. The ministries of finance, economy, foreign affairs and the interior are located in the immediate vicinity. The top commercial establishments of Athens fan out from the w and n.

The embassies of the 19thC Great Powers and the grand residences of many of the people who today command the destinies of the country are lined along **Vassilissis Sofias Ave.**, which is also the site of the acclaimed new concert hall, the **Megarón Mousíkis Athenon** (see NIGHTLIFE AND ENTERTAINMENT, page 94). Both the **Presidential Palace** and the **Prime Ministry** are located on the opposite edge of the park, on Irodotou Attikou St.

Political demonstrations and marches are traditionally held on Syntagma Square. The custom goes back to 1843 when a riot here compelled King Otto to grant the country's first constitution.

> ❖   The area extending s of the square part of the way into the park was occupied in Antiquity by the grounds of the *Lyceum* ("Wolf's Field"), a sacred grove of Apollo lying outside the city walls. Aristotle used the Lyceum to teach his philosophy. His successor Theophrastus acquired the so-called *Museum*, or Garden of the Muses, corresponding almost exactly to the present Syntagma Sq., which remained the precincts of the Aristotelian school for more than 800 years. The area was included within the city boundaries during Hadrian's extension of the walls.

Along with Omonia, Syntagma Sq. formed one of the nodal points of the new Athens that was drawn by Schaubart in 1834, but realized on a more modest scale by Leo von Klenze when the former's grandiose concepts failed to mesh with Greek realities.

The principal architectural landmark of the square is the **Parliament** *(Voulí),* formerly the Royal Palace, built by Friedrich Gaertner for King Otto in 1836–42 and used as the residence of the kings of Greece until 1924. The constitution of 1843 was promulgated by Otto from a balcony of this palace. The parliament, which was formerly housed at Stadiou 13 (now the NATIONAL HISTORICAL MUSEUM), moved here in 1935 when the monarchy was restored after an 11-year republican interregnum. Visits to the building are possible by invitation only.

Two republican guards *(évzones)* stand in front of the parliament in ceremonial uniforms of white pleated skirt *(foustanélla),* pompon slippers *(tsaroúhia)* and tasseled caps. The costume was inspired by the attire of Albanian *klephts* (bandits) who fought heroically in the Greek war of independence, and was adopted by King Otto. Other *Evzones* are posted in front of the Presidential Palace (see page 65). A **parade** (★) of *Evzones* accompanied by a military band takes place on Syntagma Sq. every Sunday at 11am.

Located a block away on the n side of the square, the stately **Hotel Grande Bretagne** was built in the 1840s by the Danish architect Theophil von Hansen as a private mansion that doubled up as a royal guest house. It was used for a time by the French school of archeology, before being converted into a hotel in 1874.

❖　Famous guests of the Grande Bretagne included Gabriele d'Annunzio, Saint-Saëns, Richard Strauss, and the Prince and Princess of Monaco. During World War II it served as the headquarters of German, then of British occupying forces. An attempt to blow it up from the sewers on Christmas Eve 1944, when Churchill was staying here, was foiled at the last moment. Constantine Karamanlis directed the restoration of Greek democracy in 1974 from temporary government headquarters on the 5th floor.

Stadiou and Panepistimiou Avenues

Stately 19thC buildings alternate with elegant and not-so-elegant shops along the two principal thoroughfares of central Athens.

The main landmarks along Panepistimiou (officially called **Venizelou**, after Eleftherios Venizelos, the leading political figure of the early 20thC) are the **Iliou Melathron** (Palace of Ilium), once the home of Heinrich Schliemann (see page 60), now the Supreme Court of Appeals; the Catholic cathedral of **St Denis**; the majestic pseudo-Classical monuments of the **Hellenic Academy** (built by Th. von Hansen in 1859–85), the **National Library** (1887–91) and the now ceremonial main hall of the **University** (Christian Hansen, 1837–42).

Klafthmonos Sq., on Stadiou, is dominated by a statue of **Kolokotronis**, the heroic bandit-leader of the War of Independence (1770–1843) who was twice condemned to death by different Greek governments. Nearby is the **Old Parliament**, which now houses the NATIONAL HISTORICAL MUSEUM.

The parks

The National Garden *(Ethnikós kipós)* and the adjoining Zápio Park extend behind the Parliament like a green oasis in the heart of the city. The **National Garden** (✩ *open dawn to dusk)* was created by the Court Gardener Friedrich Schmitt as a private garden for Amalia, Otto's queen, who raised eyebrows by dispatching the navy's one battleship on missions to bring exotic plants from all parts of the globe. The garden retains something of a German and royal character with its luxuriant vegetation, well-tended paths and strutting peacocks. Within it are a Botanical Museum and a tiny Zoo.

The **Zápio Park** *(Zappeion)* was donated to the state by the Zappas family in the 1870s. At its center stands a grand **Exhibition Hall** designed by Th. Hansen in the 1870s, with a popular outdoor movie theater and café where concerts are given on summer evenings.

On the E side of the park, across a sidewalk occupied by a colorful row of florists, is the **Presidential Palace** *(Anáktora)*. Built by Ernst Ziller, this was used as the royal residence from 1935–67 and has been the official home of the president of the republic since the establishment of that largely ceremonial office in 1975. Next door at #19 is the **Prime Ministry**, the real seat of political power.

A short walk to the S of the palace leads to the **Stadium** *(Stádio)*, a vast expanse of gleaming Pentelic marble flanked by the pine-covered hill of Arditos. The present structure was built in 1896, as a gift of the

Alexandrian plutocrat George Averoff, to host the first of the modern Olympic Games, which took place in Athens. It occupies, however, the precise location of the ancient Panathenaic stadium, and its form is a faithful copy of the original as described by Pausanias.

> ❖   The ancient stadium of Athens was built in 330BC as a venue for the quadrennial Panathenaic Games. Its length, as now, was one stade or 204m (223 yards), the standard measure of the Olympic foot race. Hadrian held the presidency of the games during his first imperial visit to Athens, and 1,000 wild beasts were set loose on the field on this occasion.

Mets

The small rectangular area circumscribed by Arditos Hill, the TEMPLE OF ZEUS and the FIRST CEMETERY is known as **Mets** (from the French city of Metz, the name of a pro-Entente café that flourished here during World War I), a quiet district of many old garden houses and a village-like character.

It has recently become a favorite residence of the Athenian literati and younger professionals, and consequently possesses a number of good bars, interesting boutiques and art stores, concentrated along Markou Moussourou, the main street.

Museums of Athens

The **National Archeological Museum**, containing one of the world's most important collections of Classical Greek art, is among the highlights of Athens and should not be missed under any circumstances. The **Benaki Museum** complements it nicely, devoted as it is to the opposite (Christian, Byzantine, Oriental) pole of the Greek cultural heritage. The **Cycladic Art (Goulandris) Museum** deserves a visit if only for the admirably clear and enlightening displays. All three museums have shops, where reproductions of excellent quality can be bought. Other museums are of secondary interest.

- The **ACROPOLIS**, **AGORA** and **KERAMIKOS** museums have been described on the preceding pages, under the entries for the respective archeological sites.

OPENING HOURS
As a rule, all museums open from 8.30am to 3pm every day except Monday. Exceptions are noted below.

BENAKI MUSEUM ☆
Vassilissis Sofias 17 and Koumbari 1 ☎ 36.11.617. Map 2D4. Open Mon–Sat 8.30am–2pm. Closed Sun.
The Museum is a fantastic, colorful treasure-trove of Byzantine, late-Greek and Muslim antiquities from all over the Near East.

> ❖ Emmanuel Benakis (1843–1929) was a Greek who made his fortune in the cotton trade in Egypt. His son Antonis (1873–1954) devoted his life to collecting antiquities, which he donated to the public in 1931 together with his Neoclassical mansion.

The large collection of **Byzantine icons** includes some excellent examples of the 15thC Cretan school, including two early El Grecos. These clearly demonstrate the cross-fertilization of Greek and Italian art in the early Renaissance, while the following centuries show a precipitous return to rigid conservatism in church art.

Other gems include several Roman-period **portraits** from Faiyoum (Egypt), fine specimens of **Iznik ceramics** and **Bursa textiles** (Turkey), and fabulous **silver filigree** and **carved wood work** from Asia Minor. A 17thC marble-inlaid Egyptian **fountain hall** has been reconstructed in its entirety. Many of these items represent cultural traditions in which Greek artisans were active, or which were influenced by, and in turn enriched, Byzantine/Greek art.

The upper floor contains the Far Eastern collection as well as old paintings, drawings and engravings of Athens. A wonderful collection of Greek **folk costumes** is exhibited in the basement. The **library**, one of the world's richest repositories of Byzantine and post-Byzantine manuscripts and archival material relating to modern Greek history, is open by permission only.

BYZANTINE MUSEUM
Vassilissis Sofias 22 ☎*72.11.027. Map 2D5* ▨ *Open Tues–Sun 8.30am–3pm. Closed Mon.*

The neo-Renaissance building now housing the Byzantine Museum was erected in 1840 as a residence for the Duchesse de Plaisance, who was one of the most eccentric figures of 19thC Athens. The museum possesses a great wealth of Byzantine **icons**. It also has reconstructions of several church interiors from various periods of Byzantine architecture, and ecclesiastical objects and embroideries that display an almost obsessive workmanship.

❖   Née Sophie de Marbois (1785–1854), the Duchesse de Plaisance married Lebrun, one of Napoleon's generals, helped finance the Greek war of independence from her personal fortune, and took up residence in Athens in 1837. She always traveled with a crystal casket containing the embalmed body of her daughter, and a pack of wild dogs that terrorized Athens. She devised a private religion that she evangelized enthusiastically, was reputed to yield willingly to brigands in mountain paths, and died reciting some verses of Lamartine.

CYCLADIC ART MUSEUM ☆
Neofitou Douka 4 ☎*72.49.706. Map 2D5* ▨ *Open Mon, Wed–Sat 8.30am–3pm. Closed Tues, Sun.*

Managed privately by the Nicholas Goulandris Foundation, this deserves to be called the only modern museum in Athens. The presentation is lucid, with expert and detailed documentation, well-designed charts and illustrations. The collection comprises a large number of artifacts from the early Cycladic cultures of 3300–2000BC, including several well-preserved marble **figurines**. The astonishing "modernity" of these idols juxtaposes interestingly with the modern artists exhibited on the upper floor.

The museum has a good, if expensive, shop selling replicas of the items on display.

GOULANDRIS MUSEUM   See CYCLADIC ART MUSEUM, above.

JEWISH MUSEUM
Amalias 36 ☎*32.25.582. Map 2E4* ▣ *Open Sun–Fri 9am–1pm. Closed Sat.*

This has a small collection of memorabilia relating to the Jewish community of Athens.

❖   The origins of Jewish presence in Greece go back to the 3rdC BC, although the modern community has its roots in the mass emigration of Sephardic (Spanish) Jews to the Ottoman domains in 1492. Under Turkish rule most Greek towns had substantial Jewish populations, and Thessaloniki in particular was an important Jewish center. These communities shrank after independence, mostly by emigration to Turkey and America, and were almost wiped out by the Nazis during World War II. Greek Jews now number less than 5,000, most of them in Thessaloniki.

KANELLOPOULOS MUSEUM

Theorias and Panos, in Plaka ☎ *32.12.313. Map 1E3. Open Tues–Sun 8.30am–3pm. Closed Mon.*

An eclectic family collection, somewhat similar in scope, although not in wealth, to that of the Benaki Museum, is housed here. As well as icons and folkloric items, there is a vast quantity of Archaic and Classical small objects, vases and jewelry, making it a worthwhile stop on a stroll from the ACROPOLIS.

MUSEUM OF GREEK FOLK ART

Kydathineon 17, in Plaka ☎ *32.29.031. Map 1E3. Open Tues–Sun 8.30am–3pm. Closed Mon.*

A small but fascinating collection of items from the Greek rural tradition, spanning mostly the 19th and early 20thC. The sometimes startlingly "primitive" or "non-European" character of Greek folk culture surprises those accustomed to the neo-Hellenic national image. Displays include a remarkable series of native costumes from various parts of the country, fabrics, embroiderics, silverware, domestic articles, carnival masks and *Karagiozis* shadow-play figures.

The upper floor has the reconstruction of the interior of a village house, with wood panels painted by the naive painter Theophilos of Lesbos (1878–1934).

The museum's **ceramic collection** is exhibited separately in the former Bazaar Mosque on Monastiraki Sq. *(☎ 32.42.066: see page 63).*

NATIONAL ARCHEOLOGICAL MUSEUM ★

28 Oktovriou (Patission) 44 ☎ *82.17.717. Map 2B4* ▩ *Open Mon 12.30–7pm; Tues–Fri 8.30am–7pm; Sat–Sun 8.30am–3pm; shorter hours in winter.*

The museum was erected in 1866–89 (extended 1925–39) to house finds from the excavations of the British, French, German and American Archeological schools and the Greek Archeological Society. As time has passed, it has grown into one of the world's leading repositories of Classical Greek art.

❖   The earliest core of the collection were the Aegina friezes, recovered by the Germans in 1833 and first displayed at the Theseum. The collection was enriched substantially by the discoveries of Schliemann at Mycenae in 1874–76, important bronze statues salvaged from the sea off Kythera in 1900 and off Euboea in 1928, and most recently by Minoan frescoes unearthed by Professor Sp. Marinatos at Akrotiri on the island of Santorini in 1967–74.

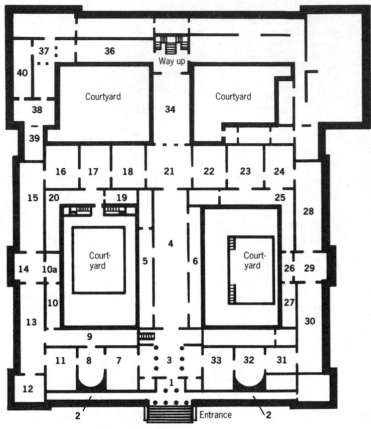

National Archeological Museum: ground floor

The **Mycenaean collection** (hall 4) is the world's richest, and includes the golden **death masks**, whose discovery prompted Schliemann to send the famous telegram, "Today, I gazed upon Agamemnon's face." The **Linear-B tablets** are among the very few that survived thanks to a fire at the palace of Pylos that baked the soft clay. The **bronze weapons** and **gold and bronze cups** are reminiscent of Homeric passages.

A small number of excellent **Cycladic figurines** are to be found in hall 5. The Minoan collection is weak, as the great majority of Minoan artifacts are kept at the Iraklion Museum in Crete.

A splendid **geometric amphora** from c.760BC is on display in hall 7. Of the great variety of **Archaic kouroi** (halls 8–13), the finest is probably the Anavysos kouros (illustrated on the opposite page), found in 1936 (hall 9); it dates from c.520BC and bears the inscription, "Stop and lament over the tomb of dead Kroiros whom furious Ares destroyed as he fought in the front rank."

Halls 14–18 and 23–24 contain **funeral stelae,** mainly from KERAMIKOS. The eloquent, subdued beauty of these sculptures was perhaps best captured by Rilke in the *Duino Elegies:*

> "On Attic stelae, did not the circumspection
> of human gesture amaze you? Were not love and farewell
> so lightly laid upon the shoulders, they seemed to be made
> of other stuff than with us? Think of the hands,
> how they rest without pressure . . . ."

Four magnificent **bronzes** deserve special notice among the many Classical and Hellenistic statues on display. The early Classical *Poseidon* in hall 14 (c.460BC) and the Hellenistic *Horse with Child Rider* in hall 21 (2ndC BC), although they are widely separated in time, were found in the same shipwreck off the coast of Euboea. The *Youth of Anakythera* (hall 28), a Peloponnesian work dating from c.340BC, has a masterfully expressive face and body, while the *Bust of Philosopher* in hall 30 is a tour de force of portraiture.

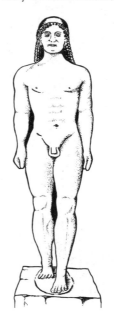

Anavysos kouros

Hall 30 is dominated by the colossal *Poseidon of Melos,* a Hellenistic work. The translucent marble group of *Aphrodite, Pan and Eros,* in the same hall, exemplifies the precious style characteristic of the Hellenistic epoch.

The vast collection of ancient **ceramics**, located upstairs, tends to be somewhat overwhelming because of the absence of any lucid and systematic documentation. The museum's rich **numismatic collection** is an object-lesson in the general decline of the quality of coins over the centuries. It includes several specimens of the Athenian silver "owl," which was the leading currency of the Eastern Mediterranean region for 200 years.

Also located on the upper floor are the splendid **Santorini frescoes**, which were buried in a volcanic eruption c.1500BC, and whose recent discovery furnished new evidence of the extension of Minoan culture beyond Crete.

NATIONAL GALLERY (Pinakothíki)

Vassileos Konstantinou 50 (opposite the Hilton) ☎ *72.17.643. Map* **2**D5
▨ *Open Tues–Sun 8.30am–3pm. Closed Mon.*
The gallery is devoted to Greek painting and sculpture in the 19th and 20thC. With the possible exception of Ghikas, none of the artists represented has a significant international following, although the collection of works by the primitive painter Theophilos holds considerable interest. There are also three paintings that are ascribed, doubtfully, to El

Greco, as well as a number of interesting minor pieces by Delacroix, Picasso, Magritte, Utrillo and Picabia.

NATIONAL HISTORICAL MUSEUM

Stadiou 13 ☎ *32.37.617. Map* **2D4** ☒ *Open Tues–Fri 9am–2pm; Sat–Sun 9am–1pm. Closed Mon.*

The collection holds various relics of modern Greek history, particularly of the war of independence. Among objects displayed are the personal effects of Patriarch Gregorios, who was hanged in Constantinople in 1821, the ashes of a nephew of Napoleon Bonaparte, an urn containing the heart of revolutionary war hero Admiral Kanaris, the death mask of the bandit-hero Kolokotronis, and a helmet and sword said to have been worn by Byron when he commanded the garrison of Missolonghi as an officer of the Greek liberation army.

❖ The building, designed by Florimond Boulanger in 1858 to house the Greek parliament, was used as such until the 1930s. On its steps Prime Minister Deligiannis was assassinated in 1905.

OTHER MUSEUMS IN ATHENS

Several other small museums in Athens are worth a visit if you are in the area:

- **Center for Popular Arts and Traditions**   Hadzimihali 6, map **1E3**. A fine old Plaka mansion devoted to the vanishing heritage of Greek village life.
- **Museum of the City of Athens**   Paparigopoulou 7, Klafthmonos Sq., map **1D3**. Old engravings, photographs and objects, housed in a stately mansion that was the first residence of King Otto and Queen Amalia in 1834–42.
- **War Museum**   Vassilissis Sofias and Rizari, map **2D5**. A collection of mementoes of Greece's various wars since 1821.

Where to stay

Making your choice

Since the early 1970s, tourism has overtaken shipping as Greece's largest industry: with around 10 million foreign visitors a year, the sector now accounts for more than a quarter of the country's GDP. The number of hotels has grown proportionately, and all parts of Greece now claim adequate accommodation to satisfy the needs and requirements of every class of international visitor.

Almost all of the country's approximately 5,000 hotels, however, have been built or modified since the mid-1960s, which means that there are practically no establishments of great tradition and character such as those to be found in some other European countries. All of the medium-to-better category hotels offer modern facilities and uniform standards of design and service, but tend to lack individual character. Modest hotels often compensate for their crumbly looks by the greater charm and friendliness of the personnel.

Mention should be made of two state-controlled hotel systems. **Xenia** hotels, operated by a state-owned agency, exist in most towns and tourist destinations (although not in Athens itself). Their architecture and style of management reflect the slightly chilling touch of public administration, but they all offer reliable standards and reasonable prices. Some, such as the Xenia in NAFPLIO (see page 154) are among the best hotels in Greece.

The newer network of **GNTO guesthouse/hotels** consists of impeccably restored historic buildings and architectural landmarks. These are generally run by young and highly educated personnel, with an excellent esthetic sense that compensates for any management deficiencies.

Another feature of the accommodation sector in Greece is a vast number of private rooms (**pensions**), which offer basic services at prices somewhat lower than those of hotels in a comparable category. They advertise themselves prominently with signs saying *enoikiazómenai domátia/rooms/zimmer;* in a pinch, a list may be obtained from accommodation agencies (in tourist centers) or from local police (in lesser towns). A good budget option elsewhere, pensions in Athens are thin on the ground and mostly unattractive.

LOCATION
There are a few hotels within the old town area, most of them relatively small and simple. A majority of the hotels favored by tourists are near the edges of the old town, around **Syntagma Sq.**, and s toward the

Dion. Areopagitou and **Syngrou** avenues. Another concentration of hotels in the middle of the range can be found in the noisy and traffic-infested area around **Aharnon** and **Liossion** streets, at the N approach to the city center.

Ilissia, the neighborhood of the US Embassy and the Hilton, where several top hotels are located, is elegant, less crowded, but quite a long walk from the main sights and shops.

A variety of down-and-out hotels, geared mainly to Greek visitors from the provinces rather than foreign tourists, are located in the market area SW of **Omonia** and in the vicinity of the rail stations. Some, although not all, of these function also as brothels.

Visitors who prefer to stay near the sea, and who can put up with inconvenient public transport and the noise of airplane traffic, might choose from a large number of hotels located between **Paleo Faliro** *(6km/4 miles from downtown Athens)* and **Vouliagmeni** *(24km/15 miles),* on the Attic coast. The northern suburb of **Kifissia** *(15km/9 miles)* is quiet, cool, and offers a variety of fine hotels.

For details of accommodation in these areas, see OUTSKIRTS OF ATHENS, pages 101–2 and 106. Hotels in **Piraeus** are not generally recommended, but if Athens is too full, or you have a boat to catch next morning, we suggest a few alternatives on page 109.

HOTEL BREAKFASTS

For most Greeks, breakfast consists of a cup of strong coffee and a pack of cigarettes. Hotels make a concession to foreign ways by adding bread, butter and a half-spoonful of bad jam; this procedure completes what is euphemistically called a "continental breakfast." If you want eggs and limp bacon, ask for "English breakfast"; it costs 800–1,000dr.

An exception to this rule is to be found in the deluxe hotels, some of which serve Lucullan breakfast buffets. Our advice: get a room somewhere without breakfast, and head for the HILTON, LEDRA MARRIOTT or ST GEORGE LYCABETTUS for your morning treat.

Alternatively, leave the hotel breakfast behind and take a morning stroll to any nearby taverna for a dish of delicious Greek yogurt, laced with honey.

SOME USEFUL ADVICE

Most Athenian hotels are afflicted by a high level of noise from street traffic, so it is usually advisable to ask for a room that does not face the street. Another prudent precaution in summer and fall is to protect yourself against mosquitoes. The most effective means of combat are the plug-in devices that use odorless tablets; they are available in every pharmacy and supermarket.

Finally, the shower curtain seems to be an unknown entity, even in some upper-range hotels.

RESERVATIONS

In August it is absolutely essential to have your accommodation in the islands arranged well ahead, and it is advisable to do so in Athens as well. At other times, you should be able to find a room without much difficulty. Many hotels outside Athens close between November and March, and on the less popular islands it may be impossible to find any accommodation during this period.

In the US, it is possible to reserve rooms in any hotel anywhere in Greece via the **Greek Hotel Reservation Center** in Los Angeles, which you can contact through your local travel agency.

You may sometimes find hotel receptionists very reluctant to give you a room unless you intend to take it for (say) three days or more. Honesty may not necessarily be the best policy in such situations, and you should not hesitate to call the police if the hotel tries to charge you for three nights if you check out after one.

PRICES

Our **price categories** for hotels reflect the cost of a double room, with bath/shower where these are available, in the high season. As a rule, prices quoted by hotels in the top categories (L, A, B) include breakfast, while in the lower categories (C, D, E) breakfast tends to be extra.

A word of caution: prices may vary depending on season (anything goes in August), time of day (rooms cost less if you arrive late at night), availability of rooms, and the haggling propensities of the manager. Off-season prices may be as much as 40 percent lower than in summer, except for the top Athens hotels, which quote a single price throughout the year.

Our price categories are based on the high-season cost, at the time of writing, of a **double room**.

Symbol	Category	Current price	(US dollars)
☐	Cheap	under 5,000dr	(up to $25)
☐	Inexpensive	5,000–10,000dr	($25–50)
☐	Moderate	10,000–20,000dr	($50–100)
☐	Expensive	20,000–40,000dr	($100–200)
☐	Very expensive	40,000dr and up	($200 and up)

LUXURY HOTELS

The Greek **L** (luxury) category equals, roughly, the international five- or four-star classification. All hotels in this group have a complement of in-house restaurants and bars. Telephone, color TV and air conditioning are standard fixtures in each room. All major charge and credit cards are accepted.

The acknowledged front-runners of the Athenian hotel scene are the **Athens Hilton**, **Athenaeum Inter-Continental** and **Ledra Marriott**, with the **N.J.V. Meridien Athens** and **Astir** following close behind. One of the finest hotels of the Athens region, the **Astir Palace**, is located in the beach suburb of Vouliagmeni, 24km (15 miles) from the center; we describe it on page 101.

Our list falls into two sections: a first-choice selection, which we describe in some detail, and a more concise listing of all the other L-class hotels in the city.

ATHENAEUM INTER-CONTINENTAL
Syngrou 89–93. Off map 1F2
☎90.23.666 ⟨Fx⟩92.17.653 ▥ *605 rms*
◀≣ ≕ ≋ ♫ ♪ ⟐ ⟐

A spacious atrium lobby is one attraction of this modern hotel, which also offers a fine choice of places to eat. The **Rôtisserie** is counted among the best French restaurants in town. The **Kublai Khan** restaurant offers a unique Mongolian barbecue and firepot, in addition to Chinese dishes; the **Café Vienna** is a favorite meeting spot.

ATHENS HILTON
Vassilissis Sofias 46, Ilissia. Map 2D6
☎72.50.200 ⟨Fx⟩72.50.300 ▥ *453 rms*
◀≣ ≕ ≋ ♫ ♪ ⟐ ⟐

The oldest of Athens' international chain hotels, the Hilton is an acknowledged hub of the capital's diplomatic and business life. Its large swimming pool is a popular social venue in summer. The **Galaxy** roof garden has a splendid view of the Acropolis. Restaurants, of which the choice is predictably wide, include the ultra-chic **Ta Nissia**, "where Athens meets for dinner."

CARAVEL
Vassileos Alexandrou 2. Map 2D6
☎72.53.721 ⟨Fx⟩72.53.744 ▥ to ▥
470 rms ≕ ≋ ♫ ⟐ ⟐

This is a modern hotel next to the Hilton, very popular with US and East Asian package groups, and noted for its excellent Anglo-American breakfast. An in-house mosque caters to Muslim guests.

DIVANI-PALACE ACROPOLIS
Parthenonos 19–25, Makrigiani. Map 1E3
☎92.22.945 ⟨Fx⟩92.14.993 ▥ *253 rms*
◀≣ ≕ ≋ ♫ ⟐

Its central, yet quiet location, with a marvelous view of the Acropolis, is one attraction of the Divani-Palace. The hotel is housed in a beautiful building, opulently furnished, with cool marble galore and a beautiful dining room. The buffet breakfast is excellent.

GRANDE BRETAGNE
Syntagma Sq. Map 2D4 ☎32.30.251

⟨Fx⟩32.38.361. In US, toll-free ☎(800) 223.6800. London offices ☎(071) 583.4211 ▥ to ▥ *394 rms and suites*
≕ ♫

The grand old hotel of 19thC Athens, located smack against the Parliament building, forms a virtual extension of its lobby. This is where Churchill stayed — and narrowly escaped assassination — when he came during the civil war in 1944, and where Karamanlis had his headquarters during the restoration of Greek democracy in 1974 (see SYNTAGMA SQUARE on page 65). A thorough remodeling in the 50s spared few traces of the original turn-of-the-century elegance, but the two bars and three restaurants of the GB retain their position among the chief haunts of the capital's political and economic elite.

LEDRA MARRIOTT
Syngrou 113–115. Off map 1F2
☎93.47.711 ⟨Fx⟩93.58.603 ▥ *256 rms*
⟐ ≕ ≋ ♫ ♪ ⟐ ⟐

Somewhat off-center in location, this is the newest, and arguably the best, of that burgeoning breed, the US chain hotels. The **Kona Kai Polynesian** restaurant, **Bali Lounge** and Sunday buffet brunch in the **Zephyros Café** are all noteworthy. Rooms have video equipment with a selection of movies.

ROYAL OLYMPIC
Ath. Diakou 28–32, Makrigiani. Map 1E3
☎92.26.411 ⟨Fx⟩92.33.317 ▥ *297 rms*
◀≣ ⟐ ≕ ≋ ♫ ⟐ ⟐

The Royal Olympic is that rare thing, a modern hotel with a human touch. The constant presence of the owner, Mr Papageorgiou, with his booming voice, adds to a distinctive sense of personal hospitality. He is backed by an experienced staff, with many years' loyal service and familiarity. A lovely view of the Temple of Olympian Zeus is another plus. The only drawback is its busy and somewhat noisy location.

ST GEORGE LYCABETTUS
Kleomenous 2, Kolonaki. Map 2D5
☎72.90.710 ⟨Fx⟩72.90.439 ▥ *150 rms*
◀≣ ⟐ ≕ ≋ ♫ ⟐

This small hotel offers luxury without the mass-produced feel, in a modern building surrounded by much greenery. In the heart of the most fashionable part of Athens, high on the flank of the pine-covered Lykavitos hill (commanding a superb view of the city), the St George Lycabettus is still only a 10-minute walk from Syntagma Sq. Its **Grand Balcon** restaurant provides gourmet dining in elegant surroundings, while **Tony's Bar** is a convivial spot for pre-dinner drinks. The full range of business and secretarial services, as well as conference facilities, are also laid on for the business market.

OTHER LUXURY HOTELS

- **Astir Palace Athens**   Panestimiou and Vassilissis Sofias ☎36.43.112. Map 2D4 ▥ to ▨ 79 rms.
- **Athens Chandris**   Syngrou 385, Paleo Faliro (near the coast) ☎94.14.824. Map **1aF3** Ⓕ94.25.082 ▥ to ▨ 386 rms.
- **Holiday Inn**   Mihalakopoulou 50, Ilissia ☎72.48.322 Ⓕ72.48.187. Map 2D6 ▥ 188 rms.
- **N. J. V. Meridien Athens**   Stadiou and Vassileos Georgiou A ☎32.55.301 Ⓕ32.35.856. Map 2D4 ▨ 183 rms.
- **Park**   Leof. Alexandras 10, Pedion Areos ☎88.32.711 Ⓕ82.38.420. Map 2B4 ▥ 145 rms.

MODERATE-TO-GOOD HOTELS

There are approximately 100 **A**- and **B**-class hotels in Athens, most of which offer more or less identical apartment-block architecture, adequate if sometimes curt service, and edible if generally characterless "international" cuisine. All rooms have bath or shower, telephone and central heating. TV sets in rooms, air conditioning and a restaurant are obligatory in class A, but not in class B.

ACROPOLIS HOUSE (B)
Kodrou 6–8, Plaka. Map 1E3 ☎*32.22.344* ▥ *19 rms.*
A charming historic house with painted halls, a cozy living room and guest rooms of varying size and furniture, but adequate standards. Its location is ideal: on a quiet Plaka side street, a stone's throw from both the lively part of the old town and Syntagma Sq. One problem is that parking in the vicinity is just about impossible.

ADONIS (B)
Voulis and Kodrou 3, Plaka. Map 1E3 ☎*32.49.737* ▥ *26 rms.*
Just across the street from the Acropolis House, the Adonis is pretty similar in scope, without the quaint architecture and decor. In its favor, however, are several family-sized suites.

ASTOR (A)
Karageorgi Servias 16 (off Syntagma Sq.). Map 2D4 ☎*32.55.555* ▥ *133 rms.*
An impressive marble lobby, comfortable rooms and a central location, in addition to a cut-rate pricing policy, make this one of the best-value A-class hotels in Athens. A number of rooms have terraces where you can catch sight of the Acropolis.

ATHENIAN INN (B)
Haritos 22, Kolonaki. Map 2D5 ☎*72.38.097* Ⓕ*72.39.552* ▥ *28 rms* ▤ ◁€ ♫
Guests in this quiet, modern hotel, on a posh residential street, have a choice of views from their rooms. Some face Lykavitos, others a splendid panorama of Athens. It also offers good buffet breakfasts and a basement bar-nightclub.

ATHENS GATE (B)
Syngrou 10, Makrigiani. Map 1E3
☎*92.38.302* ✉*32.52.952* Ⅲ *106 rms*
♨ ≋

A modern hotel facing the Temple of Olympian Zeus, with a roof-garden restaurant offering splendid views of the Acropolis.

ELECTRA PALACE (A)
Nikodimou 18, Plaka. Map 1D3
☎*32.41.401* ✉*32.41.875* Ⅲ *106 rms*
♨ ≋ ▄

This fine, modern hotel, located on a quiet street, offers the best accommodation you are likely to find in Plaka. Its roof garden with swimming pool offers a panoramic view of the Acropolis and the city. Sauna, covered garage and buffet breakfast are other attractions. The same company owns the **Electra** (A) at Ermou 5, off Syntagma Sq.

HERODION (A)
Robertou Galli 4, Makrigiani. Map 1E2
☎*92.36.832* ✉*92.35.851* Ⅲ
90 rms ≋

This long-established hotel, close to the Odeon of Herodes Atticus at the foot of the Acropolis, offers smooth and professional service and a convenient location for the Athens Festival (see page 95). The roof-terrace affords a splendid view, and the tree-shaded patio garden is a cool and pleasant place for drinks.

NOVOTEL MIRAYIA ATHENS (A)
Mihail Voda 4-6. Map 1B3 ☎*86.27.133*
✉*86.27.053* Ⅲ *195 rms* ≋ ▄

The Athens representative of the French hotel chain is a favorite with business travelers on a no-frills budget. The traffic-infested and noisy location is a liability; the roof garden with swimming pool an asset.

A- AND B-CLASS ALTERNATIVES

- **Adam's Pension** (B)   Herefontos 6, Plaka. Map 1E3 ☎32.25.381.
- **Amalia** (A)   Leof. Amalias 10. Map 2E4 Ⅲ ☎32.37.301.
- **Athens Center** (B)   Sofokleous 26. Map 1C3 Ⅲ ☎52.48.511 ≋
- **Esperia Palace** (A)   Stadiou 22. Map 1D3 Ⅲ ☎32.38.001.
- **Olympic Palace** (A)   Filelinon 16. Map 2D4 Ⅲ ☎32.37.611.
- **Omiros** (B)   Apollonos 15, Plaka. Map 1D3 Ⅲ ☎32.25.486.
- **Zafolia** (A)   Leof. Alexandras 87–89. Map 2B5 Ⅲ ☎64.49.012 ≋

BUDGET HOTELS

As in the islands, where a certain casualness can be a cherished part of the Greek experience, cheapjack hotels in Athens can be *very* bad indeed. Mass travel is the name of the game, and if you don't like your room, too bad — there'll surely be someone else who is desperate enough to take it.

Category **C** (some rooms with private bath, hot water most of the time) is usually quite acceptable for travelers on a shoestring budget. **D** (one shower per eight rooms, hot water if you are lucky) is pushing your luck, and **E** (sink, sometimes with water), pretty desperate.

The attitude of the management (friendly, indifferent or nasty) usually makes all the difference to a hotel in this bracket. Unless otherwise indicated, none of the following have air conditioning, and none take charge and credit cards, except under duress.

APHRODITE (C)
21 Apollonos, Plaka. Map 1D3
☎*32.34.357* Ⅲ *84 rms* ▦

Good and friendly service and a very good buffet-style breakfast are two of this particular Aphrodite's attractions. The top- (6th-) floor guest rooms, commanding magnificent views of either the Acropolis (to the w) or the Lykavitos (to the E), are another.

ART GALLERY (C)
Erechthiou 5, Plaka. Map 1E3
☎*92.38.376* ▭ *19 rms.*
This pleasantly furnished and friendly place, with a roof garden, is right in the heart of Plaka. A perennial favorite of backpackers.

ATHENS CONNECTION (C)
Ioulianou 20. Map 1B3 ☎*88.28.334*
▭ *26 rms.*
Between Athens Station and the NA-TIONAL ARCHEOLOGICAL MUSEUM, this is one of the best among the many inexpensive hotels in this area.

HERMION (D)
Ermou 66c, Monastiraki. Map 1D3
☎*32.12.753* ▭ *29 rms* 🔲 🔲
This is a nice old house with a friendly owner. The interior is spartan but not without character; with some luck, you might even get hot running water in your shower. The location is very central, on a noisy shopping street.

IDEAL (D)
Voreou 2 and Eolou 39, Monastiraki.
Map 1D3 ☎*32.13.195* ▭ *32 rms.*
In a central location, the Ideal occupies an attractive old building that must have seen better days, with an old keeper who stays friendly so long as you aren't too demanding.

JOSEPH HOUSE (C)
Markou Moussourou 13, Mets. Map 2E4
☎*92.31.204* ▭ *15 rms.*

A handsome Neoclassical mansion in a small-townish part of Athens, run in an informal fashion by a group of young foreigners. You can cook your own meals in the kitchen, and the communal atmosphere makes it a good place to get to know fellow roaders.

NEFELI (C)
Iperidou 16, Plaka. Map 1E3 ☎*32.28.044*
▭ *18 rms* ◄
In a very central yet quiet location in Plaka, this is a clean building, run to acceptable standards.

OMONIA (C)
Omonia Sq. 4. Map 1C3 ☎*52.32.710*
▭ *252 rms* 🔲 ◄
A vast hotel on the city's noisiest square. Charmless but reasonably clean and efficient by class-C standards, this is the one place where you are almost certain to find a room when everywhere else in Athens is full to the brim.

PELLA INN (C)
Ermou and Karaiskaki 1, Monastiraki. Map
1D3 ☎*32.12.229* ▭ *21 rms.*
Appealing mostly to backpackers, the Pella has a telephone in every room and balcony views of the Acropolis.

PHAEDRA (D)
Herefontos 16, Plaka. Map 1E3
☎*32.38.461* ▭ *to* ▭ *21 rms.*
A fairly run-down hotel located in one of the pleasantest corners of Plaka, near the Lysicrates monument.

APARTMENT HOTELS

An alternative to staying in a full-service hotel is to rent an efficiency (self-catering) apartment (in Athens) or a villa (in the countryside). Increasingly popular in recent years, these may prove an attractive option for families or small groups who are planning to stay in one place for a week or more.

Prices in Athens vary between 10,000–12,000dr per day for a double room, and around 20,000dr per day for a suite. A select few are listed here: many more can be found advertised in the local English-language press or the *Herald Tribune*.

- **Andromeda** (A)   Timoleontos Vassou 22 (near US Embassy). Off map **2C6**
  ☎64.66.361. 26 rms. Polynesian restaurant 🔲 ◄
- **Ava** (B)   Lisikratous 9, Plaka ☎32.36.618. Map 1E3. 24 rms 🔲 in some.

- **Delice** (A)   Vassileos Alexandrou 3 (near the Hilton) ☎72.38.311. Off map 2D6. 44 rms. Breakfast 🖃
- **Embassy** (A)   Timoleontos Vassou 15 (near the US Embassy) ☎64.21.152. Off map 2C6 🖃
- **Riva** (A)   Mihalakopoulou 114, Ilissia ☎77.06.611. Off map 2C6. 81 rms. Breakfast ⇌🖃🚗

YOUTH HOSTELS

To stay in any of the Greek Youth Hostels, you will require a member's card, obtainable for a small fee from the **Greek Youth Hostels Association** *(Dragatsianou 4, off Stadiou ☎32.34.107, map 1D3)*. An overnight stay costs from 500–1,000dr.

- **Youth Hostel**   Damareos 75, Pangrati. Off map 2E6 ☎75.19.530.
- **Youth Hostel**   Peoniou 57, near Athens Station. Map 1B2 ☎88.32.878.
- **YMCA**   Omirou 28. Map 2D4 ☎36.26.970.
- **YWCA**   Amerikis 11. Map 2D4 ☎36.24.291.

CAMPING

The best and nearest campsite in the Athens area is the **GNTO Camping** in the suburb of **Voula** *(16km/10 miles from downtown Athens ☎89.51.646 or 89.53.248)*. Private campsites exist in **Rafina**, **Kifissia**, **Daphni**, **Marathon**, **Sounion**, **Nea Makri** and **Varkiza**.

Camping in the open is not permitted. Throughout this book, campsites are indicated by the ▲ symbol.

Eating and drinking

Greek cuisine

Greek and Mediterranean cuisine have become massively popular in the West in the last few years, thanks to the Anglo-American craze for all things mono-unsaturated. Kalamata olives, feta cheese and tarama-saláta have invaded Western households as the antidote to an artery-clogging diet of white bread and animal fat: olive oil is promoted as the elixir of life.

The average Greek-in-the-taverna may not always share this preoccupation with "healthy" eating: the olives and cheese are more likely to be a bit of *hors d'oeuvre* to help down an early glass of *oúzo,* followed by a proper meal, consisting of a nice fat chunk of mutton in Bechamel sauce, accompanied by a chain of cigarette smoke. But the delightful informality of Greek dining ensures that you always leave the table feeling satisfied, yet light; and the ubiquitous olive oil does have the wonderful effect of making every meal taste at once rich and easy on the digestive tract.

EATING OUT IN ATHENS

Although Athens has a number of good restaurants, it has none that really merits a gastronomic pilgrimage, and most visitors on a short stay will be perfectly satisfied to sample the great multiplicity of tavernas in Plaka, on a quest to discover the most charming nook or the most outrageous waiter.

The most popular tavernas in Athens are collected in **Plaka**, of which **Kydathineon St.** forms the main axis. Expect here neither culinary excellence nor a spotless standard of service. But you will find Plaka a delightfully pleasant place to enjoy an evening meal (except in August, when it may get too crowded, and in mid-winter, when it is too cold to sit outside), with a cheerful atmosphere and many quietly beautiful corners that more than compensate for the distinctly average food and pedestrian wine.

For Greeks, dining out is a social affair. The taverna performs a function similar to the English pub or German *kneipe*. Eating, in other words, is incidental to holding forth with a group of friends or enjoying the spectacle of the world passing by. The culinary claims of the taverna are therefore, inevitably, modest. The most important considerations are such things as the quality of the setting (good view, lovely pergola, lots of action) or the charm of the host (sassy, friendly).

THE TAVERNA

The *taverna* is the heart and soul of Greek food culture: a simple restaurant with that invariably rickety look, with more tables out on the sidewalk or garden than inside, clustered together in the main square, along the harbor walk or at a beauty spot on the edge of town. Its next of kin include the *psistaría,* a taverna specializing in grills, and the *ouzerí,* an establishment primarily for drinking *oúzo* but serving a range of appetizers as well.

It is easy to find fault with the culinary dimension of things. The choice, for example, is astonishingly limited, with *all* tavernas across Greece offering an almost identical menu. The food is invariably edible and occasionally quite tasty too, but very often drowned in olive oil and sometimes smothered in tomato paste as well.

Seafood is generally fresh and tasty, but special care should be taken to ensure that it is not fried in burned or reused oil. Sauces are almost unknown. Experimenting with unorthodox tastes is as rare and shocking as a church painter fooling around with his icons.

As a rule, one orders food in a taverna after inspecting the wares in the cook's display, or even checking the boiling pots in his kitchen. A preview is especially important when ordering fish, which varies enormously in size, quality and price; it is always safest to investigate the fridge and have your choice weighed and priced before you commit yourself to any seafood.

Standard taverna fare includes "Greek salad," which Greeks call *horiatikí,* or "peasant salad"; *tsatsíki,* a yogurt and cucumber mix laced with garlic; *melitsánosaláta,* a creamy eggplant (aubergine) dip; fried squid, or *kalamária;* octopus, or *ohtopódi,* usually prepared as a salad; *mousákka,* a casserole of eggplant and minced meat; *dolmádes,* vine leaves wrapped around minced meat and rice; *stifado,* beef chunks with onion and broth; and *pastítsio,* a macaroni casserole.

In addition, there is the usual variety of grilled meats and fried fish. *Souvláki* is lamb or pork bits grilled on a skewer. *Gyro* is a big mound of meat, usually pork, wrapped around a spit, roasted and peeled off in thin slices. *Biftéki* is not what the name suggests, but a sort of breaded and grilled meatball.

Coffee, if it is available at all, is either instant or "Greek coffee," a murky concoction sipped from tiny cups. Filtered coffee is unknown except in the classiest establishments. Desserts do not form part of traditional taverna fare, although some tavernas have lately taken to including *baklavá* or ice cream *(pagotó)* on their menu. For a wider selection of desserts you must move on to a *záharoplastío,* or pâtisserie, large numbers of which exist in every town.

A typical taverna meal involving an hors d'oeuvre, salad, main course and table wine will almost always cost between 2,000 and 3,000dr. In Athens and Piraeus, as well as other major tourist destinations, there are also numerous upmarket tavernas that cater primarily to tourists. Apart from over-solicitous waiters and garish decor, these rarely offer anything more or better than an average taverna, but cost from two and three times as much.

DRINK

As with so much else in Greece, so with wine: entirely acceptable and perfectly enjoyable wines exist in great abundance, but none really deserves to be singled out for special praise. Regional character is mostly a matter of speculation; vintage is rarely indicated and rarely matters; and grape variety is practically unknown. Greeks themselves show a preference for house wine over bottled brands; this turns out to be excellent advice, especially in the SW Peloponnese and on some of the islands.

Change, however, may be on the way. **Boutari**, a venerable brand, has led the pack by greatly improving the quality and image of its wines; it now markets nearly a dozen locally denominated wines of distinctive character and well-defined vintage. **Clauss**, a rival, seems set to follow suit, although their workhorse, *Demestica,* remains a distinctly pedestrian brand. **Strofiliá**, red, white and rosé, is another name to look for. Among specialty wines, the sweet, red **Mavrodafni** of the Patras region deserves a mention. **Zitsa**, produced in Metsovo, in the NW, is the best among carbonated wines.

Finally, one should not forget the invariable companion to a taverna lunch, the *retsína*. This obtains its resin flavor from the pine casks in which it is aged, and must be drunk well chilled. The best *retsína* is produced in the Athenian hinterland of Attica.

Three brands of lager, Amstel, Kronenbourg and Heineken, brewed in Greece under license, dominate the beer market. Imported brands have become commonplace, but there are no small local brewers.

Oúzo, a colorless aniseed liquor that turns white when mixed with water, is the most popular aperitif. It is always served with *mezédes* (sing. *mezé),* elaborate hors d'oeuvres that, at their best, remain a specialty of Cypriot or Constantinopolitan-Greek chefs; *pikilía* is a plate of mixed *oúzo* snacks, served at the waiter's whim.

It is generally believed that the best way to cure an *oúzo* hangover, or for that matter any hangover, is *patsá,* a gelatinous white soup made of sheep's trotters and/or tripe. This is, admittedly, an acquired taste, but once acquired it tends to stay with you.

CHOOSING A RESTAURANT

Only a few tavernas in Plaka are singled out in our listing. The food is pretty much identical in most places, menus are prominently displayed, and part of the fun of eating out in Plaka lies in the strolling and choosing. Some tavernas offer live Greek music and dancing in the later hours. Many of these are to be found on and around **Mnisikleous** and at the edge of the **Acropolis**. Their bills amount to about double the regular tariff, or 5,000–7,500dr per person.

The *estiatório,* an eating establishment more in tune with Western concepts of a restaurant, is a recent development in Greek dining. For the present, however, it is a phenomenon more or less confined to the cities of Athens and Thessaloniki. Apart from these, there are, of course, the restaurants of the better-class hotels all around the country, most of which serve standardized "Greek and international cuisine." The best of these feature original and interesting menus, leavening Greek themes with foreign — often Italian — inspirations; the worst peddle *filet mignon* and cold potatoes at insulting prices.

The chic district of **Kolonaki** is where you will find the finest restaurants. Others line the axis of Vassilissis Sofias–Kifissias avenues, leading from the area around the Hilton hotel to the northern suburbs of **Psyhiko**, **Halandri**, **Maroussi** and **Kifissia**. In summer, most diners prefer to head toward the coast, to **Kalamaki**, **Agios Kosmas**, **Glyfada** and beyond.

Going to Piraeus for seafood and jollity is a well-established Athenian custom, and the fish tavernas at **Mikrolimano** harbor form the Piraean counterpart to Plaka. The change of setting and the cool sea breeze are welcome differences, but prices at harbor tavernas tend to be high, rarely falling below 5,000dr.

A cluster of good tavernas catering mainly to the local student and young professional clientele can be found in the district of **Exarhia**, NE of Omonia. The fine restaurants of Athens are to be found mostly in the fashionable neighborhoods of **Kolonaki**, **Mets** and **Pangrati**. A selection of favorites is listed below.

For truly "local" color, try the various working-man's eateries located s and w of **Omonia**. One type of establishment specializes only in *patsá* (see page 83). The famous MONASTIRI TAVERNA, within the meat market on Athinas, stays open 24 hours a day, dishing out the best *patsá* in town to late revelers.

PRICES AND TIPPING
Our **price categories** reflect the average cost of a full meal for one, with beer or wine, including taxes and tips. Be warned, however, that the bill can sometimes be extremely unpredictable. This is particularly true if you have fish, or if you dine in restaurants that feature a lot of music and drunken dancing.

Tips are less compulsory than in Anglo-Saxon countries. One leaves 5 to 10 percent to express appreciation for a good meal well served; in simpler tavernas, leaving the small change will do.

Symbol	Category	Current price	US$ amount
▯	Inexpensive	under 2,500dr	up to $12
▯	Moderate	2,500–4,500dr	$12–18
▯	Expensive	4,500–7,500dr	$18–30
▯	Very expensive	7,500dr and up	$30 and up

All restaurants listed below are open daily for lunch and dinner unless otherwise indicated. Reservations are generally recommended for all but the humblest tavernas.

RESTAURANTS — TRADITIONAL
We start with our selection of Athens' best traditional restaurants, and follow with a concise listing of other adequate-to-commendable representatives in this category.

APOTSOS

Panepistimiou 10 ☎*36.37.046* ▭
Map 2D4.
Traditional *ouzerí* with an excellent selection of *mezédes*, located in an arcade just off Syntagma. A favorite spot for politicians, businessmen and resident Englishmen.

BAJAZZO

Ploutarchou 35, Kolonaki (below the Lykavitos funicular) ☎*72.91.420* ▭
Map 2D5. Closed Sun ▣ ▣ ▣ ▣
An original, at times whimsical, menu includes such esoteric treats as *calamares* stuffed with pine nuts and rice, grape leaves filled with sea-bass mousse, eggplants with *oúzo*-flavored mincemeat. All of this is offered up in a converted Kolonaki mansion.

DIONYSOS (ACROPOLIS)

Robertou Galli 43, Makrigiani ☎*92.33.182* ▭ *to* ▭ *Map 1E3* ☙ ♮
Its unique panorama of the Acropolis makes this an essential stop on any sightseeing tour of Athens. Specialties of the house include charcoal-broiled shrimp, baby lamb and filet mignon in oregano sauce. The upper floor, which has a musical program in the evening, is reserved for full meals, while you can have a quick lunch or dinner downstairs or in the delightful summer garden. The **Dionysos** on Lykavitos Hill, a sister establishment, has an equally impressive view, although the menu is more limited and the service tends to be inferior.

DOURAMBEYS

A. Dilaveri 29, Piraeus ☎*41.22.092* ▭ *to* ▭ *No cards.*
This is possibly the most famous seafood place in Greater Athens, distinguished as much for its delectable fish as for its impressive presentation. The bill is also likely to impress, but it's worth it.

FORTUNA

Anapiron Polemou 22, Kolonaki ☎*72.21.282* ▭ *Map 2D5. Closed Sun.*
One of the best restaurants in central Athens for fresh seafood. The fish is on the expensive side, but you can avoid surprises by being thorough at the outset in selecting and pricing your fish.

GARDEN

Kifissias 300, Halandri ☎*68.26.759* ▭
Map 1aC5.
As its name suggests, this ultra-fashionable restaurant stands out for its greenhouse setting, filled with plants and greenery. Vegetation has a starring role on the menu, too, with an excellent salad bar, numerous vegetarian dishes and a wide variety of seafood, as well as the usual carnivorous courses. The waiters are very knowledgeable about wines and are happy to advise. Another branch has recently opened in Glyfada *(I. Metaxa 39* ☎*89.43.880);* more are likely to follow.

GEROFINIKAS

Pindarou 10, Kolonaki ☎*98.39.093* ▭
Map 2D4 ▣ ▣ ▣ ▣
The fare is more or less what you would expect to find in any other taverna, but done to perfection. Posters betray the Constantinopolitan origins of the cuisine and staff; the slightly faded ambience marks out what has been a gastronomic favorite of Athenians since the days before there were tourists in town.

IDEAL

Panepistimiou 46 ☎*33.02.200* ▭
Map 1C3. Closed Sun ▣ ▣ ▣ ▣
This classic Athens restaurant has recovered, phoenix-like, after disastrous fires that gutted it twice in two years. As many as 20 specialties every day and an old and experienced staff help maintain the Ideal's reputation as a *stéki* — a "cult meeting place."

KOSTOYIANNIS

Zaimi 37, Exarhia ☎*82.12.496* ▭
Map 2B4. Closed Sun ▣ ▣ ▣ ▣
A famous taverna with a vast selection of dishes, notable especially for its game, as well as some excellent desserts.

MYRTIÁ

Trivonianou 32–34, Mets ☎*90.23.633* ▭

Map 2F4. Closed Sun 🔔 ▣ ▣ ▣ ▣
This is the best known of several top-notch taverna/restaurants in Mets — the "Greenwich Village" of Athens. A delicious variety of traditional Greek dishes is reason enough for a visit, but it can also offer lively music and a prominent clientele. Reservations are vital (afficionados should note the new address!).

PARKO
Behind Eleftherias Park (near Athens Concert Hall) ☎ *72.23.784* ▥ *Off map 2D6.*
A bar-restaurant-café in a pleasant location, where you can go for anything from a coffee and sandwich, or a drink, to a full meal.

PLATANOS
Diogenous 4, Plaka ☎ *32.20.666* ▥
Map 1E3. Closed Sun ✿
Do not look for cloth napkins at this humble little taverna in Plaka, but for good, genuine food and honest service. This is the perfect place to take an important guest who wants to lunch in a "typical Greek taverna." The wine is homemade, and the courtyard delightful in summer.

SOCRATES'S PRISON
Mitseon 20, Makrigiani ☎ *92.23.434* ▥ *Map 1E3. Closed Sun* ▣ ▣ ▣
An amazing variety of *mezédes* is on offer here; charcoal-grilled swordfish, rolled pork with celery and carrots and roast lamb with mushrooms. A favorite with the vacation-package crowd.

STROFILIÁ
Karytsi 7, Syntagma ☎ *32.34.803* ▥ *Map 1D3.*
The only genuine "wine cellar" in central Athens. It stocks a large selection of Greek wines as well as its own excellent Strofiliá wines. The food consists of a few warm dishes, a good salad bar and various cheeses.

TA NISSIA
Athens Hilton ☎ *72.20.201* ▥ *Map 2D6. 7.30pm–12.30am daily* ▣ ▣ ▣ ▣
A chic gourmet restaurant with traditional Greek and international cuisine. Choose from a wide variety of fish and meat specialties, or from the groaning buffet board.

XYNOS
Angelou Geronta 4, Plaka ☎ *32.21.065* ▥ *Map 1E3. Closed Sat, Sun* ✿ 🔔
A traditional taverna — one of the few left in Plaka that attract Greeks as well as tourists. A wide selection of taverna fare is available. The cozy atmosphere (the restaurant is too small for package groups) is enhanced by guitarist/singers who sing old wine songs. The courtyard is pleasant in summer.

OTHER OPTIONS

- **Dekaokto**   Souidias 51, Kolonaki ☎72.35.561 ▥ Map 2D5.
- **Diros**   Xenofondos 10–12, Syntagma ☎32.32.392 ▥ Map 2D4.
- **El Greco**   Kifissias and Fthiotidos 6, Ambelokipi ☎69.30.089 ▥ Off map 2C6. Closed Sun.
- **Hermion**   Pandrossou 15, Monastiraki ☎32.46.725 ▥ Map 1D3 ✿
- **Kentriko**   Inside the arcade at Kolokotroni 3, Syntagma ☎32.32.482 ▥ Map 1D3. Closed Sun.
- **Manesis**   Markou Moussourou 3, Mets ☎92.27.684 ▥ Map 2E4 🔔 ✿
- **Palia Taverna**   Markou Moussourou 35, Mets ☎75.22.396 ▥ Map 2F4 Open daily 9.30pm–1am 🔔

RESTAURANTS — INTERNATIONAL
Formerly almost unheard-of in the Greek capital, foreign dining became the rage in the 1980s and early 90s. Still, Italian and Chinese are

the only national cuisines to be seriously represented, each with about three dozen restaurants to its credit.

Establishments that call their cooking "international" tend to specialize in culinary clichés; likewise those that are labeled "French," with a couple of exceptions noted below. A number of Arabic, Indian, Southeast Asian and otherwise exotic restaurants are to be found in the area around the airport and in Piraeus.

Apart from the occasional pizza-and-spaghetti parlor or hamburger joint, non-Greek eating is still quite unknown in the provinces.

We follow our "A-list" of international-style restaurants in Athens with a selection of other establishments that should be quite acceptable.

L'ABREUVOIR
Xenokratous 51, Kolonaki ☎ *72.29.106*
▥ *Map 2D5* ✿ ⒶⒺ ◉ ⒸⒹ ⒱ⓈⒶ
The menu may be a touch unadventurous, but L'Abreuvoir is one of the most highly regarded French restaurants in the Greek capital, with a commendable selection of wines.

BALTHAZAR
Tsoha 27, Kolonaki ☎ *64.41.215* ▥
Off map 2C6 ⒶⒺ ◉ ⒸⒹ ⒱ⓈⒶ
A renovated Kolonaki mansion houses this fashionable eatery with a famous bar, frequented by prominent personalities and beautiful people. An international menu spans the full range from Italian dishes to curries.

BOSCHETTO
Alsos Evangelismou (in the park)
☎ *72.10.893* ▥ *Map 2D5. Closed Sun.*
No culinary clichés will be found at this ultra-fashionable Italian restaurant. The food is superb, as well as being highly original. Some Greek specialties get the treatment, too.

BRASSERIE DES ARTS
N.J.V. Meridien Athens hotel, Syntagma Sq.
☎ *32.55.301* ▥ *Map 2D4.*
In an unspoken contest for the title of Best French Restaurant in Athens, this is l'Abreuvoir's chief rival, in the dazzling dining-room of one of the city's plushest hotels. For less formal meals, you could try **Le Bistrot Athenien**, in the same hotel.

CHANG'S HOUSE
Doiranis 15 (turn right at Syngrou 190)

☎ *95.95.191* ▥ *No lunch on Sun* ⒶⒺ ◉ ⒸⒹ ⒱ⓈⒶ
Regarded as the best representative of Chinese cuisine in Athens, along with the **China** restaurant *(Efroniou 72, Ilissia* ☎ *72.33.200),* which is under the same management. The 160-item menu boasts the attentions of "the best cooks from Taiwan and Hong Kong."

DA WALTER
Evzonon 7, Kolonaki ☎ *72.48.726* ▥
Map 2D5. Open 8pm–1am. Closed Sun.
Sumptuous Italian cuisine is the order of the day here: choose from specialties such as rigatoni with four cheeses or Piedmontese fillet with sauce madeira. Popular bar.

DER SPIEGEL
Frangoklisias 2, Paradisos Marousi (near the Pepsi factory) ☎ *68.46.393* ▥
Closed Mon.
A small international restaurant with a Teutonic flavor, Der Spiegel is owned and run by a German lady in impeccably formal yet pleasant style.

EDEN
Lysiou 12, Plaka ☎ *32.48.858* ▥
Map 1D3.
Opened a few years ago as the first vegetarian restaurant in Athens, this place was an instant success among tourists and locals alike. The menu contains a good selection of dishes, all superbly cooked. Moved to a new, larger location in 1993.

KUBLAI KHAN
Athenaeum Inter-Continental hotel, Syngrou

89 ☎*90.23.666* ▨▨▨ AE ⊙ ⊙ VISA
Dinner only. Closed Sun.
Delicious Mongolian dishes, cooked the traditional way with barbecue and fire-pot, make this an exciting place to eat. For less daring palates, the menu also lists some Chinese specialties.

MARE NOSTRUM
Kifissias 292, Neo Psyhiko ☎*67.22.891* ▨▨▨
The ultimate in Athenian culinary luxury is offered in this privé restaurant, serving only private groups of at least 15 persons. The menu is an ingenious *mélange* of French and Italian, with a number of *nouvelle cuisine* specialties. But lesser mortals are not totally excluded: they can dine, at a more down-to-earth cost, in the **Brasserie** that is located in the same building.

MICHIKO
Kydathineon 27, Plaka ☎*32.20.980* ▨▨
Map 1E3. Closed Sun ⬇ AE ▨▨ ⊙ VISA
Tempura, sukiyaki, sushi and *sashimi,* served in a lovely garden, provide a rare escape, in Plaka, from the *mousákka-* and-*dolmades* routine.

THE PLOUGHMAN
Iridanou 26, Ilissia (near the Holiday Inn)
☎*72.10.244* ▨▨ *Closed Sun* AE ⊙ ⊙ VISA
English food and ambience are on top of the Ploughman's bill of fare, complete with dartboard and lukewarm beer.

SYMPOSIUM
Erechthiou 46 ☎*92.25.321* ▨▨▨ *Map 1E3.*
Closed Sun AE ⊙ ⊙ VISA
Considered by many to be the best "international" restaurant in town. Good bar, view of the Acropolis.

NON-GREEK ALTERNATIVES

- **FRENCH** **Le Calvados** ▨▨▨ Alkmanos 5 (near the Hilton) ☎72.26.291. Off map **2D6**. Closed Sun.
- **INDIAN** **Curry Palace** ▨▨ Posidonos 38B, Kalamaki (near Elinikon airport) ☎98.38.889.
- **ITALIAN** **Dolce Vita** ▨▨ Dinokratous 26, Kolonaki ☎72.91.259. Map **2D5**. Closed Sun. • **Il Fungo** ▨▨ Posidonos 68, Paleo Faliro ☎98.16.765.
- **KOREAN–JAPANESE–CHINESE** **Golden Flower** ▨▨ to ▨▨ Nikis 30, Syntagma ☎32.30.113. Map **1D3**. • **Seoul** ▨▨ to ▨▨ Evritanias 8, Ambelo-kipi (near President Hotel) ☎69.24.669. Off map **2C6**.
- **MEXICAN** **Dos Hermanos** ▨▨ Kiriazi 24, Kifissia ☎80.87.906. Open Tues–Sun 7pm–1am. Closed Mon.
- **POLYNESIAN-JAPANESE** **Kona Kai** ▨▨▨ Ledra Marriott Hotel, Syngrou 115 ☎93.47.711. Closed Sun.
- **TEX-MEX** **Buffalo Bill's** ▨▨ Kyprou 13, Glyfada ☎89.43.128. Open Tues–Sat 7pm–1am; Sun from 2pm. Closed Mon.
- **VIETNAMESE** **Viet Hy** ▨▨ Posidonos 43, Kalamaki (near Elinikon airport) ☎93.80.142.

FOR A SNACK AND COFFEE
The *kafenío* is where a Greek goes to while away his excess hours over a thimbleful of coffee. You will rarely find anything to eat in a *kafenío,* and the good and genuine ones (practically none in the tourist center of Athens, but hundreds elsewhere) have a regular, all-male clientele who will gaze with unconcealed curiosity at any outsider who strays in.

Other facilities for a quick snack or coffee throng the Athenian streets under the names of café, salon de thé, *gyro* joint (see page 82), bistro, pizza parlor or *záharoplastío* (pâtisserie). And in case you wondered,

McDonald's has arrived at last. The flagship franchise of the hamburger giant opened on Syntagma Sq. *(Ermou 2)* in 1991 and has since become an Athenian fad.

The following are conveniently located to perform as what the Germans call a *treffpunkt:* a good place to meet someone, or just to keep in mind as a point of reference in a busy city.

- **Brazilian Coffeeshop**   Voukourestiou 1, off Syntagma Sq. 🖵 Map **2**D4. A stand-up coffee shop with good pastries; a perennial Athens favorite and meeting point of prominent people.
- **Caravan**   Voukourestiou 11 🖵 Map **2**D4. The very best in oriental pastries, made by a Greek of Lebanese origin. Additional branches exist in Kifissia, Halandri and elsewhere.
- **GB Corner**   Syntagma Sq. 🖵 Map **2**D4. Very "English" coffee shop in the Grande Bretagne hotel, with a separate entrance. Lunch fare.
- **Jimmy's Coffeeshop**   Valaoritou 7, Syntagma Sq. 🖵. Map **2**D4. A permanently crowded café and snack bar catering equally to students, businessmen and ministry personnel from the vicinity.
- **Orea Ellada**   Through passage at Pandrossou 36, Plaka 🖵 Map **1**D3. Pleasant café with lovely view of the Acropolis.
- **Profundis**   Hatzimihali 1, Plaka 🖵 Map **1**E3. Quaintly furnished tea parlor in the heart of Plaka.

HOTEL CAFÉS AND BISTROS
Ever popular among the café/bistros of major hotels are the **Byzantine Room** of the HILTON, **Café Vienna** in the ATHENAEUM INTER-CONTINENTAL and the **Zephyros** lounge of the LEDRA MARRIOTT.

Nightlife and entertainment

Athens after dark

Athens, as they say, lives by night. Few nations on earth are as adept as the Greeks at turning every occasion into a party. The rule is to do it in company: you go out with a bunch of friends, produce an astonishing amount of noise, and let the *kéfi* wrap its cocoon around your party until the rest of the world sinks into utter insignificance. Dinner starts around 9 or 10pm; things begin to get rolling after midnight, and sunrise is when early risers begin to take their leave.

Children of the upper-middle classes prefer Western forms and tunes, and there is a welter of rock, jazz and disco clubs and piano bars to cater to them in Kolonaki, Psyhiko, Kifissia, Glyfada and other classy neighborhoods. Ordinary Greeks share with most tourists a predilection for more "authentic" forms of Greek entertainment.

GREEK NIGHTS

The spirit of Zorba the Greek pervades **Plaka** at night. Plenty of tavernas, notably those located on Mnisikleous and at the edge of the Acropolis, offer song-and-dance programs, often inviting the active participation of patrons. Similar establishments, with varying degrees of glitz and sophistication, exist along **Leof. Syngrou**, in **Piraeus** and along the **Saronic coast**.

All of these places serve full meals along with *oúzo* and other alcohol, although the food is, as a rule, irritatingly expensive. Bashing dishes is no longer considered polite, but some establishments provide supplementary plates made of light plaster for patrons who wish to engage in this celebrated form of Greek merriment.

The categories of musical taverna, music hall and *bouzoúki* often blur. A **music hall** is, in general, a fabulously garish fun palace with a full nightly program that proceeds from bit singers, comedians and dance shows to the top stars of Greek pop singing. Dinner and *mezé* are served as part of the bill; reservations are essential, as is a fat wallet.

A club of the sort known in the vernacular as **skilládiko** ("doghouse") is a seedier version of the same: alcohol is consumed with abandon, the *artistes* sing of woe and despondence; later, they may join some of the guests at their table, or their bed.

A **bouzoúki** — from the name of a stringed instrument — is the generic title for a musical café of modest scale and few pretensions. Those that specialize in more sophisticated forms of music and attract students, leftists and the literati — the *kulturiárika* — are usually called a **buát** (as in the French *boîte*); the best of these are to be found in Exarhia, the central university district, and Mets.

GREEK MUSIC

A few words about Greek music: *laikó*, or Greek pop, is the sort of Greek song that you are most likely to encounter in tavernas and shops and taxis, with a singer of sugary voice accompanied by canned *bouzoúkia;* a less traditional, more Westernized version of it goes by the name of *élafro* ("light") *laikó*.

Both of these traditions have their roots in *rembétiko*, which some have called the Greek counterpart of the blues. *Rembétiko* was invented in the 1920s in the down-and-out clubs of Piraeus that were frequented by refugees from Asia Minor. Its bleakly pessimistic themes and expressive tunes became the badge of a subculture; banned by the military regime of 1967–74, it became immensely popular among students and intellectuals later in the 1970s.

Completely different from either pop or *rembétiko* is **demotikó,** the music of rural Greece, distinguished for its quicksilver rhythms and the dominant use of the *klarino,* a kin of the clarinet.

Popular **dances** include the *zeibékiko,* an intricate and expressive solo dance performed by men; the *tsiftetéli,* a sort of male belly dance; and the *kasápiko,* where a string of people holding hands synchronize their steps to a strongly rhythmical beat. All three have their roots in *rembétiko,* while the *sérviko,* a quick and lively dance, derives from the demotic tradition.

WHERE TO HEAR IT

All of the following establishments feature the different forms of Greek music in various measures. The popularity of any given house is, of course, subject to the vagaries of season and fashion. All of them serve full meals, unless otherwise noted, and invite dancing. Performances typically start around 10 or 11pm, but the seats will rarely fill up before midnight.

- **Athinaia**   Posidonos 63, Tzitzifies (near Piraeus) ☎94.28.777. This is one of Athens's top music halls, rivaled only by the **Neraida**, **Diogenes Palace** and **Nea Dilina**; it books some of the most talked-about singers of each season.
- **Diogenes Palace**   Syngrou 259 ☎94.24.267. Closed Mon. Popular music hall.
- **Frangosyriani**   Arahovis 57, Exarhia ☎36.00.693. Map **2**C4. Closed Thurs. A *buát* in the student district, featuring excellent *rembétiko.*
- **Harama**   Skopeftirio Kesarianis (below the Kesariani monastery, 8km/5 miles E of Athens) ☎76.64.869. Map **7**D2. Closed Tues. This delightful little *bouzoúki,* virtually unknown to tourists, is a good place to spend a jolly night with an informal group of Greek friends.
- **Kalokairinos**   Kekropos 10, Plaka ☎32.32.054. Map **1**E3. Attractive garden in Plaka featuring a program of folk dances, singers and a moderately risqué floor show, followed by guests taking to the floor in various stages of inebriation.

- **Maralinas** Vrassida 11 (near the Athens Hilton) ☎72.35.425. Off map 2D6. Greco-Arabic restaurant and night club with lots of belly dancing.
- **Nea Dilina** Akti Posidonos, Glyfada ☎89.41.300. Top-ranking music hall.
- **Neraida** Vassileos Georgiou 2, Kalamaki (near the airport) ☎98.12.004. Famous music hall.
- **Ravanastro** Dimitsanis 60, Ambelokipi ☎64.49.534. Off map 2B6. Small *buát* favored by the literati; features often unknown but brilliant singers, presenting original music as well as traditional *rembétiko* and *demotikó*. Wine and snacks served, but no full meals.
- **Rembetiki Istoria** Ippokratous 181, Exarhia ☎64.24.937. Map 2C5. Closed Mon, Tues, Wed. Popular *rembétiko* club in Exarhia.

BARS, PUBS AND BAR-RESTAURANTS

Western-style cocktail bars, very often featuring piano or guitar music, have been fashionable since the 1980s among the young urban professional classes and gilded youth of Athens. The best speckle the back streets of Kolonaki. What follows is a tiny selection of those currently considered "in." Those with a ➤ symbol offer full-scale dining as well.

- **Actuel** Kleomenous 44, Kolonaki ☎72.49.861. Map 2D5 ➤
- **Kouti** Adrianou 65, Thisio. Map 1D2. Nice little place near the entrance of the Agora.
- **Mamphis** Ventiri 5, Pangrati (behind the Hilton) ☎72.24.140. Map 2D6. Loud rock, young clientele.
- **Nick's** Spefsippou 26–28, Kolonaki ☎72.41.235. Map 2D5.
- **Ploughman** Iridanou 26, Ilissia ☎72.12.044. Off map 2D6 ➤ Best English pub in Athens. Restaurant closed Sun.
- **Radka** Haritos 30, Kolonaki ☎72.90.746. Map 2D5. Closed Sun ➤ Excellent food, interesting people.
- **Remezzo** Haritos 6, Kolonaki ☎72.28.950. Map 2D5. Closed Sun ➤ Intimate and very fashionable.
- **Rolls Music Restaurant** Anagnostopoulou 1, Kolonaki. Map 2D4 ➤

ROCK, DISCO, JAZZ CLUBS

Athens is probably the only major European city, apart from Tirana, where you could sweep the FM range and not catch a single twang of Western rock music. Still, there are some little enclaves in Kolonaki, Kifissia, etc., where Phil Collins or Dire Straits are — nearly — as familiar as Leftheris Pantazis.

AVANT GARDE
Lebesi 19, Makrigiani ☎92.42.737.
Canned rock and cocktails make a contrast from *oúzo* and *bouzoúki*. If they are your scene, this is the place to come.

BARBARELLA
Syngrou 253 ☎94.25.601 ➤
Disco music pounds out on three dance floors, where the Barbarellas of Athens strut their stuff.

9 + 9 (ENÉA SYN ENÉA)
Agras 5 (near the Stadium) ☎72.22.258. *Map 2E5.*
So sure of its leadership among Athenian discos that the name isn't even displayed. Closed in summer.

HALF NOTE
Fthiotidos 68, Ambelokipi ☎64.49.236. *Off map 2B6.*
This is the most popular jazz venue in

Athens, attracting both home-grown and foreign bands. It is now in a new location in Ambelokipi.

JAZZ BAR/RESTAURANT TSAKALOFF
Tsakaloff 10, Kolonaki ☎*36.05.889 (in*

summer, May–Oct: Kyprou 65, Glyfada ☎*89.40.050). Map 1C3.*
This is a small, intimate place with a lot of atmosphere, good live jazz, presided over by a charming hostess. Come for cocktails or a full meal.

GAY BARS

Fashions change, and much of Athens' gay scene still operates below the board, rather than above. However, the following were billed at the time of writing as some of the top gay hangouts in the homeland of Socrates and Plato.

*   **Aleko's Island**   Tsakaloff 42, Kolonaki. Map **2**D4.
*   **Alexander's**   Anagnostopoulou 44, Kolonaki. Map **2**D4.
*   **City Club**   Koryzi 4, Makrigiani (behind Syngrou 24). Map **1**F3.
*   **L.A. Bar Café**   Emmanuel Benaki 1 and Stadiou. Map **2**D4. Open Mon–Fri 9am–9pm.
*   **Spartacus Club**   Amerikis 2. Map **2**D4.

FLOOR-SHOWS AND STRIPTEASE

A number of establishments in the vicinity of **Syntagma** offer strip shows and associated pleasures. The following are considered to be reputable places. All open from 11pm to 3am and welcome charge and credit cards.

To find the less reputable places, it is sufficient to hang around Syntagma late at night and look aimless; someone is certain to approach with a proposal.

*   **Copacabana**   Kallirois 4 (across from the Temple of Olympian Zeus) ☎92.32.648. Map **1**E3.
*   **Maxim**   Othonos 6 (Syntagma Sq.) ☎32.34.831. Map **2**D4.
*   **Playboy**   Syngrou 113 ☎93.48.587. Off map **1**F2.

GAMBLING

The only legal casino in Athens is located in the **Grand Hotel Parnes** (☎*24.69.111/4),* at the top of the Mt. Parnitha funicular at an elevation of 1,100m (3,609 feet).

Performing arts and festivals

Exhaustive **listings** of concerts, lectures, art galleries, exhibitions, theater and cinema are to be found in the monthly *Athenian,* and in any of the program magazines that are on sale at kiosks.

MUSIC AND OPERA

The city of Maria Callas and Dimitri Mitropoulos was for many years a desert as far as classical music and opera were concerned. No longer: with the opening of the **Athens Concert Hall** (Palace of Music, *Megarón Mousikís Athenon,* or MMA) in 1991, Athens can boast one of the great arts centers of Europe. The opening of the dazzling marble Concert Hall *(Vassilissis Sofías and Kokkali* ☎ *72.82.000; off map* **2**D6), after nearly 30 years in construction, was a landmark event in the cultural life of the city. A ticket office is located in the Spiromilios Arcade *(Amerikis 3, off Syntagma Sq.* ☎ *72.25.511).*

For sophisticated presentations of traditional Greek (demotic) music, it is worth watching for performances of the **Domna Samiou** folk ensemble *(varying locations; check current listings).*

Greek **folk dancing** is presented at the open-air theater on Philopappus hill by the **Dora Stratou** company at 10.25pm every summer night, with additional performances at 8.15pm on Wednesday and Sunday (☎ *32.44.395).*

CINEMA

Foreign **movies** are as a rule shown in the original language with Greek subtitles. Several movie theaters in the central area change their programs daily for the benefit of a clientele consisting mainly of tourists. Most theaters functioning in summer are in the open air.

SOUND AND LIGHT SHOW

The **Acropolis Sound and Light Show** can be watched from the **Pnyx** in English from 9–9.45pm and in German or French from 10–10.45pm (☎ *92.26.210* ■). The words are so corny that it may be advisable to choose a language you don't know.

FESTIVALS AND SPECIAL EVENTS

The **Blessing of the Sea** is performed at Piraeus and other ports on January 6. A cross is immersed in the sea and retrieved by swimmers.

Carnival is celebrated throughout Greece with processions, costumes and dances during the eight days preceding Shrove Monday (February or March, usually later than in Catholic countries). Lively shows at Plaka.

St George's Day is commemorated on April 23 in many places with picturesque folk festivals involving dances, buffoonery, and blessing of cattle, notably at **Aharnes** outside Athens and at **Arahova** near Delphi.

Easter is by far the most important religious and popular feast for Greeks. The Greek Orthodox Easter does not usually coincide with the Western date, being set between one and four weeks later. On **Good Friday** bells toll and flags fly at half-mast. At night, Christ's funeral procession is carried through the main streets of every parish. Particularly impressive is the procession from the Metrópolis round Syntagma Sq. in Athens. After the **Saturday night mass**, the light of resurrection is passed from candle to candle, and taken home lit.

In Athens there is a moving spectacle from the hill of **Lykavitos**, when one church after another in the darkened city bursts into light to the ringing of bells. The fast is broken with *magirítsa* (thick soup with lamb's innards). **Easter Sunday** is celebrated with lamb roasted on the spit; rejoicing and dancing continue on **Easter Monday**.

The **Athens Festival** runs from June to mid-September, during which period the ancient Odeon of Herodes Atticus, on the s slope of the Acropolis, becomes a stage for ancient Greek drama performed in the original tongue, as well as operas, ballets and concerts performed by both Greek and foreign companies. The setting is impressive, and you don't have to be fluent in Classical Greek: just read your Sophocles beforehand and you'll be quite able to enjoy the drama. *(Information and tickets from the Athens Festival box office, Stadiou 4* ☎ *32.27.944, map 2 D4.)*

Plays ancient and modern are performed also at the open-air theater on Lykavitos hill.

Greek **folk dancing** is presented at the open-air theater on **Philopappus** hill by the Dora Stratou company at 10.25pm every summer night, with additional performances at 8.15pm on Wednesday and Sunday (☎ *32.44.395).*

The **Dormition of the Virgin** is celebrated on August 15, with important festivities in many locations around Greece, although festivities in Athens are unimpressive. A major pilgrimage takes place on the island of **Tinos**.

Shopping

What to buy, and where to buy it

Anything you might think of buying in Greece is obtainable in Athens, often more easily, less expensively and better than elsewhere in the country. Gold and silver jewelry, ceramics, antiques, *flokáti* rugs, leather, embroidery, quilts and furs are what most visitors find interesting.

Prices have gone up steeply in the 90s — scandalously, in the opinion of many Greeks — to keep up with EU single-market policies. The cost of many items now approaches Italian or German levels, not always with the corresponding levels of quality.

The habit of bargaining for prices, a relic of Greece's oriental past, is on the decline. In winter it is sometimes possible to obtain a 10- or 20-percent reduction through fast talk, charm and patience, but during the busy season few shopkeepers will bother to respond. One area where this rule does not apply is the Monastiraki flea market, where you will be pitied if you pay the first price quoted on an item.

SOUVENIRS AND HANDICRAFTS

Souvenir stores exist in great abundance in **Plaka** and **Monastiraki**, with **Adrianou**, **Pandrossou** and **Ifestou** streets forming the principal shopping axes. Before making any purchase, it may be worth visiting the **National Organization of Greek Handicrafts** (*Mitropoleos 9, map 1 D3*). This has a large, priced display of folk arts, and will provide a list of shops where purchases at these set prices can be made.

Of greatest interest is earthenware **pottery**, a field in which Athens has excelled since Archaic times. Traditional ceramics of excellent quality come from the islands of Sifnos and Skopelos; museum copies of Antique ware, as well as modern designs based on Greek themes, include some very creditable work.

Naive painting, executed on such things as shop signs, wooden chests, chairs and door frames, forms a highly original field of traditional craft. A merchant who stocks a good selection is **Sp. Aravantinos** at Nikodimou 29, Plaka (*map 1 E3*).

Flokáti rugs and *tagária* shoulder bags are produced by the Vlah villagers of central and NW Greece, using coarse sheep's wool, which is dyed a vivid color or decorated with appliqué fabrics. The trade in Athens is concentrated on Mitropoleos and Ermou, off the SW corner of Syntagma Sq. Most shops, such as **Karamichos-Mazarakis** (*Voulis 31–33, off Mitropoleos; map 1 D3*) will ship your purchase directly to your home.

Other traditional handicrafts have suffered from the rapid modernization of Greek society in recent decades. **Woodcarving** and **glassmaking** are now practically dead; **textiles** and **embroideries** have been reduced to a lamentable level of mass-produced kitsch.

ANTIQUES AND CURIOSITIES

Greek **rural handicrafts** dating from before the age of plastic and cement stand out by their quaint charm and traditional sophistication. The fact was discovered quite recently by educated Greeks and tourists alike, propelling prices of Greek antiques into the stratosphere.

The place to look for upmarket antiques is the area behind Kolonaki Sq., notably Haritos and Spefsipou streets. Some of the best-known dealers in this part of town are **Michalarias** *(on Irodotou; map 2 D5)* and **Zoumboulakis** *(antique gallery at Haritos 26, map 2 D5; modern art galleries at Kolonaki Sq. 20 and Kriezotou 7, both map 2 D4).* Other shops with a good reputation include **Martinos** *(on Pandrossou; map 1 D3)* and **Giannoukos** *(on Leof. Amalias; map 2 E4).* Each of these establishments will be able to assess any antiques you may have bought elsewhere.

A delightfully chaotic **flea market** operates along Ifestou, with its hub in the **Avisiniás** marketplace, in Monastiraki *(map 1 D2),* on Sunday morning and to a lesser extent throughout the week. Everything from second-hand clothes and spare parts to ancient phonographs and photographs is touted. The likelihood of finding a secret gem is small, but the rummaging and bargaining is nevertheless great fun.

Seekers of curiosities may discover interesting items in the shops dealing in **ecclesiastical paraphernalia**, located on Filotheis St. between the Metrópolis (cathedral) and the Archbishopric of Athens.

The **export of antiquities** from Greece is subject to draconian rules, and the penalties for attempting to smuggle an archeological object out of the country can involve prison. When buying genuine or apparent antiques, do not neglect to obtain an export certificate filled out by the shop. When in doubt, apply for written permission from the **Department of Antiquities** *(Polygnotou 13* ☎ *32.19.792; map 1 D3).*

JEWELRY

Gold jewelry forms a major category of interest because of the unique Greek designs, not because they have any claim to keen prices or superlative workmanship. The mother-houses of two worldwide jewelry chains, **Lalaounis** *(Panepistimiou 6, map 2 D4, and many branches in town)* and **Zolotas** *(Panepistimiou 10, map 2 D4, and branch at the airport),* are both located near Syntagma. Both carry a wide selection of museum reproductions, as do many lesser jewelers located in their immediate vicinity and in Plaka.

Silver filigree and turquoise jewelry, which is produced mainly in the town of Ioannina in Epiros, features Oriental rather than Classical motifs. The main concentrations of Ioannina silversmiths are along **Voukourestiou** *(map 2 D4)* and **Karageorgi Servias**, near Syntagma Sq. *(map 2 D4).*

FUR

The furs of Athens are very much in a class of their own, for no animal ever wore such coats. They are made of scraps and snippets left over from cutting, sent from all over the world to the town of Kastoria in Macedonia, where they are pieced together with a skill perfected over centuries. They are sold by the meter like any other textile, and eventually end up as mink coats, leopard jackets or beaver hats, although at much keener prices than the orthodox article.

A great variety of furriers can be found on **Mitropoleos St.** *(map 1 D3),* the heart of the fur trade in Athens. **Sistovaris** *(branches also at Ermou 4, map 2 D4, and Panepistimiou 9, map 2 D4)* is the leading establishment in Kastoria furs, sold by the meter or made up into every kind of clothing.

Fur prices have lately been depressed due to competition from Japanese synthetics and the scruples of Western zoophiles.

CLOTHING AND ACCESSORIES

Apart from souvenir shirts and whimsical beachwear, there is little reason to buy clothes in Greece. Neither price nor quality is particularly attractive, and fashions echo the West — at a considerable distance. The more elegant shops are to be found along **Stadiou** and in the area from **Syntagma** to **Kolonaki Sq.**, notably **Voukourestiou** and side streets. Less expensive clothes stores cluster together on **Ermou**, between **Syntagma** and **Monastiraki**.

Minion *(28 Oktovriou and Veranzerou, map 1 C3)* is the best **department store** in the city, with a comprehensive selection of both local and imported labels, a fine food store and a roof cafeteria.

Shopping malls of the sleek and modern sort are found in suburbs such as Glyfada, Kifissia, Maroussi or Psyhiko.

Leather goods, sold in abundance, are generally of above-average quality and reasonably priced. **Eleni** *(Kriezotou 14, off Syntagma, map 2 D4)* and **Skourletis** *(Ermou 28, map 1 D3)* are among the better shops.

BOOKS AND RECORDS

The most extensive selection of **foreign-language books** is to be found at **Eleftheroudakis** *(Nikis 4 ☎ 32.31.401, map 1 D3),* **Compendium** *(Nikis 28 ☎ 32.21.248, map 1 D3)* and also **Pentelides** *(Amerikis 11 ☎ 36.23.673, map 2 D4).* Bookstores in all luxury hotels, as well as **Reymondos** *(Voukourestiou 18, map 2 D4),* stock a variety of periodicals, books on Greece and current paperbacks.

The **Turtle Bookshop** *(Kolokotroni and Levidou, in Kifissia, map 1 A5)* has a charming collection of children's books.

The best place to look for **antique and out-of-print books** is the **flea market** along Ifestou. For specialized help, try **Pharos/Athens** *(P.O.B. 1826 ☎ 72.42.589).*

Souvenir **cassettes** of Greek music are thick on the ground in Plaka. A more extensive and sober collection can be found at **Filodisk** *(Emmanuel Benaki, off Panepistimiou, map 1 C3)* or at the commendable **Eleftheroudakis Music Center** *(Tower of Athens ☎ 77.96.589).*

Recreation

Sports and activities

GOLF

The only 18-hole course in mainland Greece is in **Glyfada** *(near the Elinikon airport* ☎ *89.46.820, par 72)*. There is also a 9-hole course in **Varibobi** *(21km/13 miles N of Athens center)*.

HORSEBACK RIDING

The **Hellenic Riding Club** has a riding range in **Maroussi** *(Paradissou 18* ☎ *68.12.506)*. Additional riding clubs exist in **Agia Paraskevi** *(* ☎ *66.11.088)*, **Ekali** *(* ☎ *81.35.576)* and **Varibobi** *(Tatoi Riding Club* ☎ *80.79.643; Varibobi Riding Club* ☎ *80.19.912)*.

SWIMMING AND WATER SPORTS

Public beaches exist all along the SW and E coasts of Attica. The sea near Piraeus is polluted. It may at times get somewhat murky as far as Glyfada and Voula, but the periodic alarms about pollution in the Saronic Gulf at large seem vastly exaggerated. (See pages 114–16).

Information about scuba diving, water skiing, wind surfing, sailing and other water sports can be obtained from the respective sport federations; these may be contacted through the **GNTO**.

WALKS AND MOUNTAIN SPORTS

Athens has fewer parks than any European city of comparable size, and the absence of other natural promenades (riverbank, harbor walk) is at times acutely felt. The **National Garden** *(map 2 E4)* and the **Pedion Areos** *(map 2 B4)* are the only options in town for a (relatively) quiet stroll amid greenery. The best place for a nature walk near Athens is **Mt. Parnitha**, which offers a 14km (9-mile) loop around its summit through woods and bush.

The **Hellenic Alpine Club** *(Karageorgi Servias 7* ☎ *32.34.555, map 1 D3)* maintains mountain refuges at a variety of places around Greece, including a 100-bed lodge at **Bafi** (alt. 1,150m/3,773 feet) on Mt. Parnitha.

Ski facilities exist on **Mt. Parnassus**, at **Helmos** (near Kalavryta, the Peloponnese), **Mt. Menalon** (near Tripoli, Peloponnese) and **Vermion** (near Veria, Macedonia); Parnassus is considered the best. The ski season lasts usually through January and February. For further information including snow conditions, contact the **Hellenic Skiing Federation** *(Agiou Konstantinou 34* ☎ *52.40.057)*.

Ideas for children

The heat and noise of Athens, it must be admitted, provide a less-than-ideal environment for children. If mutiny is threatened after an over-dose of monuments and museums, the chances are you'll want to head directly for the seaside (see the opposite page for the nearest beaches). If something less drastic than escape will suffice, here are some of the best ideas in town.

MUSEUMS
Among all the museums of Athens, three are likely to be of particular interest to most older children:

- **Goulandris Museum of Natural History** Levidou 13, Kifissia ☎80.80.254. Open Sat–Thurs 9am–2.30pm. Closed Fri; mid-July to mid-Aug. A fascinating collection of nature's curiosities.
- **Piraeus Maritime Museum** Akti Themistokleous, near Zea Marina ☎45.16.822. Open Tues–Sat 8.30am–1pm. Closed Sun, Mon. Model ships, ancient and modern, illustrate Athens' maritime history.
- **War Museum** Vassilissis Sofias and Rizari ☎72.90.543, map **2D5**. Open Tues–Sun 9am–2pm. Closed Mon. The antique and modern airplanes parked in the courtyard are guaranteed to fascinate junior aviators.

AQUARIUM
The **Aquarium** in the **Agios Kosmas sport complex** *(on the coast near the airport, open daily 10am–3pm ☎89.45.640)* has all sorts of exotic fish and seashells, as well as a crocodile.

THE GREAT OUTDOORS
The **National Garden** contains an excellent playground, a duck pond, a rather forlorn zoo, a botanical museum (alas, almost always shut), and a children's library in an ivy-covered fairytale cottage, where children between the ages of 5 and 14 can sit and read, draw or play.

The two-minute glide by **funicular** up the Lykavitos hill *(map 2 C5)* has high child-diversion potential for its novelty value and for the panoramic views of the city on the way up.

In the opposite direction from sea-level, the **Koutouki cave** at Peania *(16km/10 miles E)* is a magical place to take children, full of stalactites and stalagmites.

The outskirts of Athens

Getting out of the city

Less than an hour from downtown Athens and accessible by urban public transport are a second city (**Piraeus**), a lively seacoast (**Piraeus** and the **coastal suburbs**), three grand mountains (**Imitos**, **Pendeli** and **Parnitha**) and two important medieval monasteries (**Daphni** and **Kesariani**). There are too, it has to be said, some badly polluted wastelands (**Elefsina**, for one).

COASTAL SUBURBS ⌇

6km (4 miles) to 23km (14 miles) s of Athens. **Bus** *to Paleo Faliro, Kalamaki, Agios Kosmas, Elinikon from Syntagma Sq. (map 2D4); to Glyfada, Voula, Kavouri, Vouliagmeni, Varkiza from Leof. Olgas (map 2E4).*

The Saronic coast from Piraeus to the headland of Vouliagmeni is densely built with summer apartments, hotels, nightclubs, yacht marinas and beach and sports facilities. On summer weekends the area tends to get extremely crowded. The continuous din of the multilane highway that runs close to the shore and the noise of airplane traffic from the Elinikon Airport are disturbing factors.

The beaches at **Faliro** and **Glyfada** *(8km/5miles and 18km/11 miles respectively)* cannot be recommended, on account of water pollution, although they remain as popular as ever with Athenians. Both the setting and the sea get considerably better at **Voula** *(22km/14 miles),* while **Vouliagmeni** *(24km/15 miles)* is a highly attractive town with luxuriant park-like vegetation, elegant hotels and excellent beaches. In addition, Vouliagmeni has a small sulfurous lake with dramatically overhanging rocks, where the last spurs of **Mt. Imitos** come down to the sea; the baths are said to cure various ailments.

The best **public beaches** in the area are those operated by the GNTO, which exist at **Voula 1** *(☎89.53.248)* and **2** *(☎89.59.569),* **Vouliagmeni** *(☎89.60.906)* and **Varkiza** *(☎89.72.102).* All are well managed and have cabins, cafeterias, tennis courts and other sports facilities.

⌇ In Vouliagmeni: **Astir Palace** (L) *(☎89.60.211 ▥▢ to ▥▥ 570 rms in three separate compounds ⌇ ⌇ ⌇ ⌇ ▩ ▢)* is not only the most luxurious hotel in the area but possibly the best beach hotel in all of Greece. The three self-contained units lie in a lush park by the edge of the sea.

Of the half-dozen class-A hotels in the area, **Armonia** *(☎89.60.105 ▥▢ 67 rms ⌇ ▩ ⌇ ⌇ ▩ ▢)* is the largest and best-established.

Costi (A) (☎ *89.61.007* ▥ *18 rms* ▩ ✆ ▤), a small, attractive pension, **Greek Coast** (A) (☎ *89.60.401* ▥ *55 rms* ▭ ▩ ✆ ▤) and **Margi House** (A) (☎ *89.62.061* ▥ *to* ▥ *105 rms* ▭ ▩ ✆ ▤) also deserve a mention.

In Glyfada, Agios Kosmas, Elinikon and Kalamaki: a multitude of hotels in all categories exist along the coast to either side of the airport.

Of all these resorts, Glyfada has the best beach and, unsurprisingly, the better concentration of restaurants, bars, shops and nightlife.

Prices in coastal resorts tend to be considerably lower than in comparable hotels in central Athens. What follows is a selection of hotels to suit every budget.

Astir Hotel (L) (*Posidonos 58, Glyfada* ☎ *89.44.273* ▥ *128 rms* ▭ ▩ ✆ ✍ ⋔ ▤ ▢). Luxuriously appointed bungalows, right on the beach.

Emmantina (A) (*Posidonos 33, Glyfada* ☎ *89.80.683* ▥ *80 rms* ▭ ▩ ✆ ⋔ ▤ ▢).

Golden Sun (B) (*Metaxa 72, Glyfada* ☎ *89.81.353* ☒ *89.81.090* ▥ *to* ▥ *60 rms* ▭ ✆ ▤).

Beau Rivage (C) (*Posidonos 87, Glyfada* ☎ *89.42.307* ▥ *82 rms* ▭ ✆ ▤).

▭ Athenians like going out to dine on the coast, which lives up to its popularity with a string of fine restaurants. Notable are various attractively located and expensive fish restaurants at **Vouliagmeni** and a clutch of (for Greece) unusual cuisines (Arabic, Indian, Vietnamese, Korean) represented in **Glyfada/Kalamaki**.

ITHAKI
Apollonos 28, Vouliagmeni ☎ *89.63.747* ▥
In a lovely garden overlooking the sea, Ithaki serves excellent seafood, with piano accompaniment.

MOORING'S
Vouliagmeni Marina ☎ *89.61.113* ▥
One of the classiest restaurants in and around the capital, popular with yachtsmen and Sunday diners alike.

NIRYIDES
Kavouri port ☎ *89.61.560* ▥
Traditional cuisine on a delightful terrace facing pine groves and the sea.

SINGA
Litous 1, Vouliagmeni ☎ *89.60.676* ▥
The only Melanesian restaurant in Greece does a good Sunday buffet lunch.

DAPHNI MONASTERY ⛰ ☆
Located on Athens–Corinth highway 11km (7 miles) w of Athens ☎ *58.11.558. Map 7D1. 20mins by **bus** 026 from Syntagma Sq. (map 2D4)* ▨ *Open Tues–Fri 8am–7pm; Sat–Mon 8.30am–3pm.*

The monastery at Daphni is considered to be the most important Byzantine monument in the vicinity of Athens, on account of its brilliant but

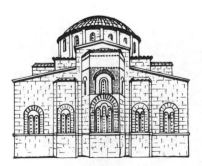

partially preserved **mosaics** of c.1100. A popular **wine festival** is held at the monastery every day from early July through late August.

The monastery occupies the site where ancient Athenians believed that the nymph Daphne, fleeing the unwelcome attentions of the god Apollo, had metamorphosed herself into a laurel tree *(daphne)*. A sanctuary of Apollo with a sacred laurel grove occupied the site until its destruction by the Goths in 395. An early monastery emerged before the 6thC, but the current edifice dates from 1080.

The Cistercian order occupied the monastery in the Frankish epoch, and several Dukes of Athens including Othon de la Roche and Walter de Brienne are buried here. Reverting to the possession of Orthodox monks under the rule of the Turks, it was abandoned at the time of the war of independence.

Neither the site nor, strictly speaking, the architecture of the monastery is very attractive. However, its Byzantine mosaics, in a sparse, severe style, are the best in Greece and among the most important in the world after those of Ravenna and Istanbul.

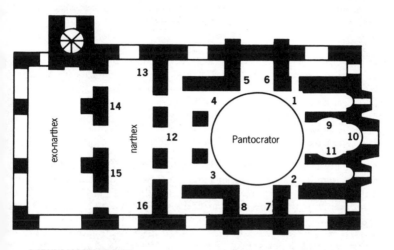

DAPHNI MOSAICS: KEY
1 Annunciation **2** Nativity **3** Baptism **4** Transfiguration **5** Entry into Jerusalem **6** Crucifixion **7** Resurrection **8** Thomas **9** Michael **10** Virgin with Child **11** Gabriel **12** Dormition of the Virgin **13** Last Supper **14** Judas' Betrayal **15** Prayer of Joachim and Anna **16** Presentation of the Virgin

The thematic arrangement of the mosaics follows standard late Byzantine practice, and reflects the heavenly hierarchies. Christ Pantocrator (Almighty) occupies the central dome surrounded by Old Testament prophets (elsewhere, these would be the Apostles); the gold background signifies Heaven. On the dome of the main apsis is the Theotokos (Mother of God) rising above the archangels. The area under the dome is reserved for mosaics illustrating the principal church festivals; in corners and on lesser surfaces are the saints and martyrs.

The narthex (the inner vestibule before the main hall) has worldlier scenes from the New Testament; over the main gate stands the theme to which the church is dedicated, which here is the Dormition of the Virgin. Depictions of sin and hell are usually found in the exo-narthex (the outer vestibule at the entrance to the church — here scrubbed clear of mosaics).

ELEUSIS (Elefsina) ⚏

*20km (13 miles) w of Athens. Map 4H7. Population 20,000. **Bus** from Eleftherias Sq. (map 1C2). **Archeological area** signposted from the highway. Open Tues–Sun 8.30am–5pm. Closed Mon* ⚏

The town of Elefsina is an industrial wasteland with a small archeological area. It will principally interest the determined scholar, or the rare romantic who is familiar with the pomp and beauty of the ancient Eleusinian Mysteries.

From the earliest (possibly pre-Greek) times, Eleusis was a sanctuary of the cult of Demeter and Kore, whose rites became one of the most important religious celebrations of Antiquity. Unlike most ancient rites, the worship of Demeter was an *esoteric* cult: that is, one in which only those initiated in its mysteries could take part. The nature of these mysteries remains unknown to the present day.

> ❖ Demeter, the goddess of agriculture, had a daughter called Persephone or Kore (Girl), who was abducted by Hades while picking flowers in a field. The goddess wandered around the world in despair, but was taken in by the kindly king of Eleusis, and here she taught mankind how to sow and reap the earth. By special dispensation from Zeus, Persephone was allowed to return to the earth for half of the year (during the time of growth and fertility), but went back to the lord of the underworld for the rest of the time.

The Mysteries were celebrated each year in March and October. For the Greater Eleusinia in October a great multitude of the initiates *(mystae)* arrived in Athens from around Greece. On the sixth day a procession, wearing myrtle branches and carrying torches and farm implements, set out for Eleusis. Here the participants stripped off their clothes and took a ritual bath in the sea. On the tenth day they were allowed into the *Telesterion,* the inner sanctum of the goddess, where the sacred cult objects were revealed to them, whose nature was a secret to be kept under pain of death.

It was at the communal bathing at Eleusis that Praxiteles, the greatest sculptor of the 4thC BC, was said to have first seen Phyrne, a priestess of Aphrodite (in other words, a temple prostitute), who inspired his *Bathing Aphrodite (the Aphrodite of Cnidus).*

The Eleusinian mysteries remained popular throughout the centuries of Roman rule. The emperors Hadrian, Marcus Aurelius and Julian were initiated, as was Cicero. A number of aspects of the rites (baptism by water, death and rebirth of a divinity, revelation of sacraments) appear to have been widely influential at around the time of the foundation of Christianity.

The colossal cult statue of Demeter was still revered at the start of the 19thC by superstitious peasants, who pasted it with cow dung to ensure a fertile harvest. It was then acquired by an English adventurer named E.D. Clarke, who planned to remove it to Cambridge, but the statue was lost with everyone else on board when the ship that was carrying it sank off the English shore.

In the archeological area one can see sad, broken bits of the **Teleste-rion** and associated buildings. The **museum** contains a variety of interesting items, including a magnificent amphora (narrow-rimmed urn) from the 7thC BC, illustrating the *Blinding of Polyphemus* in a grandly stylized manner.

FALIRO   See COASTAL SUBURBS, page 101.

GLYFADA   See COASTAL SUBURBS, page 101.

IMITOS (Hymettus)   See KESARIANI, below.

KESARIANI MONASTERY ▲ ☆
*8km (5 miles) E of Athens. Map 7D2. **Trolley #2** from Syntagma Sq. (map **2D4**) to Kesariani district, then 40min walk: easier by **taxi*** ▨ *Open Tues–Sun 8.30am–3pm. Closed Mon.*

The late Byzantine monastery of Kesariani is an intensely charming and peaceful place with a fine, distant view of the Acropolis. Although it has long been abandoned by the monks, the site retains an intimate and monastic atmosphere.

The origins of the monastery are unknown, although the main buildings date from the 11th–12thC. The name is also obscure: one explanation refers to Hadrian, the Caesar, who built an aqueduct here, another to Kesara, a daughter of the king of Eleusis, a third to a holy icon brought from Caesarea in Cappadocia (Turkey).

In 1456 the abbot of Kesariani was chosen to present the keys of Athens to Mehmed the Conqueror, no doubt reflecting the monks' predilection toward the Turks as against their Latin masters, typical of the Orthodox monastic establishment of the period. The Turks held the monastery in high regard and exempted it from taxes. In the 16th–17thC it was well known for its olive press, wine, and apiaries producing the famous Hymettian honey.

The main church, dedicated to the Presentation of Mary, is richly decorated with **frescoes** of the mid-16thC. The frescoes of the narthex are dated 1682, while the poorly preserved ones in the small side chapel go back to the 14thC. Other buildings include the refectory, living quarters (in restoration) and a Roman-type **bathhouse**, unique among Greek monasteries.

Numerous fragments, including an Ionic column near the church entrance and a ram's head fountain outside, seem to have belonged to a temple of Aphrodite known to have existed at this site in ancient times.

A road continues from the monastery to the summit of **Mt. Imitos** (Hymettus of Antiquity, 1,027m/3,369 feet), passing by the smaller Byzantine monastery of **Asteriou** (known for its frescoes). The summit is a military exclusion zone.

Hymettus was known in Antiquity for its marble and its honey, which formed a major export product of early Athens. A statue of Zeus once stood on the peak where a radar installation exists now.

KIFISSIA

*16km (10 miles) N of Athens. Map 7C2. Population 55,000. Altitude 270m (886ft). 35mins by **urban rail** from Athens.*

The most elegant of several garden suburbs located on high ground NE of Athens, with a number of sumptuous 19thC villas in Italianate style, Kifissia is home to several institutions of the Anglo-American expatriate community. Its well-endowed shops supply quality Western brands to the well-heeled and polished young people who decorate the area. The lush greenery is in welcome contrast to the parched look of most Athenian vegetation.

The **Kefalari** neighborhood at the foot of Mt. Pendeli (a 15-minute walk E from the train station) has the main concentration of soigné residences and fine resort hotels. Some of the best villas are to be found along **Tatoi St**.

Also notable are the homes of 19thC oligarchs Trikoupis *(Benaki 13)*, Deligiannis *(Levidou 19)*, Giorganda-Kolokotronis *(Kolokotroni 7)* and Pesmazoglou *(Pesmazoglou 25)*.

If time allows, visit the **Goulandris Museum of Natural History** *(Levidou 13 ☎ 80.80.254, open Sat–Thurs 9am–2.30pm, closed Fri and mid-July to mid-Aug)*, which houses the private collection of a loving and enthusiastic amateur: plants, insects, stuffed animals, fossils and rocks.

☞   **Pentelikon** (L) *(Deligianni 66, Kefalari ☎ 80.12.837 ▨ 44 rms ⇌)* occupies a magnificent old mansion, recently restored, in a sumptuous garden. One of the finest hotels of the Athens region. Open June to September.

Grand Chalet (A) *(Kokkinara 38 ☎ 80.84.837 ▨ 19 rms ⇌)* perpetuates the memories and traditions of the *belle époque* of the turn of the century. Open year round.

The summit of **Mt. Pendeli** (◀€) — Mt. Pentelicon of Antiquity — can be reached via the village of Nea Pendeli *(bus from behind the National Archeological Museum; 1hr walk, or taxi from Kifissia)*. At the end of the road is the **Moni Pendeli**, the richest and one of the largest of the monasteries currently functioning in Greece.

Signs mark the way to the **Rhododaphne Palace** (★), a sumptuous all-marble neo-Gothic villa that once belonged to the Duchesse de Plaisance (see page 68), and where she is buried. The palace was restored in later times as a royal residence and is now occasionally used for concerts.

Several paths lead farther up to ancient and modern **marble quarries**, eventually reaching a peak (1,000m/3,281 feet; the main summit is a restricted military zone) that offers an extraordinary view extending from Mt. Dirfis on Euboea to a large number of islands in the E and SE.

❖   Pentelic marble was the chief material of Attic architecture and sculpture in the Classical age and constituted an important export product of ancient Athens. Its yellowish hue is due to the presence of iron, which slowly oxidizes when it comes in contact with air. The bluish Hymettian and the translucent white Parian marbles can easily be distinguished.

THE MESOGIA

10–20km (6–12 miles) E *of Athens; access by Mesogion Avenue.* **Bus** *to Spata–Loutsa and Peania–Koropi–Markopoulo from Thision subway station (map 1D2).*

The gently sloping land behind Mt. Imitos is known as the *Mesogia* (Inland), an agricultural district of olive groves and vineyards producing the popular *retsina* wine, with the flourishing market towns of Peania, Spata, Koropi and Markopoulo forming its nodal points. Here in Antiquity the Athenian aristocracy had its rural base. The native inhabitants today are said to be of Albanian origin, although urban settlers have eroded any lingering sense of ethnic particularity.

Numerous historic churches in the area deserve to be visited on account of the vigorous frescoes of the 18thC artist Georgios Markos of Argos, the single most noteworthy painter of the Post-Byzantine era. Of greatest interest is the church of **Agia Paraskevi** in **Markopoulo** *(near main square)*, full of darkened frescoes of great force. **Koropi** has several tiny Byzantine chapels decorated by Markos.

The pleasantly wooded town of **Liopesi**, now renamed Peania after its Classical predecessor, was the birthplace of the great orator Demosthenes (c.384–322BC). The **Kanakis Taverna** *(▥ with garden)* is a well-known haunt of Athenian society. 5km (2½ miles) up from the town, the **Koutouki Cave** *(▨ open daily 9.30am–5.30pm)* is small but nevertheless quite impressive, with well-lit stalactites and stalagmites (see also IDEAS FOR CHILDREN, page 100).

MOUNT PARNITHA ◁€ ☆

35km (22 miles) N *of Athens (to the hotel). Map 7C2.* **Bus** *714 (to Agia Triada) and 736 (to the teleferique) from corner of Aharnon and Sourmeli (map 1B3).*

A most spectacular view covering all of Greater Athens, most of Attica, Euboea, the Saronic Gulf and some of the Cyclades opens up at 1,100m (3,609 feet), in front of the **Grand Hotel Parnes** (A).

The hotel *(☎ 24.69.111/15 ▥ ⇌ ≋)*, which no longer maintains the high standards of its past, contains the only gambling casino in the Athens area (see NIGHTLIFE, page 93) and is served by a **teleferique** *(8am–3am daily except Wed).*

A road continues from Agia Triada *(3km/2 miles before hotel)* to the **refuge** of the Greek Alpine Club and on to the summit (1,413m/4,636 feet) of **Karambola**.

PENDELI   See KIFISSIA.

PIRAEUS (Pireas)

8km (5 miles) SW *of Athens. Map 4H7. 20mins by* **urban rail** *from Athens. Population 200,000* **i** *at Zea Marina* ☎41.35.716 or 41.35.730.

The port of Athens, although in practice fully merged with the city, is always thought of as a separate town; it elects a separate mayor and fields its own soccer team (Olympiakos). Each of its three natural harbors is the focus of an urban area of very distinct character.

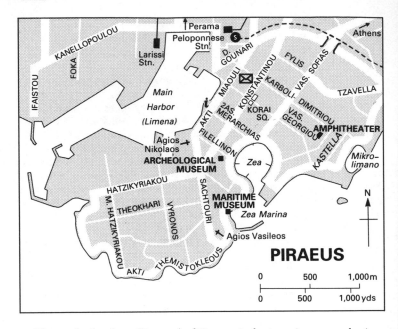

The **main harbor** *(Limena)* of Piraeus is the town's core and raison d'être. From here passenger boats depart to more than 60 islands and a dozen countries; cargo ships representing the third-largest merchant fleet in the world (second-largest, if the various flags of convenience used by Greek shipping magnates are counted in) unload their wares.

The embankment is full of a shabby and aggressive worldliness, with endless travel and shipping agencies, spend-your-last-penny-here shops, and, on some of the more discreet side streets, many bars and hotels of dubious flavor.

The **Zea harbor** (until recently called **Pashalimani**) accommodates the boats of Athens' yachted classes and is the hydrofoil terminal for the Saronic Islands, where the same classes own summer property. It is surrounded by a wall of comfortable apartment blocks, and the neighborhood possesses a great many shops specializing in imported household goods.

Mikrolimano (✪), which is popularly known by its traditional name of **Turkolimano**, and the steep hill district of **Kastella** that rises behind it, display a surprisingly cheerful small-town ambience. The harbor is full of bright fishing boats and small craft, and bristles with some two-dozen tavernas that manage to squeeze in a prodigious number of tables at the water's edge.

Many years ago, Turkolimano was where Athenians came to enjoy simple fisherman's fare. Now armies of uniformed waiters accost any passer-by with invitations in six languages, the fish is more likely to arrive by refrigerated truck than fisherman's dinghy, and the bill is far from small. But under the limb-loosening southern sky and sweet Aegean breeze, few people seem to mind all this, and Mikrolimano remains a perfectly enjoyable place for a good meal and a relaxing stroll.

Before 493BC, the Athenians simply parked their ships on the beach at Phaleron (Faliro). It was Themistocles who decided to build a fortified harbor at Piraeus to underpin the new policy of naval expansion. Pericles employed Hippodamus of Miletus to create here the second city in the ancient world to be laid out in a regular grid pattern (the first was the architect's own Miletus). By 431 the Long Walls, two parallel lines of fortification securing the Athens–Piraeus road, were completed.

Piraeus was sacked by Sulla in 86BC, and never fully recovered after this. It lay abandoned through the medieval and Turkish centuries, when the place was known as *Porto Leone* after the statue of a derelict lion lying among the rubbish. It was resettled by islanders in the 19thC, but received its real impetus for growth only with the arrival of Anatolian refugees after 1922.

The **Archeological Museum** *(Harilaou Trikoupi 31 ☎45.21.698, open standard hours)* merits a visit on account of the famous **Piraeus Kouros**, a splendid bronze statue of c.520BC discovered during sewer works in 1959.

☞ Few hotels in the harbor area are recommended for bona fide purposes. But several good B- and C-class hotels exist on the streets joining the Main Harbor to Zea, others on Kastella hill. Two examples follow:

Cavo d'Oro (B) *(Vass. Pavlou 19, Kastella ☎41.13.742 ▥ 74 rms),* commands an excellent view of the sea and Mikrolimano. **Park** (B) *(Kolokotroni 103 ☎45.24.611 ▥ 80 rms)* is a large, air-conditioned hotel three blocks from the ferry docks.

The nearest luxury hotel to Piraeus is the **Athens Chandris** *(Syngrou 385, Paleo Faliro ☎94.14.824 ▥).*

≡ It would be equally pointless to list all the fish tavernas at Mikrolimano or to single out any one of them by name. More tavernas of the same type exist along Akti Themistokleous, immediately s of Zea Marina, and on the skirts of Kastella hill, between Zea and Mikrolimano.

Altogether in a class of its own is **Vasilenas** *(Etolikou 72 ☎46.12.457 ▥).* This temple of epicurean delights counts magnates, monarchs and movie stars among its clients. Dinners consist of 16 to 24 courses served under the personal attention of the host, George Vasilenas.

The seaside town of **Perama**, about 6km (4 miles) w of Piraeus, has an attractive harbor promenade with a line-up of fish tavernas that many Athenians consider superior to those of Mikrolimano.

VOULIAGMENI   See COASTAL SUBURBS, page 101–2.

The Classical sites

Excursions

The Classical sites

Introduction

The best thing about Athens, say the Athenians, is the leaving of it. Within less than a day's journey of the capital are several magnificent sites of Classical archeology (Delphi, Corinth, Mycenae, Epidaurus, Olympia, Bassae), medieval walled towns, castles, monasteries and ghost cities (Osios Loukas, Monemvasia, Geraki, Mistra, Mani), delightful seacoast towns (Nafplio, Gythio, Methoni, Koroni, Pylos) and islands (Aegina, Hydra, Poros, Spetses, Euboea).

The landscape is some of the most dramatic in all of Europe. The pace of the villages and country towns is far removed from the Athenian frenzy, and the Greeks — all small-town people at heart — seem more at ease with themselves and with strangers than they are in the big city.

We start with four suggested itineraries: three day trips (to **Attica**, the **Saronic Gulf islands** and **Delphi**) and one longer excursion (to the **Peloponnese**). Starting on page 122, there are descriptions, in alphabetical order, of the sights and localities mentioned in these itineraries.

Excursion 1: Attica

For the Athenians, Attica equals beaches. Good beaches exist virtually everywhere along the E and SW coasts of the peninsula, and numerous sea resorts and summer colonies have sprung up to accommodate the summer crowds (see also COASTAL SUBURBS, pages 101–2). The region offers one of the most dramatically situated ancient temples of Greece, at **Sounion**, as well as the historic battlefield of **Marathon** and several Classical sights of lesser importance.

A tour of Attica can easily be completed in one day provided you travel by car and put aside a limited time for lunch and a quick swim. It may even be possible to throw in a side trip to the peak of **Mt. Parnitha**, covered under OUTSKIRTS OF ATHENS (page 107). A typical itinerary might then look like this:

Morning panorama at **Mt. Parnitha**, followed by side trip to either **Amphiaraeum** or **Ramnous**. The **Marathon** tumuli for those especially interested in antiquities. Lunch at **Nea Makri** or **Rafina**. **Brauron**. Beach at **Porto Rafti** or **Kaki Thalassa**; or side trip to **Koutouki Cave** (✿). Evening sun at **Sounion**. Back via the **"Apollo Coast."**

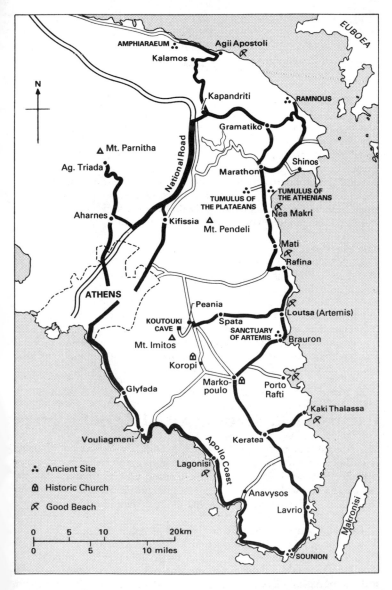

An alternative to this itinerary would be to combine the tour with a visit to the scenically impressive southern half of the island of EUBOEA, in which case you would be best advised to allow two days, perhaps staying the night in the pleasant harbor town of **Karystos**. It is possible to drive onto the island by the bridge at **Halkida** and return by ferry from Karystos, or vice versa.

Length of proposed itinerary: c.230km (144 miles), excluding Mt. Parnitha, the Koutouki Cave and Euboea. Note that, particularly in the eastern half of the peninsula, there are a great many local roads that do not appear on many maps and are very poorly signposted; so count on getting lost a few times if you are driving your own car.

The south coast

The s coast of Attica, which tourist brochures have for no apparent reason christened the **Apollo Coast**, has the more striking landscape: mountains drop quite steeply to the shore, becoming wilder toward the headland of SOUNION. The land is very arid, such that few villages existed here until recent times. The settlements that now dot the shore beyond the suburban limits of Athens are quite modest affairs, consisting of a few hotels and clusters of summer housing. A great number of small but excellent beaches are found along the way and remain surprisingly unexploited even at the height of summer.

The east coast

The E coast of Attica is flatter, more fertile and more densely populated. The towns, although more substantial than on the s coast, are all of recent growth and lack any sense of traditional charm. The stretch of the shore between BRAURON (Vravrona) and MARATHON in particular, where the best beaches are, has begun to grow into one unbroken resort conglomerate displaying an increasingly suburban character.

The landscape farther N becomes sharply mountainous, and here it is still possible to find some unspoiled corners of nature, notably near the minor historic sites of AMPHIARAEUM and RAMNOUS.

Excursion 2: Saronic-Argolid Gulf islands

The five islands of the Saronic-Argolid Gulf are near enough to be regarded as part of the Athens metropolitan region. Fast and frequent hydrofoil services from Piraeus reduce travel time to **Spetses**, the farthest island, to one hour 20 minutes. Many Athenians own or rent summer residences on the islands, and some even commute daily to work in the city.

Poros, **Hydra** and **Spetses** in particular retain the delightful traditional atmosphere of the Aegean islands, so for visitors who do not have time to make a full sea trip they provide an excellent opportunity to enjoy their Greek islands at close range. **Aegina** offers the impressive ancient **temple of Aphaia** as well as good beaches and a medieval ghost town. **Salamis** is interesting mainly for historical reasons.

Agencies in Athens offer day tours combining several islands, usually Aegina, Poros and Hydra. A typical tour will have enough time for the temple and beach at Aegina, a harborside lunch at Poros and an afternoon stroll at Hydra. This, of course, merely scratches the surface, but it may still provide an ideal way to "sample" the archipelago with a view to

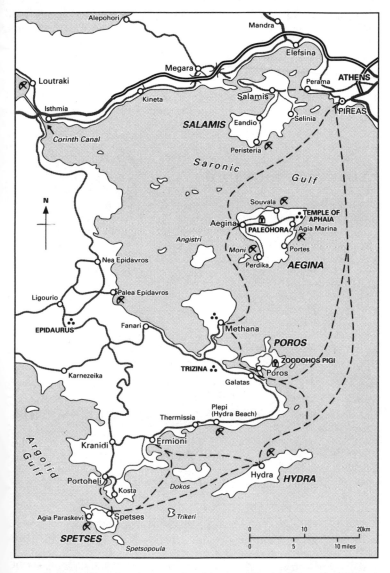

returning later for a longer stay, should any of the islands appeal. Tours usually cost the same or slightly less than the same itinerary followed independently by hydrofoil.

When traveling independently, remember that **"Flying Dolphins"** to Aegina depart from the main harbor of Piraeus, whereas those to Poros, Hydra and Spetses leave from the hydrofoil terminal at Zea Marina. **Ferries** to all islands depart from the main harbor; they cost about half

115

as much and take approximately three times longer. The islands are interconnected with frequent boats, and connected to various mainland ports including Palea Epidavros, Methana, Galatas, Ermioni and Porto Heli. *(For "Flying Dolphins" information ☎45.36.107 or 45.37.107 in Athens.)*

Cars cannot be brought into Hydra, and they require special permission for Spetses. All points of interest in Poros are within longish walking distance, and there are taxis too. Aegina has bus, taxi and rental motorcycles to choose from.

Excursion 3: Delphi

Delphi is the most strikingly evocative of Classical Greek ruin sites, and justifies an excursion in its own right. The road from Athens passes through **Boeotia**, a land full of ancient memories, but what survives by way of actual sights is of limited appeal to the nonenthusiast. Along the way, the two great mountain masses of **Parnassus** and **Helicon** offer some extraordinary scenery to those with the time and means to explore their upper reaches.

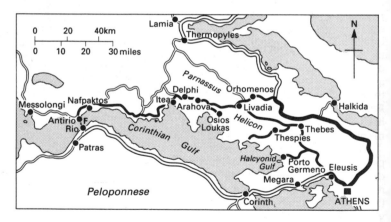

Delphi is connected to Athens by a fine highway of 167km (105 miles) in length, with an alternative route of 184km (115 miles) via **Eleusis**, making a day trip perfectly feasible. On the other hand, an overnight stay at the lively tourist village near the archeological site allows a more leisurely exploration of the sights along the way, with the bonus of an opportunity to visit the ruins during the less crowded early morning or evening hours.

Alternatively this excursion can be combined with a tour of the Peloponnese, using the Rio–Antirio ferry to cross the Corinthian Gulf on the way to or from Patras (see EXCURSION 4, page 120). In this case it is probably best to leave Delphi to the end as a fitting conclusion to a 3- to

10-day itinerary that would include (at least) Corinth, Nafplio, Mistra and Olympia.

Various tour operators in Athens organize one- or two-day excursions to Delphi, typical prices being about 7,000dr for a day trip including lunch and museum fees, or 15,000dr for a two-day tour including hotel, half-board and museum fees. Most tours feature stops at **Thebes** and **Arahova** and a side trip to the **Osios Loukas** monastery.

The same route can be followed at slightly lower cost by public bus, but in peak season you should weigh this against the likelihood that finding either bus or hotel room could prove difficult indeed.

Excursion 4: The Peloponnese

No other part of Greece can rival the Peloponnese, the huge, hand-shaped almost-island in the south, in either grandeur of landscapes or wealth of historic sights. In physical character, this is Greece's Greece: uncompromisingly mountainous, crisscrossed with the most abrupt changes of scenery, and always within sight of the sea.

Located within easy reach of Athens in the northern half of the peninsula are **Corinth** and **Olympia**, the two most substantial and interesting Classical sites of Greece besides Athens and Delphi, as are the memorable Bronze Age citadel of **Mycenae**, the spectacular ancient theater of **Epidaurus** and the lonely mountaintop temple of **Bassae**. Also here is **Nafplio**, perhaps the most attractive town in mainland Greece.

The southern half of the Peloponnese is much less touristically developed, with the result that it retains that more direct and spontaneous charm that is so often a victim of organized mass travel. Yet the sights of this area are no less impressive than those of the N: the fantastic medieval towns of **Mistra** and **Monemvasia**, the bizarre fortified villages of **Mani** and the seductive landscape of **Messenia** must surely be reckoned among the top priorities of any serious itinerary through Greece.

The seven modern provinces *(nómoi)* of the Peloponnese *(Peloponisos)* are an emulation of the seven or eight "countries" of Antiquity, each of which had its own distinct ethnic and political identity. Each province forms a physically and in part historically separate region, and it is useful to have some familiarity with their outlines (see map above).

See also color maps **5–6** at the back of the book.

117

Achaea and Corinthia

The northern seaboard of the peninsula owes its historical importance to its control over the most important waterway of Greece, the Gulf and Canal of Corinth. CORINTH flourished in Antiquity on this basis, as PATRAS does today. The pompous monuments of the former form a nice contrast with those of nearby NEMEA, which already lay in ruins when the Romans made Corinth the capital of their Greek province.

Of the celebrated "hundred gorges of Achaea," the **Vouraikos Gorge**, leading up to KALAVRYTA, is probably the most impressive.

Arcadia

Arcadia was inhabited in Antiquity by pastoral nomads who did not take to city life until forced to do so in the 4thC, and then only reluctantly. The Greeks, who had a sober opinion of country life, viewed them as uncouth brutes. The Roman poet Virgil first romanticized the singing shepherds of this land in his *Georgics,* and "Arcadia" has been a synonym for pastoral idyll ever since.

It is possible to rediscover that idyll when the treeless hills and pastures break forth in a profusion of wild flowers in springtime, but otherwise Arcadia presents few interesting sights to the tourist. The two major towns, TRIPOLI and MEGALOPOLI, seem designed to confirm the ancient Arcadians' dislike of cities.

The ARCADIAN COAST, which in Antiquity formed a separate region called Cynuria, is a beautiful stretch of mountainous seashore where hardly any roads existed until recently.

Argolis

The fertile plain of Argos is carpeted with citrus orchards, which make a visit in spring, when the trees are in bloom, a most memorable experience. This plain was the hub of the Bronze Age civilization of the Greeks: ARGOS was the leading city of Greece for centuries, while Agamemnon, the supreme leader of the Trojan expedition, was king of MYCENAE, the royal citadel that has given its modern name to that prehistoric culture.

Near the ruins of prehistoric TIRYNS stands the reminder of another age of prosperity: NAFPLIO, under the name of Napoli di Levante, was the capital of the short-lived Venetian dominion in the Peloponnese (1687–1715), and retains its delightful mix of Italian and Turkish architecture from that period.

The ARGOLID PENINSULA forms a wild and extraordinarily scenic contrast to the placid plain (and, incidentally, provides an alternative springboard for a visit to the Saronic Islands). Hidden among its pine forests, the ancient medical complex of EPIDAURUS owns the best-preserved Classical theater in Greece.

Elis

The landscape of Elis is reminiscent of northern Italy, with an intensively cultivated coastal plain and dense leafy forests in the foothills of the interior. In Antiquity it was regarded as a holy land and kept free of arms on account of the sanctuary of Zeus at OLYMPIA, the holiest site of the ancient Greek religion and the venue of the Olympic Games.

The park-like setting of the ruins of Olympia contrasts with another Classical site nearby, the temple of Apollo at BASSAE, which crowns a barren mountaintop in the middle of wilderness, and formed perhaps the single most stirring ancient monument of Greece before it was condomized some years ago in an ill-advised protection scheme.

Laconia

A land of harsh, vast mountains with the lovely valley of the Eurotas tucked in between, Laconia has a scenery ideally suited to the austere martial culture of SPARTA, whose domain it was in Antiquity. Classical monuments are all but nonexistent, but their absence is more than compensated for by several of the most striking medieval sites of Greece. The walled towns of MISTRA and MONEMVASIA and the ghost village of GERAKI date from a brief interlude at the end of the Middle Ages when a semi-independent Byzantine principality wrested this part of Greece from the Frankish baronies and produced the swan song of Byzantine art before succumbing to the Turks.

After the Turkish conquest, some of the warlike inhabitants of Laconia withdrew to the inhospitable mountains of MANI, the middle "finger" of the Peloponnese, from where they marauded Turk and Greek alike until well into the last century. The unique fortified villages of this pirate republic are among the strangest sights of Greece, and the underground lake of the Diros Cave is perhaps its most extraordinary natural prodigy.

Messenia

Nothing could be more pronounced than the contrast between wild Laconia and the soft, smiling hills and orchards of Greece's most southwestern province. The Messenians were subjected by Sparta from early on, and never really broke loose despite a regular succession of revolts. Ancient MESSENE, their beautifully situated capital, remains the least tourist-swarmed of major ruin sites in Greece.

The region also boasts some of the country's best beaches, which are punctuated by pleasant old seaside towns (PYLOS, METHONI and KORONI among others), each under the shade of a historic fortress bearing the marks of countless captures and recaptures by the Venetians and the Ottomans.

PLANNING YOUR TRIP

Vacation packages to the Peloponnese from Athens generally include only the northern half of the peninsula. A typical **4-day tour** would be: Corinth, Mycenae, Epidaurus, Nafplio (overnight), Tripoli, Bassae, Olympia (overnight), Patras, Delphi (overnight), Thebes, Athens.

Alternatively: Corinth, Mycenae, Epidaurus, Nafplio (overnight), Leonidio, Sparta–Mistra (overnight), Bassae, Olympia (overnight), Patras, Corinth, Athens.

The following **7-day itinerary** would be hectic by most people's standards. It assumes a private or rented car and makes no provision for

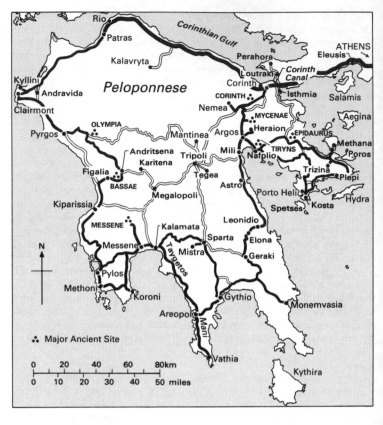

unplanned delays, laziness or lovely beaches. Total distance: about 1,350km (844 miles).

- **Day 1:** Corinth and Acrocorinth; Nemea; Mycenae; Nafplio; Epidaurus. Overnight at Nafplio *(210km/131 miles from Athens, including Nafplio–Epidaurus and back)*.
- **Day 2:** Arcadian coast to Leonidio; Geraki; Monemvasia *(189km/ 118 miles; slow driving most of the way)*.
- **Day 3:** Gythio; tour of the Mani; night at Gythio *(211km/132 miles; leave enough time for the Diros Caves and stopovers in villages)*.
- **Day 4:** Sparta; Mistra; Kalamata; then either visit ancient Messene and spend the night at Kiparissia *(201km/126 miles)*, or choose one of the following: Koroni *(164km/103 miles)*, Pylos *(160km/100 miles)* or Methoni *(175km/109 miles)*.
- **Day 5:** Up to Bassae by the (partly bad) w road via Figalia; down via Andritsena; night at Olympia *(198km/124 miles from Pylos)*.
- **Day 6:** Fast drive to Patras; ferry from Rio to Antirio; Nafpaktos; night at Delphi — see EXCURSION 3, pages 116–17 — *(225km/141 miles)*.
- **Day 7:** Back to Athens *(167km/104 miles)*.

Gain a day by cutting out Messenia: drive from Sparta to Megalopoli (direct route via Perivolia, slow but scenic), catch the sunset at Bassae, and arrive in Olympia after dark. Alternatively, **add a day** for a tour of the Argolid Peninsula, with visits to one or two islands: day one, continue from Epidaurus to Poros; day two, visit Hydra, return to Nafplio at night.

TRANSPORT

Buses to all points in the Peloponnese leave Athens from the KTEL terminal at Kifissias 100. As a rule, take the bus to the provincial capital (Corinth, Patras, Argos, Tripoli, Pyrgos, Sparta, Kalamata; direct buses also to Nafplio, Gythio and Pylos), then change to the local bus.

Ten trains a day run from Stathmos Peloponnisou in Athens to Corinth, then direct or via a connection to Patras–Pyrgos–Kiparissia–Kalamata *(7 trains a day)* and Argos–Tripoli–Kalamata *(4 trains a day)*. Nafplio and Olympia are served by local spurs from Pyrgos and Argos, respectively.

"Flying Dolphin" hydrofoils serve Leonidio and Monemvasia twice a week *(Tues and Sat 9am)* from the Zea Marina at Piraeus. For hydrofoils to the Saronic islands and mainland points across, see EXCURSION 2.

Car rental is available at Patras, Nafplio, Porto Heli, Olympia, Monemvasia and Gythio. A daily Olympic flight links Athens with Kalamata.

SIGHTSEEING

For the best **beaches**, choose from the Messenian towns of Pylos, Methoni and Koroni. For grand **scenery**, drive the Argolid and Arcadian coast routes. For unspoiled and pretty **Classical ruins**, try Nemea and Messene.

In any event, never contemplate missing: **Nafplio**, **Mistra**, **Mani** or **Olympia**. If you plan to explore the **mainland** N of the Corinthian Gulf, see EXCURSION 3.

A to Z of Classical sites

For each significant town and point of interest covered in the suggested excursion routes, we give a brief description, background and notes on accommodation. Our listings include the generally recognized "top" hotel of the locality, and a few representative hotels in categories C and above. Hotels in lower categories, or pensions, are occasionally listed when they have been found by personal experience to be especially attractive or well-managed establishments.

The traditional small-town taverna, to be found all over Greece, can be relied upon (with few exceptions) to offer informal, affordable dining. Because of the remarkable uniformity of taverna fare, quality and price, few hints on dining are given in this chapter. An in-depth guide to that quintessentially Greek institution, the taverna, is given on page 82.

AEGINA (Egina) 𝚰𝚰𝚰 ◁€ 🐾 ★

*Map **4**H7. Resident population 12,000 (Aegina town 6,000) ☎ code: 0297*
*𝒊 22.391. **Hydrofoil** from Piraeus main harbor 8–10 times daily, 30mins; Palea Epidavros twice daily; Methana. Some direct **boats** from Agia Marina.*

Most visitors go to Aegina for the ancient **temple of Aphaia**, although the magnificently mountainous island also conceals an abandoned medieval town and numerous Byzantine churches and monasteries that command extraordinary views. The main town with its busy harbor possesses considerable charm.

Aegina was the powerful and bitter rival of Athens until Pericles engineered the capture of "the eyesore of Piraeus" in 457BC. At the outbreak of the Peloponnesian war in 431, the Athenians deported the island's inhabitants in a disgraceful episode that Thucydides recounts as a parable in political cynicism.

After a long career in sea piracy under the auspices of Venice, Aegina was captured and devastated by the Turkish admiral Barbarossa in 1537. The Venetians then made several attempts at recapture, and succeeded temporarily in 1687–1718. In 1826–28 the island served as temporary headquarters for the Greek independence movement under the presidency of Kapodistrias.

> ❖ Pistachio cultivation forms the main source of income besides tourism and shipping, and Aegina counts, after California and Turkey, as one of the world's leading producers. The harvest, which takes place in August, is interesting to observe and gives a chance to buy the fresh nuts at a penny a pound. In recent years, however, the intensive irrigation required for the trees has drained the underground water and created an increasingly disastrous drought.

SIGHTS AND PLACES OF INTEREST

Aegina town has a beach (beyond the archeological area), but the island's most popular beach resort is located at **Agia Marina** (*12km/8 miles E*) at the foot of the Aphaia temple. Less crowded beaches exist at

Souvala *(8km/5 miles NE)* and at the pleasant fishing village of **Perdika** *(10km/6 miles S)*.

With time to spare, it is worth making a trip to the steep and thickly wooded isle of **Moni** *(motorboat 10mins from Perdika)*, where there is a campsite, a taverna and a very pretty bay with crystal-clear water. It is often referred to as the best beach within an hour's radius of the capital.

Aegina Town 🐟 ☆

The harbor with its churches, narrow alleys, tavernas, horse-drawn carriages and colorful fishermen's boats forms the picturesque hub of the town. On a hill W of the harbor is the **archeological area** with the single standing column of a temple of Apollo and the floor mosaics of an early medieval synagogue. The town **museum** *(standard opening hours)*, which originally housed the first high school of modern Greece, contains some interesting specimens of early pottery.

Temple of Aphaia 🏛 ◁ξ ★

12km (8 miles) E of town. Open daily 8.30am–sunset 🚌

The temple of Aphaia, one of the most famous Classical sites of Greece, enjoys a matchless situation on a wooded mountaintop 200m (656 feet) above the sea. The spectacular view takes in the Acropolis of Athens, the Acro-Corinth and several of the Cyclades.

The temple's Doric structure, of undistinguished local limestone, dates from the early part of the 5thC BC and remains in a reasonably good state with most of its 32 columns standing; colored fragments indicate that the temple was once fully painted. A reconstruction of the temple is illustrated on page 23.

Aphaia was a goddess worshiped, under different names, in Aegina and Crete alone, with apparently very ancient origins in the Minoan religion. Some later accounts made her a sister of Artemis and Apollo.

The superb sculptures of the temple were discovered nearly intact amid the rubble by the English architect Charles Cockerell and the German antiquarian Haller von Hallerstein on a weekend's digging trip in 1811.

At the ensuing auction, the agent of the British Museum failed to arrive on time, and Crown Prince Ludwig of Bavaria, father of the future King Otto of Greece, was able to acquire the sculptures for 120,000 marks. Now at the Glyptothek of Munich, they count among the most important surviving works of Archaic Greek sculpture. Some fragments remain at Athens' NATIONAL ARCHEOLOGICAL MUSEUM.

Paleohora 🔺 ☆

8km (5 miles) E of town, left turn on the Aphaia road. Contact tourist police in Aegina for access to churches.

To escape piratical raids, the main town of Aegina was moved to the mountain site of Paleohora ("Old Town") in the 8th–9thC, where it remained until the early 19thC. The site is now deserted. The houses were removed stone by stone, but some 30 churches still stand. They represent nearly every architectural period between the 13thC and the late 18thC; some have kept their frescoes. One is used occasionally for church services.

Below Paleohora on the Aphaia road is the **Monastery of Agios Nektarios**, commemorating the only canonized saint of modern Greece (died 1920). His tomb attracts many pilgrims, who put an ear to his sarcophagus to hear the holy man chattering inside. His feast is held on November 9.

Just outside Aegina on the road leading to Paleohora can be seen **Omorfi Eklesia** (Pretty Church), a charming edifice of 1282 built of Antique materials.

In **Aegina town**: **Archontiko** (A) (☎ 24.156 ▥ 12 rms and suites 🍴 ▤) is housed in a delightful old mansion.

In **Agia Marina**, a large number of hotels, mostly C, include **Ble Sintrivani** (A) (☎ 32.052 ▥ 23 rms) and **Apollo** (B) (☎ 32.271 ▥ 107 rms), both open April to October.

In **Perdika**: try the **Aegina Maris** (B) hotel and bungalows (☎ 25.130/2 ▥ 164 rms 🍴 ≈ 🦞).

▲ Near the archeological site in **Aegina town** and on **Moni island**.

AEGOSTHENA   See PORTO GERMENO, page 162.

AMPHIARAEUM (Amfiareo) 🏛 ◁€

*49km (31 miles) N of Athens. Map 7B2. **Bus** to Kalamos from Mavromateon and Leof. Alexandras (map 2B4); then taxi or 25min walk. **Archeological site** open daily 8.30am–6pm ▣ ☎(0295) 62.144.*

The ruins of this ancient temple and spa complex, which are dedicated to the hero-seer Amphiaraos, are worth a visit less for their archeological value than for their strikingly beautiful natural setting at the foot of a forested ravine. Sadly, however, a disastrous forest fire in 1992 partly diminished their attraction. Along the way, the **Kapandriti–Kalamos–Agii Apostoli** road offers some magnificent and unspoiled views toward **Euboea**.

❖   The seer Amphiaraos of Argos fought as one of the "Seven against Thebes," and perished here when his chariot was swallowed up by the earth. A local cult associated with an oracle and a curative spa grew around his name. Pilgrims sacrificed a ram, wrapped themselves in its fleece for the night, and their dreams, interpreted by priests, advised them how to achieve a cure.

The very partially preserved **Doric temple** of the 4thC BC is a simple *prostyle* (one with only a row of columns in front of the entrance). Farther on are the remains of what must have been an impressive **colonnade** with attached **thermal baths**, and a charming **theater** behind. Across the brook were patients' chambers and perhaps medical quarters.

6km (4 miles) down from Kalamos, the resort village of **Agii Apostoli** offers a good beach, hotels (B, C, D) and tavernas.

ARAHOVA ◀€
*8km (5 miles) E of Delphi. Map 3G5. Population 3,000. On Athens–Delphi **bus route**.*

Arahova occupies a panoramic position (altitude 940m/3,084 feet) on the flank of **Mt. Parnassus**, and forms the starting point of excursions into the mountain. The village has been famous for its hand-woven fabrics since Turkish times, although current products tend to be gaudy affairs of technicolor dye and crass design. They cover every wall and shop window along the main street, giving the town a distinctly psychedelic atmosphere.

A road leads N *(26km/16 miles)*, via Kalivia, to the **ski center** of Mt. Parnassus at 1,500m (4,921 feet) *(⇌ no ☜ ski equipment available at Arahova)*. From here it is possible to drive to within an hour's walk of the summit (2,457m/8,061 feet). The view from the top takes in nearly all of continental Greece from **Mt. Athos** in the N to **Mt. Taygetos** in the S.

The ancient Greeks believed the summit of Mt. Parnassus to be the abode of the god Dionysus, where he held orgiastic feasts with his wine-crazed Maenads. Later poetic tradition transferred the Muses from Mt. Helicon (see THEBES, pages 168–9) to Parnassus, and in Latin and post-Renaissance literature the mountain came to represent both the source and perfection of artistic achievement. The frightfully barren, craggy peak of reality bears little resemblance to the idyllic *Montparnasse* of 18thC painters and poets.

ARCADIAN COAST ◀€ ☜ ☆
Map 6I5–6.

The E coast of the Peloponnese between the Argolid Plain and **Leonidio** is a wild, sparsely inhabited region with several pretty villages and many deserted beaches. Before the construction of the road in the 1960s, it was one of the least accessible parts of Greece. An ethnological curiosity still exists in the upper valley of the Vrassiotis Stream, where the **Tsakon** villagers (six villages accessible by poor road from Astros or Ag. Andreas) speak a Slavic language apparently descended from the early medieval Slav invasions.

The coast has a handful of beach resorts in the earliest stages of development, the beaches of **Astros** and **Tyros** being the main ones. Astros (population 2,500) also owns the beautiful and little-visited 11thC Monastery of Christ the Savior, or **Loukous** (4km/2½ miles NW).

With a population of 3,500, **Leonidio** *(hydrofoil from Piraeus and Monemvasia)* is an attractive town with many medieval buildings and narrow lanes. Driving down from the N, it strikes the visitor as being the first pleasant town in Greece not entirely to subsist on tourism.

The road farther S to GERAKI follows the extraordinary gorge (◀€) of the Dafnon Stream and climbs to over 1,000m (3,300 feet) at the lovely village of **Kosmas**.

☜   Choose from any one of a bunch of modest hotels at the beaches of Astros and Tyros, or more simple accommodation in Leonidio. **Kamaria** (C) in Leonidio

(☎ (0757) 22.757 ▢ to ▥ 22 rms; open Apr-Oct) occupies an attractive house in the village.

▲   7km (4 miles) s of Ag. Andreas.

ARGOLID PENINSULA ◁Ξ ☜ ☆
Map 6I6.

The drive from EPIDAURUS to Methana may be the most dramatic in Greece, with a magnificent island-speckled sea bursting unexpectedly into view at a height of 600m (1,950 feet). The N coast is especially attractive, with rich vegetation and extensive citrus orchards. Although the peninsula is ringed with several rapidly growing beach resorts, the spaces between them remain surprisingly unspoiled.

Some ancient and medieval ruins are visible at the unexcavated site of **Troezen** *(Trizína, near the village of Damala; turnoff s 7km/4 miles w of Galatas),* more interesting for their peaceful rustic setting than anything else. The city was important in Mycenaean times but played a secondary role in later Antiquity.

The small port of **Ermioni** is the subject of Strabo's curious remark that, the passage to Hades from this country being a short cut, the inhabitants did not put passage-money in the mouths of their dead. The passage in question remains undiscovered.

The principal resorts, **Palea Epidavros** *(not the ancient ruin site, which is 13km/8 miles inland),* **Nea Epidavros**, **Galatas**, **Plepi** (Hydra Beach) and **Porto Heli/Kosta** offer precious little beyond beaches and acceptable hotels. They are unremarkable as towns, particularly the last four, which grew only recently to accommodate the spillover from the Saronic Islands. **Methana**, which is older and nicer, is very popular with Athenians because of its hot sulfur baths.

❧   A large number of hotels are to be found in Palea Epidavros (B, C, D), Ermioni (B, D, E) and Porto Heli/Kosta (A, B, C, D). For accommodation in Galatas, see under POROS.

The largest and classiest resort complexes on the coast are located in Plepi, on the mainland across from HYDRA: **Kappa Club** (A) *(☎ (0754) 41.080 ▥ 272 rms and bungalows, open Apr-Oct);* and **Porto Hydra** (A) *(☎ (0754) 41.112 ▥ 271 rms and bungalows, open Mar-Oct)* both have ⇌ ⋙ ☜ ℘ ♫ ▦

Hinitsa Beach (A), in Porto Heli, is a good, fully equipped, modern beach hotel *(☎ (0754) 51.401 ▥ 206 rms ⇌ ⋙ ☜ ℘ ♫ ▦).*

Other good, B-class choices are: **Marialena** *(Palea Epidavros ☎ (0753) 41.090 ▥ 12 furnished apartments, open year round);* **Cap d'Or** *(Kosta ☎ (0754) 51.360 ☒ (01) 72.25.334 ▢ 147 rms and bungalows ⇌ ⋙ ☜ ℘ Apr-Oct);* and **Costa Perla** *(Ermioni ☎ (0754) 31.112 ▢ 191 rms and bungalows ⇌ ⋙ ☜ ℘ Apr-Sept).*

ARGOS ☷
140km (88 miles) sw of Athens. Map 6I5. Population 20,000 ☎ code: 0751.

Argos is one of the oldest cities of Greece and one of the very few that has had a more or less continuous history under the same name, but its historic sights are few and not of great interest. The town thrives as the chief market of the fertile plain of the same name, which produces a large slice of Greece's orange yield; the central produce market and "bazaar" streets are worth a visit for their colorful commotion.

HISTORY AND LEGENDS

Argos was the chief city of Greece in the Heroic Age, and Homer uses "Argive" as a synonym for Greek. It was established by the semilegendary **Pelasgians**, a pre-Hellenic people who introduced the cult of Hera. The royal line was founded by **Danaos**, an Egyptian who was a son of Io, the Holy Cow. His 50 daughters (the Danaids) murdered their husbands on the night of their collective wedding and threw their heads in the marshes of Lerna, for which ghastly act they were condemned by the god of the underworld to carry water forever in a leaking vessel.

The successors of Danaos included **Perseus**, king of Mycenae and Tiryns, who slew the snake-haired Medusa and married the Ethiopian princess Andromeda, and **Amphitryon**, who was the father of Heracles. The kingdom then fell to the descendants of Pelops, the eponymous ruler of the Peloponnese, who ruled from the citadel of MYCENAE; **Agamemnon** was his grandson.

In historic times Argos was taken by the Dorians, who invaded the Peloponnese c.1200BC, and was generally overshadowed by Sparta. In 272BC, the Macedonian king Pyrrhus, he of the Pyrrhic victory, was killed in Argos after being hit by a tile thrown by an old woman from a rooftop. The city had some importance through Roman, Byzantine and Frankish rule, losing primacy to Nafplio only during the Venetian-Turkish centuries.

SIGHTS AND PLACES OF INTEREST

There is a rather fine Hellenistic-Roman **theater** at the sw edge of the town; with a capacity of 20,000 spectators, it is one of the largest in Greece. More interesting is the **Kastro** (◀€), a Byzantine–Frankish–Venetian–Turkish citadel that encloses **Larissa**, the ancient acropolis of Argos.

🐚 **Telessila** (C) (☎ 28.351 ▯ 32 rms) is a decent hotel, but with NAFPLIO only 13km (8 miles) away, there is little reason to stay in Argos.

ENVIRONS

The massive but completely destroyed ruins of the Argive **Heraion** (temple of Hera) occupy a bald solitary hilltop 6km (4 miles) NE of town. They are certainly worth a visit for the splendid view. Not a trace has been found of the famous paintings of Polyclitus, which Strabo tells us were the most beautiful in the world.

> ❖ Hera, the jealous wife of Zeus, was the principal deity of the Argives and thus the main protector of the Greeks during the Trojan War. She was born at the **Stymphalian Lake** *(35km/22 miles NW, near NEMEA)*, whose waters were believed to communicate by an underground channel with the **Erasinos Spring** *(in the village of Kefalari, 5km/2½ miles s of Argos).*

BASSAE (Vases) 🏛 ⬿

47km (29 miles) from coast (mostly unpaved road); 14km (9 miles) from Andritsena. Map 5I4. No public transport (only tour buses). Free entrance.

The road climbs through a forested valley to increasingly barren and desolate mountains. Each turn reveals a higher range of gray cliffs, with only a few stray goats and a solitary hovering eagle to accompany the wild oaks. Joachim Bocher, who in 1765 became the first Westerner to get this far, was overwhelmed to discover on top of the highest peak of the range, at 1,150m (3,773 feet), a nearly intact **Temple of Apollo** from the finest era of Classical architecture.

The modern experience is somewhat less stirring: at the end of the gruelling drive the visitor is regaled with the sight, gleaming in the distance, of a vast, white circus tent.

It was the idea of some benighted archeologist, eager to protect his little domain against the depredations of sun and wind, to clothe the temple of Apollo in a plastic sack. The temple itself, which is as good as any other temple (Doric, 6 x 15 column peristyle, stylobate of three steps, etc.), once derived its tremendous majesty from a setting that inspired divine awe. It now has the appearance of a dinosaur skeleton trapped in a sterile museum.

The temple is described by Pausanias as a work of Ictinus, the architect of the Parthenon, although modern opinion gives it a somewhat earlier date. The frieze of the cella, which had survived wholly intact, was removed by Charles Cockerell in 1811–12 and forms one of the prize exhibits of the British Museum.

There is no food or shelter at the site. 14km (9 miles) down the way is the attractive mountain village of **Andritsena**, which has adapted itself to tourism in a so-far-pleasant way; there are several tavernas.

⬿   **Theoxenia** (B) *(in Andritsena* ☎*(0626) 22.219* ⬜ *33 rms* ⇌ *open Mar-Oct)* rents rooms.

BRAURON (Vravrona, Vraona) 🏛

*38km (24 miles) E of Athens. Map 7D3. **Bus** to Markopoulo from corner of Mavromateon and Leof. Alexandras (map 2B4); then 8km (5 miles) taxi or walk. **Archeological site** open Tues–Sun 8.30am–3pm; closed Mon ▨ ☎(0294) 71.020.*

The sanctuary of Artemis Brauronia was one of the most ancient holy places of Attica, with many Archaic and violent myths associated with it. The heavily ruined remains of the sanctuary lie on a pleasant knoll at the edge of a marsh.

The oldest Brauron myth concerned a bear, an animal sacred to Artemis, that killed a girl. Legend also said that Iphigenia, the daughter that Agamemnon wanted to sacrifice to the gods, came here with a sacred idol of Artemis and later died here. The most unusual aspect of the Brauronian cult was the company of little Athenian girls called *arktoi* (she-bears) who lived in the sanctuary until puberty, wore saffron robes, and performed the bear-dance on certain occasions.

❖ Peisistratus, the first nonaristocratic ruler of Athens (ruled c.560–527BC), was a native Brauronian. He came to power by coup and ruled autocratically, but was supported by the popular classes.

The sanctuary consisted of a tiny **temple** and a large colonnaded enclosure that contained the living quarters of the *arktoi*. A small late-Byzantine **church** was erected beside the temple ruins. The **museum** contains numerous nondescript articles and an interesting reconstructed model of the sanctuary.

500m (550 yards) away on the road to Markopoulo one can see the ruins of a 6thC **church** of substantial size, one of the very few in Greece that date from the early Byzantine period. It appears to have been destroyed very shortly after its construction.

An excellent GNTO public beach exists at **Porto Rafti**.

☞ A large **tourist complex** close to the archeological site, an A-class hotel in the beach resort of **Porto Rafti** and numerous modest hotels in **Artemis**, a popular resort (formerly named Loutsa) are the main accommodation alternatives in Brauron.

Artemis (A) in Porto Rafti (☎ (0299) 72.000 ⬚ *32 furnished apartments* ⇛ ⚏ ⚏ ⊞ *open year round).*

Another good A-class hotel to try is the **Vraona Bay** in Vravrona (☎ (0294) 88.454 ⬚ *352 rms and bungalows* ⇛ ⚏ ⚏ ♒ ⋔ ⊞ *open Apr-Oct).*

CORINTH (Korinthos) 🏛 ⛴ ★
Town 80km (50 miles) w of Athens. Map **6H6**. *Population 22,000* ☎ *code: 0741.* **Archeological site** *6km (4 miles) sw of town; open daily 8.30am–3pm* ▨

The modern town of Corinth was founded in 1858 after an earthquake destroyed the older site, which had grown among the ruins of ancient Corinth. It is a colorless place, overshadowed on the one hand by the popular beach resort of **Loutraki** (5km/2½ miles N) and on the other by the lively touristville that has again sprouted near the ruins.

HISTORY AND LEGENDS
The name of Corinth indicates a pre-Greek origin. In the 7thC BC, under the enlightened rule of the tyrant Periander, the city became one of the leading maritime powers of Greece, with colonies as far afield as Corcyra (Corfu) and Syracuse (Sicily).

Overshadowed by Athens for several centuries, Corinth returned to prominence in the 3rdC BC as the leader of the Achaean League, which was the last independent Greek power to emerge during the decline of the Macedonians. Its tense relationship with Rome led finally to its complete eradication by L. Mummius in 146BC.

Corinth was rebuilt in 44BC by order of Julius Caesar and repopulated with Roman legionnaires and freedmen who, according to Strabo, looted a huge amount of art from the rubble, swamping Roman markets with Corinthian antiquities. In 29BC Augustus created the province of Achaea, comprising all southern Greece except the "free" cities, with Corinth as its proconsular seat. It was richly embellished by various emperors.

St Paul arrived in Corinth after Athens and lived here for 18 months plying his trade as tent-maker *(Acts 18.1-17)*. His epistles to the Corinthians contain one of the most famous and moving passages of the New Testament, the so-called Hymn to Love *(I Corinthians 13):*

> "If I speak with the tongues of men and angels, and have not love, then I am become as sounding brass or a tinkling cymbal. And if I have the gift of prophecy, and understand all mysteries, and all knowledge; and have all faith so that I could remove mountains, and have not love, I am nothing. And though I bestow all my goods to feed the poor, and have not love, it profiteth me nothing . . . For now we see the world through a glass darkly; but then we shall see it face to face."

The magnificent fortress of the Acrocorinth, being a key to the control of the Peloponnese and of the trade route through the Isthmus, allowed the city to maintain some importance during the Middle Ages. Under Frankish-Venetian rule it was the principal export point of Greek products to the West, including a type of raisin that obtained the name "currant" from its port of shipment.

Ancient Corinth

The archeological area excavated by the American School comprises the **Roman Agora** (Forum), a vast and monumental space with the ruins of numerous public buildings surrounding it. The heavily ruined shells of a Greek-Roman **theater** and an **odeon**, the latter a gift of the ubiquitous Herodes Atticus, are seen outside the site. Soon after the main entrance, note the **Corinthian capitals** placed on the re-erected columns of an unidentified temple, recalling the architectural order that the city pioneered in the 4thC BC. (An explanation of the Classical Orders is given on page 24.)

The agora of Corinth is dominated from a prominence on the N by the 6thC BC Doric **Temple of Apollo**, whose seven standing columns are not only all that remain of the pre-Roman city, but the only relatively well-preserved specimen of an Archaic Greek temple as well.

Several **stoas**, which in their own day must have been a glorious sight indeed, surround the marketplace, interspersed with the memorials of various Roman worthies, Mummius and Caesar among them. The ceremonial **Lechaion Road** was, as customary in wealthier Hellenistic and Roman cities, lined with marble colonnades to either side surmounted by rows of statues.

Some of these statues, mostly Roman works with the characteristic mixture of pomp and realism, can be seen at the site **museum**. The museum also contains interesting late Roman mosaics and a wealth of Latin inscriptions.

The attractive village of **Arhea Korinthos**, with its old rustic houses set among orchards, derives its livelihood exclusively from tourism. A derelict mosque and several old churches are reminders of the town's history before 1858.

Acrocorinth

The acropolis of Corinth was famous in Antiquity for its **Temple of Aphrodite**, which owned more than 1,000 sacred prostitutes, slaves dedicated to the goddess by both male and female citizens. According to Strabo, the city was crowded with visitors and grew rich on account of these women. Sailors freely spent their money on them, whence the proverb, "Not for every man the voyage to Corinth."

Acrocorinth was besieged without success for five years by Guillaume de Champlitte, Geoffroi de Villehardouin and Othon de la Roche before it fell to the Franks in 1210.

The dizzying 575m-high (1,886-foot) rock says a lot for the vigor of those men of ancient times who came to pay their respects to the goddess. The top is enclosed by a **triple fortification**; the first gate through is Turkish, the second Venetian, the third, with flanking towers, from the 4thC BC, when a Macedonian stronghold was erected here as one of the key supports of Philip's hegemony over Greece.

The remains of an old **Turkish quarter** (with mosque, minaret and baths) are prominent within the citadel. Traces of the Temple of Aphrodite are visible at the highest point — and one of the most memorable views in Greece.

☞ A number of good hotels are located on the seashore in **Loutraki** and **Isthmia**. **Corinth**-town has a dozen modest (C- and D-class) hotels, while the archeological site (**Arhea Korinthos**) offers many private rooms and inexpensive pensions in a pleasant setting.

King Saron (A) (☎ (0741) 37.201 ▥ to ▥ 161 rms ≋ ⚬ ⚌ ⚏ ♪ ⊞)

is a very good hotel on the beach in Isthmia.

Xenia (A) (☎ (0741) 31.208 ▥ ≋), in Arhea Korinthos, is mainly a restaurant, but also rents out three charming guest rooms.

Ephira (C) (Vassileos Konstantinou 52 ☎ (0741) 22.434 ▥ 45 rms) is an adequate hotel in Corinth-town.

CORINTH CANAL

The canal was built by a French company in 1882–92, but was not a new idea: Periander, tyrant of Corinth, one of the Seven Sages of Antiquity, attempted to construct one about 600BC. Defeated by technical obstacles, he created instead a paved road on which light craft were hauled over wooden rollers until the 12thC.

Alexander, Caesar and Caligula toyed with the project, and finally Nero inaugurated work with a golden pick-axe. Some 6,000 slaves brought from Jerusalem dug several sectors, until civil war in AD68 caused the work to be abandoned.

The modern canal, 6km (4 miles) long and 23m (25 yards) wide, runs through a cutting 87m (285 feet) deep at its center.

ISTHMIA

Despite vast amounts of money and publicity poured in by the American School, little remains to excite the visitor at the **Temple of Poseidon**, near the Aegean end of the isthmus, or at the **theater** and the **stadium** in which were held the biennial Isthmian Games, the most important in Greece after those of Olympia.

Fresh from his victory over the Macedonians, the Roman consul T. Quinctius Flaminius (see bust at OLYMPIA museum) proclaimed the Liberation of Greece at the Isthmian Games of 196BC. It was a short-lived freedom that ended 50 years later when Mummius wiped out Corinth in retaliation for the maltreatment of Roman envoys, who were showered with excrement in the streets of the city. Nero, not one to be outdone by precedent, announced the independence of Greece again at the Isthmian Games of AD67. No one took him seriously.

Heraeum of Perachora

The remote and wild site of the **Temple of Hera**, situated in an olive grove on the steep headland to the NW of Corinth, makes it a worthwhile excursion for lovers of dramatic scenery. Not much is left of the temple today, but there is a delightful deserted **cove** nearby with transparent waters, and the views along the way, especially at sunset, are truly spectacular.

DELPHI 🏛 ⋞ ★

*167km (104 miles) NW of Athens. Map **3**G5. Population of village: 2,000*
*☎ code: 0265 ℹ 82.220. **Bus** 5 times daily from Athens (KTEL terminal at Liossion 260) via Thebes; 3 times daily from Lamia; 3 times daily from Nafpaktos. **Museum and archeological site** open Mon–Fri 7.30am–6pm; Sat–Sun 8.30am–3pm (museum closed Mon morning).*

Delphi holds an awe-inspiring position in the fold of two immense rose-gray cliffs, the **Phaedriades**, which climb toward the wild crags of Mt. Parnassus and command a majestic panorama over the aptly named "Sea of Olives" which stretches as far as the Gulf of Corinth below a drop of several hundred meters.

The Sanctuary of Delphic Apollo was one of the most sacred places of ancient Greece, forming, like Olympia, one of the focal points of a common Greek cultural identity. The Delphic oracle played a prominent part in nearly every historic event from before the recorded era until the final victory of Christianity in the 4thC. Greek cities from Italy to the shores of the Black Sea vied with each other to win the oracle's favor by embellishing the sanctuary with costly gifts; they turned Delphi into a showcase of ancient art and architecture.

LEGENDS

Delphi was originally a sacred place of Mother Earth (**Gaea**), who lurked in cracks and pits in the rock, protected by her son **Python**, the snake. Also here was the **Omphalos**, the Navel of the Earth (not the sculptured Omphalos now exhibited in the museum, which is evidently a much later cult object).

Apollo, who was born on the island of Delos in the Aegean, was brought here by some Cretans to whom he appeared in the guise of a dolphin *(Apollo Delphinios)*. He dispersed the underworld deities and killed Python, but thereafter adopted the snake as one of his symbols *(Apollo Pythios)*.

HISTORY

The arrival of the cult of Apollo implies Minoan origins and so must be placed sometime before 1500BC. By 1000BC a league comprising the representatives of all Greek tribes and cities (the Amphictyony) was entrusted with the administration of the site. The quadrennial Pythian Games were instituted early in the 6thC BC by the Athenian noble family of the Alcmaeonids, who were then influential at Delphi; they also built the early temple of Apollo and perhaps played a role in introducing the subordinate cult of Athena. The current temple of Apollo was erected in 366–329BC after an earthquake had destroyed the previous edifice.

The earliest recorded gift to the temple was that of the Lydian king Croesus c.550BC. By Roman times, the number of statues in the sanctuary alone exceeded 3,000. Some of these were carried off to Rome by Nero; the serpent column erected in 479BC to commemorate the Greek victory at Plataea was taken by Constantine to his new capital and now stands at the Hippodrome in Istanbul. The immunity of the holy site, however, was generally respected during the sundry wars and invasions of Antiquity, excepting an attack by the Gauls in 279BC, which was repulsed by an intervention of the god in person, reputedly in the form of a cataclysmic thunderstorm.

Delphi was abandoned after the outlawing of the oracle in AD391 and lay half-forgotten for 1,400 years. The village of **Kastri** (Towers) emerged among the ruins; villagers put the ancient marbles to good use as building material, and the precinct of the Athena Temple (see pages 135–36) now acquired the graphic name of **Marmaria**, or "Where You Get The Marble." The investigations started in the 1860s by the French School of Archeology soon brought to light the **Naxian Sphinx** and the **Stoa of the Athenians**, thereby persuading the French government to put up the money needed to remove Kastri to its present location 1.5km (1 mile) to the w. Systematic excavations conducted in 1892–1903 by Th. Homolle recovered the ruins of Delphi more or less as they stand now.

THE ORACLE

Pilgrims came to Delphi from all parts of the Mediterranean world to consult the oracle about marriages, business loans, voyages, elections, conspiracies and wars. The **Pythia**, the priestess of Apollo who was a peasant woman of over 50, drank from the Castalian spring to purify herself. She then inhaled the apparently hallucinogenic fumes that emanated from a chasm in the temple's crypt, took her seat on a tripod and delivered her advice in mumbled utterances. These were interpreted and put into hexameter verse by priests, who included such influential personalities as the historian Plutarch.

Lycurgus and Solon sought the oracle's advice about their constitutions of Sparta and Athens respectively. Colonies were never founded until it had been consulted. When Croesus wanted to know if he should go to war against Persia, he was told that if he did he would destroy a great kingdom; he did, and destroyed his own. In both the Persian and Peloponnesian wars the oracle tended to side with the enemies of Athens.

Julian the Apostate (AD361–363) was the last pagan emperor to honor the Pythia. His messenger was told:

> "Go tell the king — the carven hall is felled;
> Apollo has no cell, prophetic bay,
> Nor talking spring; his cadenced well is stilled."

The museum

It may be best to start a tour of Delphi with the museum, if only for the sake of the excellent graphic **reconstruction**, which gives a good idea of the splendor of the site as it must have appeared 2,000 years ago.

The highlight of the collection is the bronze **Charioteer**, one of the great surviving masterpieces of Antiquity. This was part of a group marking a racing victory of Polyzalos, the tyrant of Gela in Sicily (473BC), and it is sobering to think that it constituted no more than a minor piece among more than 3,000 such gifts.

The immense **Naxian Sphinx** was presented in 560BC by the people of Naxos. The primitive, almost "Egyptian" monument of **Kleobis and Biton** represent two priests of the Argive Hera who were deified after their death. The graceful statue of **Antinous**, the lover of Hadrian who was similarly deified posthumously, belongs to a different artistic era about 750 years down the way.

Other noteworthy exhibits include fragmentary **friezes** of the Athenian, Siphnian and Sicyonian Treasuries, which the respective cities built to house the gifts of their pilgrims, and the **Omphalos**, which was kept in the crypt of the temple and marked the center of the earth.

The Sacred Precinct

The **Sanctuary** or **Temenos of Apollo** forms a rectangle 180m x 130m (590 x 426 feet) in size, which contained, as well as the temple itself, various administrative buildings, the treasuries of the city-states, numerous votive monuments and a theater. The **stadium** where the Pythian Games were held is located a short distance above the sharply sloping enclosure.

The paved square in front of the main gate was the **Roman Agora**, where pious offerings could be bought in the shops of the stoa. Other Roman buildings outside the enclosure, mainly baths, are recognizable by the use of brick.

The various **monuments** that survive in the form of bare pedestals, if at all, commemorated a full spectrum of events and personalities, sublime as well as workaday. There were trophies marking the battles of Marathon and Plataea and the campaigns of Alexander, while the **Bull of Corcyra** celebrated a particularly good tuna catch, and the **Treasury of Siphnos** immortalized the proceeds of a satisfying gold mine.

The **Temple of Pythian Apollo**, a Doric peripteral structure with 6 x 15 columns, replaced the earlier temple of the 6thC at a time of transition when the Classical Doric Order was already past its prime, but the brilliant refinements of Hellenistic architecture were as yet unborn. Six of its strong, squat pillars have been re-erected and give a sense of the temple's

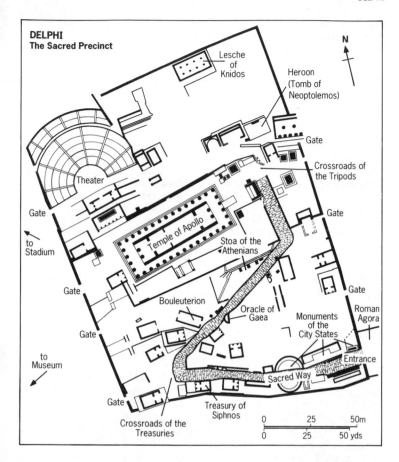

DELPHI
The Sacred Precinct

N

Lesche of Knidos

Heroon (Tomb of Neoptolemos)

Gate

Crossroads of the Tripods

Theater

Gate

to Stadium

Gate

Temple of Apollo

Stoa of the Athenians

Gate

Bouleuterion

Oracle of Gaea

Monuments of the City States

Roman Agora

Gate

Gate

to Museum

Entrance

Sacred Way

Gate

Treasury of Siphnos

Crossroads of the Treasuries

0   25   50m
0   25   50 yds

former majesty. Below its front revetment, a pile of stones marks the site of the prehistoric sanctuary of Gaea.

The **theater** commands a marvelous view over the site, the olive-clad plains and the sea beyond. Here morality plays were staged re-enacting the battle of Apollo and Python, and musical performances honored the god of the lyre and the flute. Nero probably took this stage to display his talents in singing, playing instruments, heraldic speech and numerous other skills in which he earned the unanimous approval of the jury.

The Castalian Spring and Marmaria

A short walk w along the Arahova road leads to the **Castalian Spring**, which wells up in the wild ravine between the Phaedriades. Here ancient pilgrims purified themselves before approaching the temple grounds.

Marmaria, consisting of a platform among olive groves below the road, holds the ruins of two **temples of Athena**, both erected by Athenians, the older one in the 6thC BC and the newer, smaller one in the 4thC. Beside them stands perhaps the most attractive of Delphi's monuments, the **Tholos**, or Rotunda, a circular structure of 20 Doric columns of which six have been re-erected. The original use of the building is obscure, although it is not too far-fetched to think that sheer beauty may have been one inspiration.

✎   The tourist village of **Delphi** has hotel capacity far exceeding its resident population. There are five A or B hotels, a great variety of C and D hotels, private rooms and a **youth hostel**.

Amalia (A) (☎ 82.101 Ⅲ 185 rms ☴ ♫ ◢ 🍴) is a large modern hotel; **Vouzas** (A) (☎ 82.232 Ⅲ 58 rms; terrace ☴ dramatic ◖) is the nearest to the archeological site; also A-class, **Xenia** (☎ 82.151 Ⅲ 44 rms ☴ ♨)

occupies an isolated spot at the w end of the town; the B-class **Delphi Panorama** (☎ 82.437 Ⅲ 15 rms 🍴) is a pleasant pension; or try **Parnassos** (C) (☎ 82.231 Ⅲ 23 rms ◖).

Additional hotels exist in abundance at **Itea**, a port and resort town of no special merit, but considerably less crowded and less expensive than Delphi. **Nafsika** (B) (☎ 33.300/4 Ⅲ ☴ 🍴) is the best of the bunch.

▲   At the campsite outside the w end of Delphi village.

DIROS CAVES   See MANI, page 145.

EPIDAURUS (Arhea Epidavros) 🏛 ☆
28km (18 miles) E of Nafplio. Map 6I6. Local bus to Ligourio (3km/2 miles) or tour bus. Open Mon–Fri 8.30am–6pm; Sat–Sun 8.30am–3pm 📷

The sanctuary of Asclepius, one of the most famous medical centers of Antiquity, was set in the tranquil atmosphere of pine- and oleander-clad hills not far from the coastal city of Epidaurus. The sanctuary itself now consists of a heap of jumbled stone, but its 14,000-seat theater has been preserved almost intact, and as such forms one of the foremost Classical attractions of Greece. In size or architecture it will not exactly overwhelm a visitor who is familiar with Verona or Aspendos; but the site is truly pleasant, and the performances of Classical drama mounted at the theater evoke an extraordinary sense of Antiquity.

❖   The cult of Asclepius probably originated in Thessaly, although its most important sanctuary was at Epidaurus. The god of healing was born of Apollo and a mortal Thessalian woman by the name of Coronis (Crow), who was slain for sleeping with another man while pregnant with Apollo's son, bringing eternal disgrace upon the bird of her name. The boy was trained by Chiron the Centaur, and eventually wound up at Epidaurus, where he incurred the displeasure of Hades by going so far as to raise men from the dead.

The Asclepian method of treatment involved an elaborate mixture of ritual, suggestion and psychological care besides baths, medicinal plants and surgery. The sick would perform ritual purifications, and wait for the god to prescribe a cure in their dreams. Artistic and intellectual pursuits were considered essential to the treatment, hence the theater, the odeon and the profusion of (now vanished) works of art. Payment was through the sacrifice of a cock and the presentation of a votive offering, usually a replica of the part of the body that was cured.

The **theater** dates from the 4thC BC, the earliest date when theaters were built of stone, and seems to have maintained its original structure without later alterations. The shape of the auditorium is designed for maximum acoustic effect, which can be tested by standing on the top row and listening to tourists' chatter some 25m (27 yards) down on the stage.

The only noteworthy structure among the ruins of the sanctuary itself is a **tholos**, a large circular colonnade rather like the one at Delphi and similarly obscure in its original use.

Some ruins of the ancient city of Epidaurus can be glimpsed beneath the transparent sea at **Palea Epidavros**, 13km (8 miles) E (see ARGOLID PENINSULA).

The only accommodation at the site itself is in **Xenia** (B) (☎ *(0753) 22.003* ▥ ☲), 24 stone bungalows hidden among the pines. Visitors more normally stay at either NAFPLIO or Palea Epidavros (see ARGOLID PENINSULA).

EUBOEA (Evia) ◁€ ☙

*Map **4**. Island population 170,000 ☎ code: 0221. Capital: Halkida, 88km (55 miles) N of Athens; population 45,000. **Access: bridge** at Halkida; **car and passenger ferries** Rafina–Karystos (once daily, 1hr 40mins), Rafina–Marmari (thrice daily, 1hr 10mins), Agia Marina–Nea Styra, Skala Oropou–Eretria (20–25 times daily, 25mins), Arkitsa–Loutra Edipsou, Glyfa–Agiokambos; **bus** to Halkida from KTEL terminal at Liossion 260.*

Greece's second-largest island is wildly mountainous, and except for the coastal area around Halkida remains comparatively unaffected by the modern world — in marked and refreshing contrast to neighboring Attica. Its towns are architecturally uninteresting, but this is made up for by their calm pace and often dramatic setting.

The three major cities of ancient Euboea, Chalkis (now Halkida), Eretria and Cyme (Kimi), enjoyed a certain importance in the early Archaic period, with colonies in Southern Italy and the Black Sea. They declined under Athenian and Theban dominance in later Antiquity. In the Middle Ages the island was known as Negroponte, a corruption of *Euripos Bridge* (see page 89).

From 1210–1470 it was governed as a Venetian colony by Italian and Frankish barons. Under the Turks the population consisted mainly of Muslims, who were obliged to leave after the annexation of Euboea by Greece in 1830.

SIGHTS AND PLACES OF INTEREST

Halkida is situated on both sides of the Euripos channel separating Euboea from the mainland. A toy bridge, hardly 40m (44 yards) long, spans the narrowest point. The unique position of the town gives it an attractive aspect; lively promenades lined with some fine 19thC residences occupy both shores. The landward side is dominated by the **Karababa**

Fortress, a Turkish structure of 1687. Also noteworthy are a handsome **mosque** and the medieval church of **Agia Paraskevi**.

❖ The Euripos has been noted since Antiquity for its strong current, which abruptly changes direction several times a day. The phenomenon is still not adequately understood. Aristotle, who died in Chalkis in 322BC, is said to have drowned himself in despair over his inability to solve the puzzle.

Eretria has some ancient ruins but attracts visitors primarily as a fast-growing although still pleasant beach resort. Farther s, the **road to Karystos** *(128km/80 miles from Halkida)* certainly qualifies as one of the most spectacular in Greece, notably along the **Styra–Marmari** stretch, which rises to 600m (2,000 feet) above a deeply indented coastline.

The landscape is dotted with small fortresses dating from the baronies of the Venetian period. **Karystos** itself occupies a splendid location at the foot of **Mt. Ohi** (1,400m/4,600 feet), with a small fertile plain and a fine beach. The town is modern but tidy; antiquities include the imposing **Castel Rosso** on the mountain and a smaller **fort** in town, both of Venetian origin.

The northern half of the island is much greener than the s, with dense forests of chestnut and plane. **Loutra Edipsou** is renowned throughout Greece for its thermal sulfur baths. **Mt. Dirfis** (1,743m/5,718 feet) can be climbed with a relatively easy $1\frac{1}{2}$-hour hike from the alpine refuge above Steni; the view covers all of Euboea, Attica and Boeotia, as well as a large sweep of the Aegean Sea.

☞ In **Karystos** *(☎ code 0224):* the **Apollon** (A) and the **Apollon Resort** (B) *(☎22.045 ⬚ to ⬚ 115 rms);* in both ≡≞ ☏ In the town center: **Hironia** (C) *(☎22.238 ⬚)* is simple and charming.

In **Marmari** *(☎ code 0224):* try **Marmari Bay** (C) *(☎31.301/3 ⬚≡ ≋),* a large modern hotel.

In **Eretria** *(☎ code 0221):* **Eretria Beach** (B) *(4km/2$\frac{1}{2}$ miles w of town on the beach ☎62.411 ⬚ ≡≞ ☏ ≋).*

In **Halkida** *(☎ code 0221):* **Lucy**

(A) *(☎23.831 ⬚ 92 rms ☏),* on the mainland; **Paliria** (B) *(☎28.001/6 ⬚),* at the heart of the harbor walk. Numerous moderate-to-good beach hotels exist along the coast to Eretria.

In **Loutra Edipsou** *(☎ code 0226)* a very large number of A, B, C and D hotels, and pensions, include **Aegli** (A) *(☎22.215 ⬚ ☏),* a large old hotel with a stately appearance but decaying plumbing, and **Galini** (C) *(on Ag. Nikolaou St. ☎22.448 ⬚),* smaller and more modern.

GERAKI ▲ ⬛ ☆
42km (26 miles) E of Sparta. Map 6J5. Population 1,600.

On a bare hill almost untouched by tourism stand the deserted and half-destroyed shells of medieval Geraki (locally Pirgos, or "Tower"), topped by a crumbling fortress that was once the seat of one of the 12 Frankish baronies of the Peloponnese. The fort was built in 1254 by Jean de Nivelet, a knight from the Franche Comté. The ruins include more than a dozen late medieval churches, some of which (notably **Ag. Georgios**, within the fortress) retain considerable frescoes.

The site is particularly attractive in springtime when **Mt. Taygetos** rises snow-capped on the W horizon. The newer village of Geraki is a pleasant place, 2km (1 mile) to the W, with some tavernas. Those wishing to see the interior of the churches should apply here for keys.

GYTHIO 🏛 🕿 ★

47km (29 miles) S of Sparta. Map 6J5. Population 4,000 🕿 code: 0733.

Gythio is a very attractive port town with much old architecture as yet unspoiled by modern encroachments. Until a decade ago it was practically untouched by tourism, although the recent popularity of the MANI, for which Gythio forms the best base of exploration, has begun to bring in a steady stream of visitors.

The town offers few specific sights. A tour of reconnaissance should include the harbor promenade, the first parallel street up (with many old houses) and the ruined castle (◀€). On the islet of **Kranai** (reached by causeway), where Helen and Paris are said to have spent their first night together after eloping from Sparta, there is a Mani-style **tower house** (one of which is illustrated on page 145), now converted into a museum of Mainote folklore *(unfortunately, usually closed)*.

10km (6 miles) W of town is the ruined castle of **Passava**, built in the 13thC under the name of *Passe-avant* by barons of the de Neuilly family.

The twice-weekly ferry to **Crete** via the island of **Kythera** departs from Gythio Wednesday 11am and Thursday 11pm.

🕿 **Gythion** (A) (🕿 *23.523* ▢ 7 *rms* ▦), the best hotel in town, is in a fine 19thC building on the harbor. Next door, in a similarly charming but slightly rundown house, is the D-class **Aktaion** (🕿 *22.294* ▢), also the studio of local artist and poet N. Zografakis.

On the beaches on either side of town, a few decent hotels worth trying are: the **Lakonis** (A) (🕿 *22.666* ▥ 74 *rms* ⚞ ◈ *꙰*); the **Belle Helene** (B) (🕿 *22.867* ▥ 98 *rms* ◈ ⚞) and the **Laryssion** (C) (🕿 *22.021/6* ▢ 78 *rms* ⚞).

▲ On the beach NW of town.

HYDRA (Idra) 🏛 🕿 ★

Map 6I7. Resident population 3,000 🕿 code: 0298 ℹ 52.205. **Hydrofoil** *from Piraeus (Zea Marina) 8–10 times daily, 1hr; Poros 5–7 times daily; Ermioni 4–6 times daily.*

Hydra has a picture-perfect semicircular harbor, with the stately houses of 19thC seamen forming an amphitheater on the steep slopes. The town's enticing scenery made it popular with foreign — mostly English — artists and writers in the 1950s and '60s, and has attracted mass tourism (mostly young people) since the 1970s.

In the competition for tourist money, peddlers of kitsch have replaced the artists, and simple fishermen's tavernas and cafés have been driven upmarket, yet the pleasant harmony of Hydra's site and architecture remains unimpaired, outside the peak season. The car-less streets contribute hugely to the effect.

The barren island (the name, meaning "watery," is evidently ironic) was uninhabited in Antiquity and the Middle Ages. Albanian settlers arrived during the centuries of Turkish rule to profit from the great boom in Mediterranean piracy. A British connection cultivated during Napoleon's continental blockade (1806–14) put their buccaneering talents to good use in running the contraband trade to English ports. This brought the immense wealth and the overseas ties that made Hydriote captains such a crucial component of the Greek War of Independence.

Most of the naval chiefs whose names are now prominent on the streets and squares of Greece (Koundouriotis, Kriezis, Miaoulis, Tombazis, Voulgaris among others) were sons of Hydra. Their descendants included four prime ministers and one president of Greece. The "Hydriote cabal" was instrumental in forcing King Otto to accept the constitution in 1843 and in finally overthrowing him in 1862.

The island itself declined from a population of 20,000 in 1821 to a state of virtual desertion by the mid-20thC, when tourism engendered a rapid recovery.

SIGHTS AND PLACES OF INTEREST

The residences of the old merchant sailors are relatively simple on the exterior but sumptuously decorated inside. The finest are the two **Koundouriotis houses**, which can be toured on application to the owners. The **Tsamados house** has been converted into a merchant marine academy, while the **Tombazis house** accommodates a school of fine arts. In the district of **Kalo Pigadi**, high above town, there are several 18thC houses.

The coast around the town is steep and rocky, so the best way to go swimming is to rent a boat. A 40-minute walk E leads to a popular beach at **Mandraki**. Several monasteries are located in barely accessible parts of the mountain.

The major local event is the *Miaoulia*, celebrated with naval parade and mock battles on June 20.

Accommodation in town consists mainly of pensions and private rooms in converted old buildings, which are generally delightful places, faulty plumbing and all. Finding a room in July–August is not easy: it might be better to try **Ermioni** or **Hydra Beach** on the mainland.

Typical of the mansions-turned-pensions in **Hydra town** are **Miranda** (B) (☎ *52.230, 14 rms*), **Hydroussa** (B) *(formerly called Xenia* ☎ *52.217, 36 rms)* and **Hydra** (C) (☎ *52.102, 12 rms).* Another possibility is **Sophia** (D) (☎ *52.313, 5 rms).* Bear in mind that, in this type of hotel, the listed prices (moderate to inexpensive) tend to bear little relation to what is actually charged (potentially outrageous).

Miramare (A), at **Mandraki**, is the island's top modern hotel (☎ *52.300/1* ▥ *28 rms* ▱ ▰).

KALAMATA
260km (163 miles) sw of Athens. Map **6J5**. *Population 40,000* ☎ *code: 0721.* **Air connection** *daily at 7.50pm* **from** *and at 9.10pm* **to** *Athens, with added flight Sat–Sun (* ☎ *22.376 or 22.724).*

This southern Peloponnesian town is mostly uninteresting except as the producer of the excellent olives that have made its name famous around the world. Its broad main avenue shows the hand of the French engineers who designed the town after 1829.

Traces of the 1981 earthquake, which caused extensive damage in Kalamata, are still very much in evidence, with fascinatingly graphic if unfortunate examples of the destructive mechanics of how a quake affects buildings. The town has a somewhat prosaic 13thC **citadel** with several fine 19thC houses, and a Byzantine church nearby. A coastal boulevard continues E of the port to a mini pleasure port with tavernas, and on to a long pebble beach lined with hotels.

Elite (A) (☎ 25.015 ▥ ☎); **Filoxenia** (B) (☎ 23.166/8 ▥), considered the best, isolated site at the far end of the beach; **Haikos** (C) (☎ 82.886 ▢). Several inexpensive hotels are near the railroad station.

KALAVRYTA ◁€ ☆
78km (49 miles) SE of Patra (28km/18 miles from the coast). Map 6H5. Population 2,000 ☎ code: 0692.

This pleasant summer resort is worth a visit for the spectacular scenery of the **Vouraikos Gorge**, through which a quaint 19thC miniature train huffs and puffs its way up to a green and watery spot at 750m (2,460 feet). The town was rebuilt after being wiped out by the Nazis in reprisal for partisan activities during World War II.

Near the N end of the gorge *(9km/6 miles N of Kalavryta)* is the **Monastery of Mega Spileo**, an astonishing complex perched at the edge of a cavern at the foot of an immense perpendicular cliff. The history of the monastery is lost in medieval lore, and the current buildings date from only 1934. Pride of place among the monastic possessions goes to an icon of the Virgin painted by St Luke the Evangelist himself, and the skull of St Euphrosyne, who discovered the aforementioned icon miraculously preserved in this cavern.

Another monastery nearby, the **Agia Lavra** *(7km/4 miles SW of Kalavryta)*, occupies an important place in modern Greek history as the place where on March 25, 1821, Germanos, Archbishop of Patras, raised the banner of revolt against the Turks. The otherwise attractive site is marred by an excess of gushing patriotism.

Filoxenia (B) (☎ 22.422 ▢); **Maria** (C) (☎ 22.296 ▢).

KORONI ▥ ☎ ☆
53km (33 miles) s of Kalamata. Map 5J4. Population 2,000 ☎ code: 0725.

Koroni is a pleasant little port town, consisting of whitewashed houses with pink roofs surrounded by a generous landscape of vineyards and olives. Its **Venetian castle** stands out of all proportion to the village, a reminder of the time (1206–1500) when Coron, as it was then called, and nearby Modon (METHONI) were the chief strategic assets of the Italian city-republic in the Peloponnese.

The citadel was occupied by the Turks, by the Venetians again (1687–1715), and then a second time by the Turks; it still contains some inhabited houses and semiruined churches. Beyond it, a tawny sand **beach** extends for miles, with only a decent number of locals and some independently traveling tourists around to enjoy its pleasures.

☜ Practically every other house in Koroni rents rooms. The only hotel in town with any pretensions is **Auberge de la Plage** (B) (☎ *22.401* ▥ *32 rms* ⇶ ☏ *).*

KYLLINI 🏰 ☏
53km (33 miles) SE *of Patras. Map* **5***H3.*

The western "spur" of the Peloponnese is formed by the fertile alluvial deposits of the Peneios River. **Andravida**, the chief market of the district, retains few clues to its mighty past as the seat of the Frankish Princedom of Achaea. The rich and proud medieval port of **Clarence** (Glaréntsa), which once stood at the NW tip of the peninsula, is now reduced to a few indefinite bits of stone at the western edge of the nondescript beach resort of Kyllini.

On a lone prominence dominating the entire plain, 5km ($2\frac{1}{2}$ miles) inland, is the **Castle of Clairmont** (Hlemoutsi, or Castel Tornese), the best-preserved Frankish monument in Greece, a building of huge size and barbaric splendor. It contains a little Gothic church, and a maze of parapets and bastions pervaded by a melancholy air.

The plain belonged in heroic times to the kings of Elis, who were famous for their innumerable herds of cattle. One of the twelve labors of Heracles (see NAFPLIO) involved cleaning the stables of Augeias, King of Elis, which had grown so thick with manure that the land could no longer bear fruit. The hero accomplished his task by bringing the rivers Alpheios and Peneios together to flush the plain clean, and "cleaning the Augean stables" has been a metaphor ever since for a bold attack on a long-neglected sore.

The Principality of Achaea (or Morea) was created in 1205 by Geoffroi de Villehardouin, a knight of the Champagne, and held suzerainty over the 12 Duchies of the Frankish Peloponnese. It was later conquered by Mahiot de Coquerel and the Chevalier de San Superan, acquired by the Kingdom of Navarre, sold to the Counts of Cephallonia, and finally abolished by the Despots of MISTRA in 1432.

❖ The Duchy of Clarence was the allodial (absolutely owned) domain of the Princes of Achaea, from whom it passed by marriage to the family of Hainault. The title was revived by Edward III of England and his Queen, Philippa of Hainault, in favor of their second son, Lionel, and remains one of the most illustrious titles of the English nobility to this day.

☜ There are numerous beach hotels at **Loutra Kyllinis**, 9km (6 miles) to the s of Kyllini on the opposite shore of the peninsula. Some simple hotels can be found in **Kyllini** itself.

LAVRIO
Map 7E3.

The otherwise undistinguished town of Lavrio was famous in Antiquity as the site of the most extensive lead and silver mines of the Mediterranean world. More than 2,000 ancient mine shafts are prominent on the hills behind the town. Lavrio now possesses a refugee camp for asylum seekers and undocumented aliens, which explains the Iranians, Turks, East Europeans, Africans etc. who are sometimes in evidence.

The barren island of **Makronisi** has gained notoriety for its prison camp where communist suspects, among them the great poet Yannis Ritsos, were detained during the civil war of 1944–49.

LEONIDIO   See ARCADIAN COAST, page 125.

LIVADIA 🏨
122km (76 miles) NW of Athens. Map 4G6. Population 18,000 ☎ code: 0261.
Frequent bus from Athens (KTEL terminal at Liossion 260) or Thebes.

Livadia grew in importance during the Turkish era as Thebes declined, and the modern town keeps something of the spirit, if not the architecture, of a Turkish market town with busy narrow streets and diminutive shops. The **citadel** (Kastro), which was built by the Catalans after 1311 and used as the residence of the pasha later on, occupies a steep hill behind the town. At its foot, in a pleasant wooded area with a picturesque Turkish bridge and two springs, which apparently correspond to the ancient fountains of **Mnemosyne** (Memory) and **Lethe** (Forgetting), is the cave of the oracle of Trophonius. The method of consulting the oracle is described in fascinating detail by Pausanias.

🍴 **Levadia** (B) (☎ *28.266* 🔲 *); **Helikon** (C) (☎ *28.520* 🔲 *).* The **Xenia** restaurant and guesthouse located over the springs of Memory and Forgetting provide a nice spot to stop for lunch on the Athens–Delphi route.

ENVIRONS
Livadia lies at the edge of what used to be **Lake Kopais**, which was drained between 1887 and 1931 by the British Lake Copais Co. The reclaimed fertile plain is planted with cotton fields.

Along the former lakeshore, 13km (8 miles) NE, is **Orchomenos** (population 5,000), where in 2000–1700BC flourished the civilization of the Minyans, a Middle Helladic people who may or may not have been Greek. They were distinguished for a special type of pottery (Minyan ware), and successfully drained Lake Kopais — a technical feat that eluded the repeated efforts of later Antiquity. Besides numerous Neolithic, Bronze Age and Classical traces, the site also possesses the monastery **Church of the Dormition**, which is possibly the oldest standing Byzantine edifice in Greece, dating from the year 873.

On the Lamia road 14km (9 miles) NW of Livadia, a giant lion marks the site of the **Battle of Chaeronia**, where in 338BC the Macedonian army

143

under the 18-year-old Alexander put a definitive end to the ancient Greek system of independent city-states.

The town of **Chaeronia** (with a small rock-carved theater) is the birthplace of the historian Plutarch (c.AD46–125).

MANI ⛰ 🏛 🏠 ⋞ 🍽 ★
Areopoli (main village) 82km (51 miles) SE of Kalamata, 28km (18 miles) SW of Gythio. Map 6J–K5. Population of the peninsula: c.2,000 ☎ code: 0733.
Bus *from Kalamata to Areopoli; from Gythio to all villages.*

The mountain fastnesses of the middle "finger" of the Peloponnese, called Mani after the Frankish castle of Le Grand Maigne or Maine near Cape Tenaro, were the refuge of Laconian fugitives during the centuries of Turkish rule. After Independence, much patriotic mileage was made out of the claim that Mani constituted the only part of the Greek fatherland never to have been subjected to the Turk; the prosaic truth seems to have been more like certain parts of the Bronx that New York police write off as beyond saving.

Unlike the Bronx, however, the Mainote bandits had the esthetic sense to dot their eyries with incredibly picturesque fortified villages, so that their strange and eerie land is now one of the most rewarding to tour in Greece. To be sure, Mani is no longer the lost world so lyrically described by Patrick Leigh Fermor in the 1960s; there is no shortage of tour buses that ply its precipitous lanes; but they have not yet fully eradicated that awesome sense of crossing the farthest edge of the continent.

SIGHTS AND PLACES OF INTEREST
The only substantial village in Mani proper, that is, the only one with more than two shops, is **Areopoli**, which must constitute the beginning and end of a tour *(86km/54 miles)* of the peninsula.

> ❖ Areopoli was renamed after Ares, the god of war, in memory of its most famous son, Petrobey Mavromichalis, hereditary chieftain of Mani during the War of Independence. Of godlike beauty with black bushy eyebrows, and armed to the teeth with scimitar and carbine, he took part in 49 battles, not all of them against the Turks. Imprisoned by the revolutionary government, he responded by having Kapodistrias, the first president of Greece, assassinated. On his mother's side, he reputedly descended from a mermaid.

There are some 40 villages in the shadow of the **Kakovounia** (Evil Mountain, 1,214m/3,983 feet), consisting mostly of a few **tower-houses** huddled together (one is illustrated opposite). Nearly all bear the stamp of the Middle Ages, and it is hard to pick one that is more picturesque than others: **Kita** (population 100), which was the stronghold of the notorious Nicli clan, and **Vathia**, which was deserted by its inhabitants before the GNTO restored it as a rustic hotel-hamlet, yield the best photographs. **Tsikalia** and **Lagia** have memorable settings. The little gloomy port of **Gerolimenas** is the only village set directly on the shore.

A dozen or so villages own quaint little late-Byzantine churches, and the **Ag. Iannis** of Areopoli contains some naive wall-paintings that show a vivid imagination.

In all, some 800 tower-houses have been counted. Their formidably rugged architecture testifies to centuries spent warding off the forces of law and the no less dangerous rapacity of neighbors, rivals, kinsmen and blood-foes. Most of the tower-houses are more or less abandoned, but some of the few that remain in use are veritable museums of folk art, and people who own such houses (such as in Areopoli and Kita) are usually eager to show them off to curious visitors.

Tower house, Mani

Cape Tainaron (Tenaro), the tip of the peninsula, was known in mythology as the spot where Heracles descended into the underworld to steal Cerberus, the three-headed dog of Hades. The ride across the ridge from Gerolimenas to **Kokala** offers the most extraordinary scenery.

Small beaches of dazzling white pebble exist all around the peninsula, notably near the **Diros caves** (see below), at **Mezapos**, below **Vathia** and at **Kotronas**.

Diros caves ★ ▧

The **Glyfada Cave**, at the seashore below Pirgos Dirou, must count as the most extraordinary natural sight of Greece and is bound to impress even the most jaded cave-goer. The cave is in fact an underground lake 5km ($2\frac{1}{2}$ miles) long and 5 to 25m ($5\frac{1}{2}$ to 27 yards) wide, with an enormous wealth of stalactites. Visitors are taken on a 45-minute rowboat ride through scenery of terrifying beauty, which cannot fail to evoke images of Charon and the Styx. Even the silliest tourists are reduced to awed silence after the first few minutes of the ride.

Located about 200m (220 yards) along the seashore from the entrance of the Glyfada Cave, the **Alepotrypa Cave** is reputedly just as impressive, although in order to safeguard the numerous Paleolithic and Neolithic finds inside, it remains closed to visitors.

Exo Mani ◁≡

The w slopes of **Mt. Taygetos** along the coast between Areopoli and KALAMATA, known as the Outer Mani, are traversed by a magnificent road with fabulous views. The scenery changes rapidly from the scrub-covered gray hills of the s to a delectably lush environment of vineyards, palms and dark cypresses. Instead of the grim pride of Mani proper, villages present the smiling countenance of agreeable little squares with cafés set under ancient plane trees, pergolas of climbing rose, and pomegranate trees of dazzling color. There are deserted inlets for swimming, and the usual complement of Byzantine churches in practically every village. The pleasant fishing port of **Kardamyli** is a good place to stop for lunch or a beach break.

❖ In 1675, the inhabitants of Oitylo (or Itilo) emigrated en masse to Corsica. There is a persistent legend that the family of Napoleon Bonaparte descended from these emigrants, and that its name was a literal translation of Kalomeris, Greek for "Goodland."

❧ **Inner Mani:** The GNTO have restored tower-houses in **Areopoli**, **Gerolimenas** and **Vathia**; they are all wonderfully atmospheric places to stay, but the villages do become somewhat lonely at night, so many will prefer to set up base at GYTHIO. In addition, a number of basic hotels or pensions exist at **Itilo**, **Areopoli**, **Pirgos Dirou**, **Gerolimenas** and **Kotronas**.

GNTO guesthouses in historic towers: in Areopoli, **Pirgos Kapetanakou** (A) (☎ (0533) 51.233 ▥) and **Vathia**

▲ At **Stoupa**, beside the beach.

Traditional Village (A) (☎ (0533) 54.244 ▥ 15 rms in 6 towerhouses, by prior reservation only). In Gerolimenas, **Pirgos Tsitsiri** (B) (☎ (0733) 54.297 ▥ 20 rms ⇌ open Apr-Dec).

Outer Mani: there are decent places to stay in **Itilo**, **Ag. Nikolaos**, **Stoupa** and **Kardamyli**. On Neohori Beach, near Stoupa, **Lefktron** (B) (☎ (0721) 54.322 ▥ 32 rms) is a good choice. **Theano** (C) (☎ (0721) 73.222 ▥ 9 rms ✿ ✍), in Kardamyli, is another possibility.

MARATHON (Marathonas) 🏛
38km (24 miles) NE of Athens. Map 7C3. Bus from Mavromateon and Leof. Alexandras (map 2B4). Tomb and museum open Tues–Sun 8.30am–3pm; closed Mon 🔳 ☎(0294) 55.155.

In 490BC a small force of Athenians under Miltiades, aided by a unit of Plataeans, won a heroic victory at Marathon against a much larger Persian army. The runner Pheidippeides, who brought the news of the victory, collapsed and died on his arrival at the Athenian Agora. The "Marathon run" was revived at the first modern Olympics of 1896 with a Marathon–Athens race that was won by an itinerant Athenian waterseller named Louis.

❖ The actual distance to the battlefield along the modern road is a little less than 42km (26 miles); the ancient road was somewhat shorter. The official marathon course of 42km, 195m (26 miles, 213 yards) is in fact equal to the distance between Windsor Castle and the royal grandstand at Shepherd's Bush, the start and end points of the race as it was run at the London Olympics of 1908.

The 12m/39-foot-high **tumulus** where the 192 Athenians who died in the battle were buried rises amid orchards 4km (2½ miles) s of the modern town of Marathonas. The smaller **tumulus of the Plataeans** *(4km/2½ miles inland near the village of Vrana)* is nearer the actual battlefield. Nearby, a concrete structure gives protection to a **Bronze Age cemetery**.

where the complete skeletons of remarkably small men and horses can be seen in open graves. A small **museum** is located in the town itself. A single ticket gives access to all sights.

✍ Marathonas itself offers only a couple of downmarket pensions, but a plethora of adequate hotels can be found along the coast, from Shinias (to the N) to Ag. Panteleimonas, Nea Makri, Zouberi and Mati (to the S). A few recommendations follow:

Golden Coast (A) at Marathon beach (☎ (0294) 92.102 ⬚ 543 rms ═ ⌂ ⬥ ⌐ ⌂ ⊞ open Apr-Oct).

Mati (A) in Mati (☎ (0294) 71.511 ⬚ 70 rms ═ ⌂ ⬥ no AC, open year round).

Marathon Beach (B) in Nea Makri (☎ (0294) 91.255 ⬚ 166 rms ═ ⌂ ⬥ ⌂ ⊞ open Mar-Oct).

MEGALOPOLI
37km (23 miles) sw of Tripoli. Map 6I5. Population 5,000 ☎ *code: 0791.*

The only sight of even moderate interest in Megalopoli is the half-ruined ancient **theater**, which was once the largest in Greece, with a seating capacity of more than 20,000.

❖ The city owes its outsized name and appointments to the grandiose concept of Epaminondas, who herded together the inhabitants of 40 Arcadian communes in 371–368BC to create Megali Polis (Great City) as a strategic bulwark against Sparta. A hundred years later the place lay dead and deserted. Its one famous son was Polybius the historian (204–122BC), the man who gave the Romans their first taste of Greek civilization.

✍ **Leto** (C) (☎ 22.302 ⬚) is a reasonable, medium-category place to stay.

MESSENE (Arhea Messini) ▥ ☆
26km (16 miles) N of Messini town (37km/23 miles NW of Kalamata). Map 5J4.

The ruins of ancient Messene lie scattered in a beautiful countryside against the imposing backdrop of Mt. Ithomi (800m/2,625 feet); the village of **Mavromati** occupies part of the ancient site. Much of the old buildings lie half-buried in soil and overgrown with vegetation, and the absence of overt archeological activity forms a welcome contrast with other Classical locations.

The city was built after 370BC at the instigation of Epaminondas, who liberated Messenia from its long subjection to Sparta and encouraged its inhabitants to build cities. Pausanias called its walls the most powerful he had seen, not excluding those of Babylon. Messenians believed that Zeus was reared on Mt. Ithomi by a nymph. A hymn referred to —

> "Zeus of Ithomi whose heart the muse pleased,
> With her pure strings, with her free sandals."

The ruins are to be found in a wide arc below the village. They include a substantial portion of the walls that so impressed Pausanias (the

Arcadian Gate, about 1km/$\frac{1}{2}$ mile NW of the village), a large and a small **theater**, and an **agora** containing traces of a sanctuary of Asclepius.

On the peak of **Mt. Ithomi** *(20min climb)*, abandoned monastic buildings occupy the site of the former Temple of Zeus, commanding extraordinary views over the surrounding countryside. The **Vourkano Monastery**, on a SE spur of the mountain with buildings dating from the 18thC, provides room for travelers. Further accommodation and a railroad station exist at the village of **Meligalas** (Milk-and-Honey), 13km (8 miles) NE.

METHONI 🍴 🏖 ☆
65km (41 miles) SW of Kalamata. Map 5J4. Population 1,750 ☎ code: 0723.

Of the Messenian ports of Methoni, KORONI and PYLOS, each having the similar attractions of a pleasant village, Venetian castle and beach, Koroni boasts the quaintest village, Pylos the best beach and Methoni the finest castle. The harbor has been sanded up, and where Venetian galleys once dropped anchor, small numbers of beach-goers enjoy the sun.

The **castle**, a magnificent structure with moats and drawbridges and parapets, has traces of the pre-Independence town (ruined baths, mosque, church) within its vast enclosure. The two bastions on either side of the main landward gate bear the proud Venetian names of Bembo (15thC) and Loredan (1714); beyond them is a Gothic inner gate from the 13thC. The graceful fortified tower (**Boúrtsi**) on an islet at the seaward entrance is a Turkish addition (16thC). Cervantes was kept in the fortress as a prisoner after his capture at Lepanto (see NAFPAKTOS); otherwise it shares the history of its twin at Koroni.

The uninhabited islands of **Sapienza** and **Schiza** are within rowing distance of the coast.

🍴 Methoni is much better equipped with adequate hotels than Koroni. **Methoni Beach** (B) (☎31.455 or 31.544 ▥ compulsory half-board 🍽 12 rms) has a prime location between the castle and beach; other good choices are **Alex** (C) (☎31.219 ▯ 18 rms); **Phoenix** (D) (☎31.390 ▯).

▲ On the beach SE of town and at **Finikounda**, 14km (9 miles) E.

MISTRA ⛰ 🍴 ◁ ★
8km (5 miles) W of Sparta. Map 6J5. Site open daily 8.30am–3pm, sometimes until 6pm 📷

On a nearly vertical mountain face in the eastern foothills of Mt. Taygetos stand the spectacular ruins of the medieval walled city of Mistra, where for a brief Indian summer in the 15thC the Byzantine civilization experienced its last and in some ways most interesting flowering.

The churches, monasteries and palaces are unique in Greece in that they surpass the unambitious scale usually associated with Byzantine buildings in this part of the empire; they reflect the taste and wealth of the Constantinopolitan court, which briefly took refuge in this wild mountaintop before being swept away under the Turkish wave.

HISTORY

The fortress of Mistra was built by Guillaume de Villehardouin in 1249. After changing hands several times in the following 100 years, it became in 1349 the seat of a semi-independent Byzantine governor by the title of Despot (Lord) of Morea, who managed to retake the Peloponnese from the Franks piecemeal over the next 80 years.

The despotate was usually held by a brother or son of the reigning Byzantine emperor, and reached its apogee under Theodore II Paleologue (reigned 1407–43). The Despot Constantine Dragazes (reigned 1443–48) later ascended the imperial throne as Constantine XI, the last emperor of Byzantium.

The most famous resident of Mistra was **Gemistus Plethon** (c.1360–1450), who has been called the originator of Platonic studies in the West. Born in Constantinople, he spent some time in the Ottoman court in Edirne before taking residence in Mistra. Here he all but renounced Christianity, devoting himself to Platonic philosophy and to the idea of reviving the ancient Greek spirit.

He had enormous influence in the courts of Renaissance Italy: inspired by Plethon's lectures during the Council of Florence (1439), Cosimo de Medici went on to found the celebrated Platonic Academy, which revolutionized European philosophy. Sigismondo Malatesta, the famous *condottiere* who attempted to recapture Mistra from the Turks in 1464 on behalf of Venice, transferred Plethon's mortal remains to Rimini.

> ❖ Faust, transported to medieval Sparta in Part II of Goethe's play,
> imagines a Germanic revival of Greece with Mistra at its vanguard.

Mistra came under Turkish rule in 1460. It experienced a period of revival during the Venetian occupation of 1687–1715, but was sacked by the Mainotes in 1770 and by Turkish troops during the War of Independence, and gradually abandoned after the refounding of Sparta in 1834. Remaining families were expelled by the archeologists in 1952.

SIGHTS AND PLACES OF INTEREST

Sightseeing involves a very steep climb between the lower entrance (360m/1,181 feet) and the citadel (620m/2,034 feet). There is an upper entrance below the citadel. The six major churches and the Despots' Palace deserve full attention; numerous minor churches, a mosque, and the ruins of both patrician and humble houses lie scattered over the rest of the space.

The **Metropolitan** (Cathedral) was built in 1309, with frescoes executed at that time, but the domes were added in the 15thC. A lovely courtyard, containing an ancient sarcophagus and a 19thC fountain, commands a good view over the Eurotas Valley.

The **Vrontochion Monastery** contains two churches, the **Ag. Theodore** and the architecturally unique **Panagia Odigitria** (Virgin Guiding the Way), which was built in 1310. The frescoes of the latter, notably those in the narthex depicting the miracles of Christ, compare in quality with the best work of the contemporary early Florentine and Sienese masters.

Theodore II, who is buried in a side chapel, is represented in one mural in the habits of despot and monk.

The delightful **Pantanassa Monastery**, founded in 1428 by John Frangopoulos, the chief minister of the Despotate, whose house survives a short distance below the monastery, is still occupied by some elderly nuns, who sell their intricate embroideries. Among the frescoes is a fine 15thC portrait.

The **Perivléptos Monastery** is a 14thC edifice, although its architecture is reminiscent of the tiny 11thC churches of Athens. Its frescoes are among the most complete and expressive of those in any Byzantine church in the world.

The **Agia Sophia**, in the upper town, was built in 1350 and used as the palace chapel. Theodora Tocco and Cleopa Malatesta, wives of two successive despots, are buried here.

The impressive **Despots' Palace** is a rare specimen of Byzantine secular architecture. The E wing, dating from the 13thC, is probably Frankish and shows Gothic influences; the w wing was built in the 15thC and is preserved in its three stories.

☙   There is one small but fine hotel — **Byzantion** (B) (☎ *(0731) 93.309* ⅏ *22 rms* ⇌*)* — and several pensions in the pleasant village below the ruins. For more accommodation, see SPARTA.

MONEMVASIA ⛰ 📷 🏨 ≪ 🍴 ★
100km (63 miles) SE of Sparta. Map 6J6. Population 600 ☎ code: 0732.
Hydrofoil *from Piraeus, Tues and Sat 9am.* **Bus** *from Sparta.*

Monemvasia, the walled medieval town whose name means "Single Exit," occupies a seaside ledge at the foot of a huge rock, on account of which it has often been called the Gibraltar of Greece. Once a famous city from which the Malmsey wine obtained its name, it was reduced to obscure penury in modern times, until less than 100 inhabitants remained to live among its decaying houses.

More recently, tourism has created a modern hodgepodge town (called **Gefira**) on the mainland opposite the rock, while the strange ghost town within the walls has slowly begun to return to life with restored tourist shops, replanted gardens and reconsecrated churches. The pace of revival, however, has not been so fast nor so rash as to destroy the evocative, melancholy atmosphere of the place.

A stupendous **fortress** rises vertically above the town to the summit of the rock, where the fine 12thC church of **Agia Sophia** stands at the edge of a vertiginous terrace. There are four historic churches within the town itself, although none of great distinction.

The history of Monemvasia echoes that of Mistra. The city grew in significance as a Greek redoubt during the medieval Slavic invasions of the Peloponnese. It was taken by Villehardouin and retaken by the despotate. It became a Venetian property after the rest of Greece had fallen to the Turks, and remained so until 1540, whereafter the Turks and the Venetians changed place several times again.

❖   Yannis Ritsos (1909–90), perhaps the greatest poet of modern
Greece, was a native of the old village of Monemvasia. Members of
his immediate family still live there.

In ancient mythology the wild peninsula s of Monemvasia was known
as the last home of the centaurs, men with horses' bodies.

☞   There are five pensions in the
historic area of Monemvasia, all of
which are in judiciously restored old
buildings, all of them equally lovely:
GNTO-operated **Kellia** (A) (☎*61.520*
▥ 12 rms); **Malvasia** (A) (☎*61.323*
▥ 26 rms in two houses); **Vizantino**
(A) (☎*61.351* Ⓕ*61.331 ▥ 13 rms);*
Panos (B) (☎*61.480 ▥ 9 rms ▦)*
and **Theofano** (B) (☎*61.212 ▢ 3
rms, open May-Oct).*

A great number of C–D hotels, and
pensions, have emerged recently in **Gefira**, across the causeway.

▲   **Paradise**, on the beach 5km (3 miles) s of town.

MOUNT HELICON (Elikon oros)   See THEBES, page 169.

MOUNT PARNASSUS   See ARAHOVA, page 125.

MYCENAE (Mikines) 🏛 ◁€ ☆
*12km (8 miles) N of Argos. Map **6**H6. **Bus** from Argos and Nafplio. **Site** open
daily 8.30am–3pm, sometimes until 6pm* 📷

The imposing hilltop stronghold of the Bronze Age kings was already a
vaguely noticed ruin in Classical times. Its discovery by Schliemann in
1874–76 and the unearthing of the various royal treasuries buried
within were among the finest hours of modern archeology. The grim
splendor of the site cannot fail to impress the modern visitor.

The legendary history of Mycenae is inextricably confused with that
of ARGOS. The citadel was said to have been founded by Perseus, and
appears to have controlled the Peloponnese toward the end of the
'Mycenaean" era.

Its last important ruler was **Agamemnon**, who led the Greek armies
against Troy in a war that was precipitated by the abduction of Helen,
the wife of Agamemnon's brother Menelaus, king of Sparta. He returned
from the war with a mistress, Cassandra; his wife Clytemnestra had in the
meanwhile also taken a lover, Aegisthus by name, and contrived to
murder the king at his return banquet. She was in turn despatched by her
son Orestes, aided by Electra, his sister.

Archeological evidence suggests that Mycenae was inhabited from
c.5000BC, with a time of highest civilization around 1600–1200BC. The
culture of this period shows clear Egyptian influence, which accords with
the Egyptian origins of Danaos, the legendary founder of Argos, and with
various references in Homer to relations with Egypt. The royal palace was
destroyed by fire c.1200BC, during the supposed era of the Dorian
invasions.

SIGHTS AND PLACES OF INTEREST

The **citadel**, a mighty structure of irregular "Cyclopean" masonry, is entered through the **Lion Gate**, its massive lintel supporting a slab with a relief of two rampant lionesses.

15thC BC **death mask**

Just past the gate is the **First Circle of Royal Tombs**, where Schliemann discovered six graves containing the royal death masks and the spectacular gold jewelry now displayed at the Athens National Archeological Museum. Schliemann thought he had found the grave of Agamemnon, but the tombs, which date from the 16thC BC, are in fact much older than he suspected.

The **Palace**, which is based on the design of the Minoan palaces of Crete, consisted of two terraces connected by stairways that gave access to the *megaron,* the throne-room, whose form later provided the basis for Greek temple architecture. The E spur of the citadel yields a good view over the site, with a panorama extending over the Plain of Argos.

A **Second Circle of Royal Tombs**, located outside the citadel near the entrance to the archeological site, was discovered by accident in 1951. Its contents, dating from the 17thC BC, are also in Athens.

By far the most interesting tomb architecturally is to be found beside the road about 1km ($\frac{1}{2}$ mile) below the site. This so-called **Treasury of Atreus** consists of a huge underground chamber *(tholos),* 14m (46 feet) high and 15m (49 feet) in diameter, which was topped by a colossal stone block weighing 120 tonnes. The inhabitant of the tomb, whose identification with the father of Agamemnon has no basis in fact, lived in the 14thC BC; most of his belongings are at the British Museum. Eight other *tholos* tombs have been discovered in the vicinity of the citadel.

A tourist-trap village, although not unpleasant, has grown up some distance below the site.

☜ There are about a dozen simple hotels and pensions in the village. **Agamemnon**, **Menelaus**, **Helen**, **Clytemnestra**, **Electra** and **Orestes** are all represented, so is **Schliemann**. A cut above is **La Petite Planete** (B) (☎ *(0751) 66.240* Ⅱ *13 rms* ⇌).

NAFPAKTOS ☙ ☞

97km (60 miles) w of Delphi; 264km (165 miles) w of Athens. Map 3G4. Population 9,000 ☎ *code: 0634.* **Bus**: *3 times daily from Athens via Delphi; 4 times daily from Patras.*

Nafpaktos is a pleasant small town with a tiny circular harbor enclosed by the crenelated walls of a Turkish naval fort and a mighty Venetian-Turkish citadel looming on the hill above. A few attractive back streets and a fine beach E of town make this a worthwhile stopover on the Patras–Delphi route. The town is better known in the West by its medieval name of **Lepanto**.

> ❖ The naval battle of Lepanto, in which an allied fleet led by Don Juan of Austria smashed the Turkish navy (October 7, 1571), is a turning point in modern European history comparable in scope to Salamis in Antiquity. The Ottoman Empire was late to develop as a marine power, but the navy created in the 1520s by Suleyman the Magnificent was soon able to establish its mastery over the Mediterranean. After Lepanto, it never recovered. One ironic effect of this was the power vacuum and the resulting proliferation of piracy that devastated the Mediterranean for the next 250 years.

Cervantes, the author of *Don Quixote,* lost an arm at the Battle of Lepanto and was taken into captivity by the Turks.

🏨 **Xenia** (B) (☎ 22.301/2 ▢) by the beach E of town. There are also C and D hotels in town.

Reasonable beach hotels exist at convenient intervals along the beautiful Nafpaktos–Itea stretch; notably at **Paralia Tolofonos**, **Agii Pantes** and on lovely **Trizonia island**.

▲ By the beach 3km (2 miles) w of Nafpaktos town.

ENVIRONS
11km (7 miles) w of Nafpaktos, another substantial Turkish fortress stands at the ferry port of **Antirio**, dating from the year 1499 like its twin at **Rio**, across the narrowest point of the Gulf of Corinth. *(Continuous ferry service, passage 15mins.)*

NAFPLIO 🏨 📷 � ★
153km (96 miles) sw of Athens; 13km (8 miles) se of Argos. Map 6I6. Population 10,000 ☎ code: 0752 ℹ 24.444. **Hydrofoil** *daily in summer from Zea Harbor, Piraeus. Frequent* **bus** *from Argos; some direct routes from Athens (KTEL terminal at Kifissias 100).* **Train** *from Corinth and Argos.*

With its color-washed, balconied houses and flower-filled back streets, Nafplio is one of the most beautiful towns in Greece. On a vertical rock behind the town rises the dizzying 18thC Venetian fortress of Palamidi. An islet facing the port is occupied by the pretty 15thC bastion of the Bourtzi. The attractive setting of the Argolid Gulf, surrounded by high mountains, and the presence of excellent beaches nearby make Nafplio a good place to spend an extended vacation.

The ancient history of Nafplio (Nauplion) is of marginal interest except for the hero Palamedes, a clever fellow who was credited with the discovery of dice, navigational instruments and certain letters of the alphabet, and who was stoned to death at Troy on false charges of treachery concocted by Ulysses.

The city remained in Venetian hands until 1540, 80 years after the rest of Greece had come under Turkish dominance. It acquired prominence as a seaport during the second Venetian occupation (1687–1715). It was Greece's main town at Independence, and as such became its first capital (1828–34) until Athens was resuscitated to fulfill that duty.

SIGHTS AND PLACES OF INTEREST

A walking tour of Nafplio reveals street after street of pure visual delight. Many of the buildings in the old town are of Venetian origin, with perhaps a more generous share of Turkish contributions than official guides would admit. The **Venetian Arsenal** on the main square dates from the prolific governorship of Agostino Sagredo (1711–14), and now houses the **museum** (▨ *standard opening hrs* ☎ *27.502),* which has unusual Mycenaean idols from Tiryns.

In the larger of the two **mosques** on the same square, the first National Assembly met in 1825–28, and met again to confirm Otto's election as king in 1832. Before the gate of the church of **Ag. Spyridon** (built 1702), John Kapodistrias, the first president of the transitional government of Greece, was assassinated in 1831.

> ❖   John Kapodistrias was born in Corfu, entered the Russian diplomatic service, and served as the Czar's Minister at the Congress of Vienna. He was elected president by the National Assembly in 1827, and struggled in vain to impose some discipline over the various bandit chiefs and warring clans that constituted the Independence movement. He was assassinated by the henchmen of Petrobey Mavromichalis (see page 144), whom he had imprisoned.

Across the street from Ag. Spyridon, a fountain bears an inscription in Turkish, dated 1734–35, inviting whoever drinks to pray for the soul of the founder, a certain Bektash. The Byzantine church of **Ag. Nikolaos** contains frescoes by an 18thC Italian painter. A fine **mosque** of white stone, farther uphill, was converted into a Catholic church in 1840 for the benefit of Otto, who was a Catholic; it contains a Raphael copy that was presented to the young king by Louis Philippe of France.

The **Palamidi Fortress** is accessible by a discreet back road, although some may prefer to take up the challenge of the 857 steps, which Otto's Bavarian courtiers had to negotiate daily to visit the king-elect at his modest residence within the fort. The **Lower Fortress**, also called *Its Kale* or *Acro-Nafplio,* now enclosing the luxury bungalows of the Xenia Palace hotel (see below), is of much older construction and displays the proud Lion of St Mark.

↝ XENIA PALACE (L)

☎(0752) 28.981 ▨(0752) 28.987 ▥
106 rms and bungalows ⇌ *small* ☏
within walking distance ⇝ ♪ ▦ ♿
Surrounded by luxurious bungalows, set in the citadel of Acronafplio, the Xenia Palace is not only the sole L-class hotel in the Peloponnese but also one of the finest hotels in all of Greece.

The **Xenia** (A) next door (☎ *(0752) 28.991)* is a good alternative. Others: **Amfitryon** (A) (☎ *27.366/7* ▥ *48 rms*⇌ *),* a beautiful modern hotel with a lovely harbor view; **Agamemnon** (B) (☎ *28.021* ▥ *40 rms* ⇌ *);* **Helena** (C) (☎ *23.888* ▥ *77 rms);* **Amymoni** (☎ *27.219* ▭ *),* inexpensive, in a stately but decaying 19thC house.

ENVIRONS

The archeologically important but visually unexciting ruins of the Mycenaean citadel of **Tiryns** (Tiryntha) lie directly by the Argos road 4km (2½ miles) N of Nafplio (☎ *open daily 8.30am–3pm).*

Tiryns figures prominently in legends of the Heroic Age, where it appears to have been as powerful a place as Mycenae and Argos. **Heracles** inherited the kingdom of Tiryns from his mother, but was cheated out of his inheritance by Eurystheus, who then set up a series of impossible tasks for the hero.

> ❖   The Twelve Labors of Heracles were: slaying the Nemean lion and the many-headed Hydra; capturing Artemis' stag, the Eryman-thian boar and the Cretan bull; cleaning the Augean stables; hunting the Stymphalian birds; taming the man-eating horses of Diomedes; stealing the girdle of Hippolyte the Amazon and the cattle of the three-bodied Geryon; finding the apple of the Hesperides; and bringing Cerberus, the black dog of Hades, back to earth. He also sailed with the Argonauts to capture the Golden Fleece, held the earth up to give Atlas a rest, and helped Apollo and Poseidon build the walls of Troy. He was made immortal, but his end was tragic: his wife Deianeira gave him a poisoned mantle, which once worn could never be taken off. In agony, Heracles built a funeral pyre on top of Mt. Oita, and perished in the flames.

1.5km (1 mile) outside Nafplio on the Tolo road, the monastery of **Agia Moni**, with a 12thC Byzantine church, occupies a pretty site beside the **Kanathos spring**, in which Hera, to the envy of mortals and immortals, annually renewed her virginity.

Farther SE, past the insignificant ruins of ancient **Asine**, is the long sandy beach of **Tolo**, 11km (7 miles), lined by a string of hotels and fish tavernas.

☞   There is a large number of medium-category hotels in the beach resort of Tolo, most of which are C-class. Good ones include: **Sophia** (B) (☎ *59.567* 🔲), **Epidauria** (C) (☎ *59.219* 🔲) and **Minoa** (C) (☎ *59.207* 🔲).

NEMEA 🏛 ☆

*32km (20 miles) sw of Corinth. Map **6H5**. **Site and museum** open daily 8.30am–3pm; restricted hours on Sun; other hours on Sat. **Museum** closed Mon, sometimes Tues. Different schedules for off-season and half-season* ☎

The three slender columns of the **Temple of Nemean Zeus** stand in a peaceful, evocative valley, surrounded by hills and rarely disturbed by the torrents of tourism flowing between CORINTH and MYCENAE. In this corner of apparent rural calm, Heracles once slew the ferocious Ne-mean lion (see above), who was in fact a creature of Hera and was therefore translated to the heavens to form the constellation Leo.

The temple was built in 340–320BC in a solitary sacred precinct of Zeus, which hosted the biennial Nemean Games, the fourth most prestigious in ancient Greece after those of OLYMPIA, DELPHI and ISTHMIA.

The **stadium** of the Games is visible on a hillside some distance from the temple site. The local **museum** is certainly worth a visit for its well-organized and well-documented displays, the work of the American School. A few attractive tavernas exist some distance farther on at modern **Nemea**, formerly the Turkish village of Kuçuk Vadi ("Little Glen").

OLYMPIA (Olimbia) 🏛 ★
278km (174 miles) sw of Athens; 18km (11 miles) E of Pyrgos. Map 5H4.
Population of village 500 ☎ code: 0624. Train 5 times daily from Pyrgos.
Site *open weekdays 8am–5pm; Sat–Sun 8.30am–3pm* 📷 **Museum** *open*
Tues–Sun as site hours; Mon 11am–5pm 📷

Olympia, set amid the pastoral gentleness of Elis, makes a striking contrast with the dramatic grandeur of DELPHI, the only other archeological site in Greece to which it compares for importance. The beautiful lichen-gray ruins of the Sanctuary of Olympian Zeus, the most important holy site of ancient Greece and the home of the Olympic Games, cover a wide park-like area shaded by venerable pines, plane trees and evergreen oaks.

THE OLYMPIC GAMES
In one account Zeus himself instituted the Games after he had overthrown his father Cronos to become lord and master of the gods in a wrestling match here at Olympia. The height flanking the sanctuary was known as Cronos Hill (Kronion), pointing to a very ancient tradition. The more common account honored Pelops, the Lydian hero who conquered Elis and became the master of the Peloponnese, as the founder of the Games.

From 776BC, when written records began, the Games were held on the August full moon of every fourth year for over 1,000 uninterrupted years. The Olympiad formed the basis of the Greek calendar. A truce was declared during the games to allow participants to travel freely from all parts of the Greek world. The territory of Elis, which administered the Games, enjoyed permanent neutrality; those who violated it were placed under a curse and suffered eternal ignominy; armies entering it had to lay down their arms and received them back only after they left.

Only men whose native tongue was Greek could compete (Nero was the first non-Greek to take part), although barbarians were allowed in as spectators. Slaves and married women were excluded from the precinct under penalty of death. The principal event was the "stadium" race over 204m (223 yards), the name of whose winner became the designation of that particular Olympiad. Other competitions were held in wrestling, boxing, *pankration* (an all-out fight), horse and chariot racing, and the pentathlon, which in turn comprised the stadium run, wrestling, long jump, discus throw and javelin.

Winners were crowned with a branch of wild olive, feasted at public expense, praised by famous poets (in Pindar's *Odes*, for example), and given the option of erecting a statue at the sanctuary (Pliny counted 3,000 of these in the 2ndC AD). There were never any second prizes. Many famous political careers were launched by an Olympic victory: the earliest written record about Athens concerns one Cylon, the victorious Olympic runner, who attempted a coup d'etat c.640BC.

The Games were erratically recorded in the 3rdC AD, and were banned by the Edict of Theodosius in 391. The modern Olympic Games were initiated by Baron de Coubertin at Athens in 1896.

The Sanctuary (Altis)

The sacred precinct of Olympia, which had been overlaid with sand and debris up to a height of 6m (20 feet), was excavated in 1874–81 and 1936–41 by, successively, Ernst Curtius, Wilhelm Doerpfeld and Emil Kunze under the auspices of the German Archeological Institute. The trees, which form one of the attractions of the site, were planted by the Germans.

The present entrance is across the stoa of a 3rdC BC **gymnasium** adjoined by the double colonnade of a **palaestra**, a broad courtyard that was used for athletic training. The **Prytaneion** was the banqueting hall where the victors were entertained. In front of it, a small circular structure with Ionic columns was erected by Alexander the Great to commemorate the victories of his father Philip.

The **workshop** where Phidias created his spectacular statue of Zeus between 456 and 447BC was described by Pausanias some 600 years later

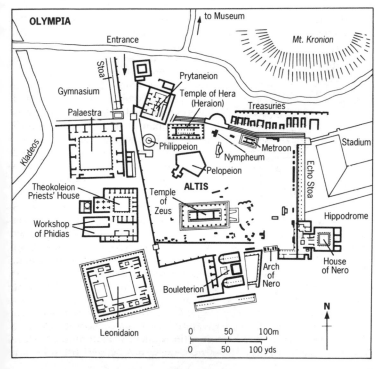

and has been identified with certainty by the discovery of a jug bearing the name of the sculptor and the molds he used for Zeus's cloak. The **Leonidaion** was built by a certain Leonidas of Naxos as a residence for distinguished guests, and later accommodated the Roman governors of Greece.

The **Bouleuterion**, dating in part from the Archaic period, was the meeting place of the Olympian senate, elected from the aristocracy of Elis. The **Arch** and **House of Nero** commemorate the scandalous extra Olympiad ordered on the occasion of the emperor's visit in AD67.

As at Delphi, Nero competed in all regular and several irregular events, and was declared the winner in all; his name was later expunged from the Olympic records.

The **Temple of Zeus**, occupying the center of the Altis, was built in the Doric style by Eleians in 470–456BC; its foundations and the lower drums of the 6 x 13 columns survive.

The temple's chief claim to fame was Phidias's colossal **statue of Zeus**, which was considered one of the Seven Wonders of the World, the only one to be so distinguished in mainland Greece.

The statue was in gold and ivory, and painted in bright colors by the sculptor's brother Panaenus. Pausanias, who saw it in its original position in the temple, confessed that merely to note its measurements could give no idea of its awe-inspiring scale, and Quintilian reported that to gaze upon it enhanced men's understanding of religion. Strabo, on the other hand, thought that Phidias had gotten his proportions wrong, as the god's head almost touched the roof and seemed ready to hit it if Zeus wanted to stand up.

Statue of Hermes, Olympia

A few fragments of the statue said to belong to the god's throne wound up in Rome, and are now at the Hermitage Museum of St Petersburg.

The **Temple of Hera** is in a better state of preservation than that of her husband, despite being the oldest structure in the Altis. It was erected in the early 6thC BC with wooden Doric columns, which were gradually replaced with stone over the centuries.

Next to this temple, Herodes Atticus erected a **Nymphaeum**, or public fountain, in the sumptuous style of the 2ndC AD (see drawing of reconstruction, in the museum); ranged beside it are the remains of the **treasuries** of various Greek cities, and the foundations of a small **temple** dedicated to Cybele, the Mother of the Gods. A small excavation in front of the fountain reveals the signs of Neolithic occupation found beneath the Classical level of the sanctuary, perhaps going back to the age when the low hill flanking the Altis at this point received the name of Cronos, the ruler of the pre-Olympian generation of gods.

The **Olympic Stadium** is a large open space where excavations undertaken on Hitler's personal orders revealed the start and finish lines of the races, as well as a wealth of trophies now exhibited in the museum. The **Echo Stoa**, so called because of its famous sevenfold echo, separated stadium and Altis.

The museum

Instituted by the German archeologists, the museum is next only to the Archeological Museum of Athens in the wealth and quality of its collection. The most memorable displays include the colossal **pediments** of the Temple of Zeus, and the statue of **Hermes** attributed to Praxiteles (illustrated opposite). The *Hermes,* if it indeed belongs to the 4thC master as Pausanias claims, is the only surviving original work of a great sculptor of Antiquity. The pediments, which are well-preserved and extremely powerful, represent the horse-race of Pelops and Oinomaos (E) and the battle of Centaurs and Lapiths (W).

> ❖ Pelops was the son of Tantalus, the king of Lydia in Asia Minor. He sought the hand of Hippodamia, the daughter of Oinomaos, king of Pisa in Elis, who challenged suitors to a chariot-race between Olympia and the Isthmus against his invincible horses, and nailed the heads of the losers to his palace gate. Pelops won with the help of Hippodamia, killed the nefarious king, instituted the Games, and gave his name to the Peloponnese ("Pelops' Island"). His children and grandchildren (who included Agamemnon and Menelaus) ruled Mycenae, Tiryns, Troezen and Sparta, as well as Elis.
>
> Perithoos, king of the Thessalian tribe of Lapiths, invited the Centaurs, the race of half-horse half-men, to his wedding. The Centaurs got drunk and attempted to abduct Lapith women, unleashing a famous war.

Other interesting items at the museum include a remarkable Archaic terracotta **statue** of *Zeus Abducting Ganymede,* and numerous memorial statues spanning the 1,000-year history of Olympia. A fascinating 3-D reconstruction of the **Altis**, a gift of Kaiser Wilhelm II from his postwar exile, and another one incorporating the latest archeological evidence, are displayed in the entrance hall.

OTHER PLACES OF INTEREST

The **International Olympic Academy**, a short distance beyond the museum, and the **Olympic Museum**, located in the village, are quaint relics of the era when modern Olympics had yet to grow into the media and business extravaganza they are today.

The **village** of Olympia, consisting of some two dozen blocks of hotels, pensions, tavernas, discotheques and souvenir stores amid profuse flowers and greenery, comes alive each summer evening with a multitude of tourists from every Western country.

The densely forested hills of the surrounding area are ideally suited for nature walks.

There are two A, seven B, nine C hotels and scores of pensions and simple accommodation in the village. **Amalia** (A) (☎ *22.190/1* ⊞ *147 rms* ≡ ⚞ ⊞) has an attractive setting in the woods; **Europa** (A) (☎ *22.700* Fx *23.166* ⊞ *30 rms* ⚞ ⚞ ⊞) overlooks the village from high up on a hill; **Xenia** (B) (☎ *22.301/2* ⊞ *36 rms* ≡) offers excellent value in its price range; alternatively, you could try **Apollon** (B) (☎ *22.522* ⊞ *86 rms* ≡) or **Ilis** (C) (☎ *22.547* ⊞ *57 rms*).

A dozen C- and D-class hotels exist in **Pyrgos**, 18km (11 miles) w, including **Letrina** (C) (☎ *23.644* ⊞).

▲ On the hillside behind the Olympic Games Museum and a short distance w of town on the Pyrgos-Patras road.

ORCHOMENOS   See LIVADIA, page 143.

OSIOS LOUKAS MONASTERY ▲ ⚞ ☆
*35km (22 miles) sw of Livadia, 10km (6 miles) from road junction. Map **4**G6. Occasional **bus** from Distomo. Included in most sightseeing tours of Delphi.*

At the Triple Way where Oedipus slew his father, a road branches through the village of **Distomo** to the w slopes of Mt. Helicon. The valleys are still as lonely as they were in the 10thC when Blessed Luke, a local monk, retreated to them to weather the darkest days of Slav migration and Bulgar oppression. His solid faith in the Byzantine cause did not go unnoticed, his hermitage grew into a monastery, and a church bearing his name was erected c.1030. Its Byzantine **mosaics**, probably the work of imperial artists from Constantinople, are the most important in Greece after those of DAPHNI.

The **main church** (🔀) is similar in structure to that of Daphni: a cross-in-square plan round a central dome. Between the arched windows of the drum stand 16 mosaic prophets; the subordinate arches have fine mosaics of angels, saints and the languages and nations, while the recesses contain scenes from the life of Christ; the Virgin occupies her usual space in the apse.

The adjoining **Church of Theotokos** is still used for church services by the few remaining monks. The broad terrace with ancient plane trees and partly ruined monks' cells can be a delightfully pleasant place when not overrun by bus-loads of sightseers.

PATRAS (Patra)
*208km (130 miles) w of Athens. Map **3**G4. Population 140,000 ☎ code: 061 i 420.304. **Bus** from Athens (OSE and KTEL, frequent), Pyrgos, Nafpaktos, Tripoli (twice daily) and elsewhere. **Train** from Corinth and Kalamata. Terminal for most ferries from Italy, Corfu, Ithaki, Kefalonia.*

The third-largest city and second-largest port of Greece has practically nothing to show for its pre-Independence history except for a meager citadel (**Kastro**) of Byzantine-Frankish-Venetian-Turkish lineage and a rather attractive Roman **Odeon**. The **harbor**, which is the only part of the city that most visitors see, is a busy international ferry port cum bus terminal cum railroad station. A short walk inland, however, reveals unexpectedly pleasant, even elegant, sections around **Vassileos Georgiou Sq**. and at the edges of the Kastro.

The principal monument is the church of **Ag. Andreas**, a devotional, if not architectural, masterpiece that was completed in 1979 to house the relics of St Andrew, returned by the Pope shortly before that date to the town of their origin. A pilgrimage takes place here on November 30.

❖ The Apostle Andrew is said to have traveled to Patras, where he was martyred in the reign of Nero by being crucified on an X-shaped cross, which explains the origin of the St Andrew's Cross. His relics were removed to Constantinople in the 4thC to buttress that city's claim to apostolic blessing; they were also removed by St Regulus to the monastery of St Andrews in Fife, furnishing Scotland with its patron and protector. Still undiminished in either quantity or efficacy, the saint went on to save Patras from a Slavic invasion, and was finally carried off to Rome when Thomas Paleologue, the last despot of Mistra, fled before the Turks in 1460.

☞ Many hotels in all price categories exist around the port. A few of the best are: **Astir** (A) *(Agiou Andrea 16* ☎ *276.311* ⅢⅢ *120 rms* ⇥ ⇗ *on roof* ▦ *);* **Galaxy** (B) *(Agiou Nikolaou 9* ☎ *275.981/3* ⅢⅢ *53 rms* ▦ *)* and **Mediterranée** (C) *(Agiou Nikolaou 18* ☎ *279.602* ⅢⅢ *96 rms).*

The coast to either side of Patras is peppered with middle-range beach resorts, notably **Bozaika** and **Lakopetra** in the s and **Rio** and **Arahovitika** in the NE, each of which has an abundance of adequate hotels.

The best beach hotel in the area is **Porto Rio** (A) *(in Rio* ☎ *922.212* ⅢⅢ *209 rms and bungalows with all amenities).*

ENVIRONS

The fast-growing beach resort of **Rio**, 9km (6 miles) NE of Patras *(continuous ferry to Antirio),* has a powerful **Turkish fortress**, built in 1499 to guard the entrance of the Gulf of Corinth. It is still used as a prison.

POROS ▣ ⬱ ☆
Map 4I7. Resident population: 3,500 ☎ *code: 0298* *i* *22.462.*
Hydrofoil *from Piraeus (Zea Marina), 5–7 times daily, 50mins. Frequent **ferry** from Galatas, 2mins.*

Poros town is located on the very narrow channel *(poros)* separating the island from the mainland, and its position helps to give it an immensely appealing, intimate look. The architecture of individual houses may be undistinguished, but the ensemble cascading down the hill framed by pine forests forms an attractive sight.

The long harbor promenade is lined with a great variety of boats and tavernas, but somehow maintains a sleepy feel that adds to the satisfaction of a long afternoon stroll.

The insignificant remains of a **temple of Poseidon** are located at a spot c.550m (1,804 feet) high, with the usual extraordinary view. In this temple, in 322BC, Demosthenes committed suicide after having led Athens and Greece into disaster by inciting yet another fruitless revolt against the Macedonians.

The best beach is 4km (2½ miles) E of town below the pine-encircled monastery of **Zoodohos Pigi** *(take a bus)*. From the mainland town of **Galatas**, effectively a suburb of Poros, it is possible to make an excursion to the ruins of ancient **Troezen** (Trizina) *(8km/5 miles SW; see ARGOLID PENINSULA, page 126)* and the vast citrus plantations of the **Lemonodasos** (Lemon Forest).

⚓ Accommodation in **Poros town** is limited to relatively simple hotels and pensions, such as **Latsi** (B) *(☎ 22.392 ▥)*, or **Manessi** (C) *(☎ 22.273 ▥)*, in a pleasant old building on the waterfront.

A much larger number of hotels (C, D) exist in **Galatas**.

Sirene (B) is set on a beautiful beach, just below the monastery of Zoodohos Pigi *(☎ 22.741 ▥ 120 rms ⊟ ≋ ♪)*.

Stella Maris (B) *(☎ 22.562 ▥)*, on the beach 5km (3 miles) NE of **Galatas**, is the most adequate modern hotel in the vicinity.

PORTO GERMENO (Aegosthena) ⇇ 🐟 🏛
*65km (41 miles) E of Athens. Map 4H6. **Bus** from Thisio subway station (map 1D2).*

The **Halcyonid Gulf** (Kólpos Alkyonidón), the extremely indented and mountainous NE branch of the Gulf of Corinth, is an area of great beauty that remains relatively unspoiled despite its nearness to Athens. A half-dozen rather long and curvy but spectacularly scenic roads descend to the coast at various points.

Of these, the town of Porto Germeno (renamed Aegosthena to conform with Classical precedent) has a couple of hotels, a string of fish tavernas and a lovely pebble beach with crystal-clear water. The mighty square towers of a 4thC BC **fortress**, which is considered to be the best-preserved example of Classical defense architecture in Greece, dominate the site.

To the N of Porto Germeno is the 1,409m (4,623-foot) peak of **Mt. Kythairon**, which features prominently in mythology. It was here that the seer Tiresias was blinded for seeing the goddesses bathe naked, Pentheus was torn to pieces for observing Dionysus in orgy with his Maenads, and the infant Oedipus was left to die so he would not grow up to kill his father. A driveable gravel road leads all the way to the summit of the mountain.

Other roads lead down to **Ag. Vasilios**, **Aliki**, **Ag. Ioannis** and **Paralia Prodromou**, little hamlets with deserted beaches and a taverna or two which may not always be open. A boat may be rented at Porto Germeno to explore the coast with greater ease.

⚓ **Egosthenion** (C) *(☎ (0263) 41.226 ▥ 80 rms)*, buried in pine groves 1km (½ mile) from the seacoast.

PYLOS 🏨 🦐 ☆
50km (31 miles) w of Kalamata. Map 5J4. Population 3,000 ☎ code: 0723.

The capital of Homer's "wise old Nestor" commands the Bay of Navarino, one of the most beautiful natural harbors of Greece. Gently rising hills form a vast amphitheater around it with as many as 20 villages smiling from afar among the rich vineyards and olive groves of the Messenian landscape.

The attractions of the town itself include warm and sleepy streets full of whitewashed houses and little tavernas, a quaint fortress, and a spectacular 6km (4-mile) beach lying between the mirror-smooth sea and a lagoon.

> ❖ At the Battle of Navarino on October 20, 1828, an allied British-French-Russian fleet annihilated the Turkish navy of Ibrahim Pasha, which was lying at anchor in the bay, in a surprise attack not unlike Pearl Harbor in conception and result. This action marked the formal entry of the European Powers into the fray of the Greek revolt, and forced a Turkish capitulation within a short time. Some of the 53 Turkish ships sunk at Navarino are still visible under the surface of the water.

The substantial **fortress**, at the southern edge of the town, is a Turkish structure of 1573 with modifications carried out by the French in 1829. The interior *(open 8.30am-3pm, closed Mon)* has a mosque converted into a church and excellent views of the bay.

The steep, uninhabited island of **Sfaktiria**, which hems the bay in almost completely, contains monuments to various heroes of Navarino and the tomb of Paul-Marie Bonaparte, a nephew of Napoleon. At its southern end, a great hollow rock known by the unusual name of ***Tsishli Baba,*** or Isle of the Blessed Pisser, blocks the harbor entrance. At the N end, where the deserted far end of the beach comes within wading distance of the island, a ruined Venetian **castle** *(Paleókastro)* marks the medieval (and possibly Mycenaean) site of Pylos.

Pylos has five B- and C-class hotels, in addition to numerous pensions. **Karalis Beach** (B) *(☎ 23.021/2 [Fx] 22.970 Ⅲ ⇌ ≈ 🦐)* occupies an isolated site between the fortress and the sea at the edge of town. **Neleus** (B) *(☎ 22.518 Ⅲ)* is a charming pension. **Karalis** (C) *(☎ 22.960 Ⅲ)* has a nice site overlooking the harbor.

▲ Lovely spot near the beach at **Gialova**, 6km (4 miles) N.

ENVIRONS
The so-called **Palace of Nestor** *(open 8.30am–3pm, closed Mon 🎫),* located by the roadside 13km (8 miles) N of Pylos, is considered the second most important Mycenaean find after Mycenae itself. What remains of its foundations will not overwhelm the casual visitor, although the ground pattern is decidedly curious.

The palace, whose superstructure was built of wood, was occupied c.1300–1200BC and burned down at the end of that period. The single largest cache ever found of tablets containing the Mycenaean "Linear B" script were baked into brick in that fire and were thus saved for posterity. The association of the palace with the legendary king Nestor of Pylos has no basis in fact.

Nestor, the amiably long-winded old warrior, appears in the *Iliad* as the commander of the second-largest Greek fleet and a ruler whom Agamemnon respects in his own right. In the *Odyssey,* Telemachus visits Pylos to find out the whereabouts of his father Ulysses, and is treated by the old king to a banquet on the beach — perhaps that at the N end of Navarino Bay.

The road continues N through a beautiful land of farms and orchards, which yield the largest share of Europe's dried raisins. The market town of **Gargaliani** has its assured niche in history as the ancestral home of former US Vice-President Spiro Agnew, né Agnostopoulos. **Kyparissia**, a pleasant oldish town with an excellent beach, perches on a hillside with a ruined Franco-Venetian castle.

RAMNOUS 𝕞

58km (36 miles) NE *of Athens. Map* **7**B3. **Bus** *to Agia Marina from Mavromateon and Heiden (map* **2**B4); *then 6km/4 miles (3km/2 miles from road junction) by taxi or on foot.* **Archeological site** *open Tues–Sun 8.30am–3pm; closed Mon. Free entrance* ☎*(0294) 63.477.*

The scant remains of a **Temple of Nemesis**, measurer of destiny and punisher of hubris, are situated on an isolated hillside near a deserted shore. The even scantier ruins of a **Shrine of Themis**, an Archaic earth-goddess, lie nearby. About 1km ($\frac{1}{2}$ mile) down the rocky valley is an overgrown **fort** (4thC BC) enclosing some ruins on a steep hillock directly by the seashore. The site has little history and lies undisturbed by tourist buses.

> ❖   The fort is locally known as "Jew's Castle," a name it shares with
> a great number of minor strongholds on both sides of the Aegean.
> The origin of the term is obscure.

SALAMIS (Salamina)

Map **4**H7. *Resident population: 20,000* ☎ *code: 01. Frequent* **ferry** *from Perama (***bus** *from Eleftherias Sq., map* **1**C2).

Immortalized by the historic naval battle that turned the tide of the Persian invasion of Greece, Salamis today forms part of the industrial periphery of Athens and is heavily polluted by spillovers from the factories on the mainland. Nonetheless, there are some good beaches on the SE coast of the island, popular with Athenian vacationers.

In Mycenaean times Salamis was the seat of an important kingdom. It took part in the Trojan war with a significant force under the dim-witted giant Ajax, son of Telamon.

In 480BC, after occupying most of mainland Greece and devastating Athens, Great King Xerxes attempted to deal the final blow to the

Athenian navy gathered near Phaleron (Faliro). The Athenians withdrew to the Gulf of Ambelakia, between Perama and the narrow headland of Cynosura on Salamis, and then annihilated the Persian armada with a gallant sortie. Xerxes is said to have watched the disaster from a throne set up in the (then forested) hills of Perama.

The battle vindicated Themistocles, who had advocated a policy of naval build-up with Churchillian tenacity. It marked the turning point of Persian expansion and the start of the age of Athenian supremacy. Deprived of naval support, the Persian army was defeated at Plataea the next year.

SOUNION 🏛 ◀ε ★

69km (43 miles) SE of Athens. Map 7F3. Bus from Mavromateon and Leof. Alexandras (map 2B4); numerous organized tours. Temple open daily 10am–sunset ▨ ☎(0292) 39.363.

The Temple of Poseidon on the barren promontory of Cape Sounion remains one of the most deeply moving sights in all of Greece, despite the inescapable multitude of sightseers who throng it daily. The temple is built in the purest white marble and stands about 60m (200 feet) above the sea at the edge of a cliff. About half its 34 Doric columns stand at full height (some re-erected), although the cella is gone. The view over the sea, particularly at sunset or in the moonlight, is striking. Byron rhapsodized it thus:

> "Place me on Sunium's marbled steep,
> Where nothing, save the waves and I,
> May hear our mutual murmurs sweep;
> There, swan-like, let me sing and die."

Cape Sounion was (and is) the last glimpse of the mainland for sailors departing from Athens and the first that would greet them on the journey home, so it made an obvious choice of location for a shrine to the god of the seamen. The present temple was erected c.440BC to replace an earlier one left unfinished by the Persian invasion.

For many centuries the secluded coves of Sounion were notorious as a pirates' haunt. As late as the end of the 19thC a group of English tourists were abducted by pirates at this spot, giving rise to the celebrated incident of the "Dilessi murders."

The temple ruins *(interior closed to visitors)* are completely covered with incised graffiti of visitors from the early 18thC to the present day. Some of the earlier inscriptions are elegant to the point of being worthy of the temple itself; but more recent efforts display a drastic and steady decline in the quality of the visitors. Among the famous signatures is that of Byron himself.

🏨 Sounion itself has thee A- and numerous B- and C-class hotels. The best hotel in the area is located in Lagonissi, on the "Apollo" coast:

Xenia Lagonissi (L) hotel and bungalows (☎(0291) 23.911 ▦24.534 ▥ 357 rms ⇋ ≋ ⧉ ♒ ♪ ▤ *open Apr-Oct).*

165

For A-class accommodation in the vicinity of Sounion, the **Belvedere Park** (A) (☎ *(0292) 39.102* ▥ *90 rms in bungalows* ⇌ ⚬ 🔥 ▦ *open Mar-Oct)* and **Cape Sounion Beach** (A) (☎ *(0292) 39.391* ▯ *188 rms in bungalows* ⇌ ⚬ 🔥 ▦ *open Apr-Oct)* are recommended.

▲   Pleasantly situated site on the way toward LAVRIO.

SPARTA (Sparti)
230km (144 miles) sw of Athens. Map 6J5. Population 12,000 ☎ code: 0731.

"The sober, hard,/and man-subduing city, which no shape/of pain could conquer, nor of pleasure charm," was abandoned at the end of Antiquity in favor of the eagle's nest of MISTRA, nearby. Modern Sparti was raised on empty ground after 1834; its broad avenues, the lush green of the Eurotas Valley and the looming presence of **Mt. Taygetos** conspire to make it a more attractive place than most other Greek towns of comparable newness.

Today there is hardly any trace of the city's past greatness, fulfilling Thucydides' prediction that future ages would be puzzled that Sparta once counted as an equal of Athens, for while Athens would leave splendid monuments in marble, Sparta, whose buildings were all of wood, was to vanish completely.

Sparta, also called Lacedaemon, was already an important city in the Mycenaean epoch, when Menelaus ruled and Helen was called the most beautiful of mortal women. The Dorians who invaded it c.1200BC enslaved the local population *(helots)* and developed the proverbially frugal culture of their small warrior aristocracy. Spartan boys were taken from their families at the age of 7 and raised in harsh conditions designed to instil physical courage and contempt of luxury. Those who failed were left in a gorge of the Taygetos to die; those who passed the initiation rites of adulthood were expected to kill or die without flinching.

In a series of wars between 461 and 403BC, Sparta successfully checked Athens' ambition to be the dominant power in Greece. Its own era of de facto mastery was brought to an end in 371BC by Epaminondas of Thebes. The city was nevertheless highly regarded by the Romans, and maintained an important position through the imperial period.

🐾   **Menelaion** (B) (☎ *22.161/5* ▯ *48 rms* ⇌ ▦), a fine Neoclassical building in the center of town; **Sparta Inn** (C) (☎ *21.021/6* ▯ *147 rms* ⇌ ▦).

ENVIRONS
6km (4 miles) s of Sparta, a few dressed stones and a small isolated church on a low hill commanding a lovely landscape of orange and banana groves mark **Amyklai** (Amiklés), the ancient cult site of Apollo's lover Hyacinth.

Hyacinth was a mortal youth of untold beauty with whom Apollo fell in love; theirs was the first love between man and man. Zephyr, the west wind, was jealous; when she blew, a discus that the god had hurled went off and killed the youth. Out of his blood grew the flower that bears his name, and Apollo ordained the feast of the Hyacinthia in his memory.

SPETSES ▣ ⬥ ☆

Map 6I6. Resident population: 2,500 ☎ *code: 0298* **i** *73.100.* **Hydrofoil** *from Piraeus (Zea Marina) 5–7 times daily, 80mins; Hydra 5–7 times daily; Porto Heli twice daily.* **Ferry** *from Kosta, 4–5 times daily, 15mins.* **Taxi boats** *available at Kosta.*

The attractive island of Spetses, with steep hills covered by pine forest, is one of the favorite summer resorts of wealthier Athenian families. The main town, also called **Dapia**, is practically free of road traffic and maintains its well-proportioned traditional architecture. Several stately 19thC mansions and decorated pebble-mosaic streets complete a pleasantly low-key picture.

The pride of Spetses is the revolutionary war heroine **Laskaréna Bouboulína**. A cynic could hardly fail to note the similarity of her cult to that of the local goddesses of the ancients and the saints of the Christians. In real life, Laskaréna, the daughter of a Hydriote pirate, was born in prison in Constantinople, and became the widow of two captains who were either pirates, or were murdered by pirates, or both.

During the war, she fought the Turks with a private battle fleet of her own, engaging in various acts of reckless heroism. She was shot in her home in 1825 when a son seduced the daughter of a rival clan. Her statues in various heroic poses speckle the island. Her **home** is Spetses' main architectural landmark, and her ashes form the *pièce de résistance* of the local museum.

Each year on September 8, the anniversary of the **Battle of Spetses** is celebrated with fireworks, dance and music.

Spetses' most popular beach is E of Dapia at **Agia Marina**, where much of the island's day and night life unfolds in summer. Magnificent, less crowded beaches are to be found at **Agii Anargyri** and **Agia Paraskevi** on the s coast, reached by taxi-boat or a scenic 2-hour walk over the hill. In between these two is the interesting sea cave of **Bekiris**.

The islet of **Spetsopoula** off the SE coast of Spetses belongs to the shipping magnate Niarchos, who is rumored to pursue there a life of unimaginable luxury.

⬥ **Spetses** (A) (☎ *72.602* ▥ ⤳ ▦ *)*, the top hotel on the island, in a nice building; **Kasteli** (A) (☎ *72.311* ▥ *hotel and bungalows* ⬥ ▦ *)*; **Roumanis** (B) (☎ *72.244* ▥*)*; **Faros** (C) *(on the main plaza* ☎ *72.613/4* ▥ *)*; **Acropole** (D) (☎ *72.219* ▥ *).* **Pension Kardiasmenos** (☎ *73.741* ▢ *)* is a lovely old mansion on the main plaza, simple but well kept.

THEBES (Thive)

77km (48 miles) NW of Athens. Map 4G6. Population 18,000 ☎ *code: 0262.* **Bus** *frequently from Athens (KTEL terminal at Liossion 260).* **Train***: 10 times daily from Larissis station.*

Thebes, the hometown of Oedipus and Antigone, one of the great cities of Greece during both the Mycenaean and Classical ages, is today a sleepy provincial town with very little to show for its long history. The **Archeological Museum** has a superb 6thC BC *kouros* and some interesting Mycenaean items.

HISTORY AND LEGENDS

The city was founded in mythic times by Kadmos, a Phoenician, who sowed the dragon's teeth from which Thebes' noble families sprang. His descendants included Laios, who was told by an oracle that his son would grow up to kill him and marry his mother. The infant Oedipus was sent to die, was saved, grew up unaware of his identity, killed his father in a quarrel, saved Thebes from an evil sphinx, was elected king and married the widow of Laios, Jocasta, his own mother. When the truth came out, he put out his own eyes and went into voluntary exile.

Oedipus's sons Eteocles and Polynices quarreled, bringing about the disastrous siege of the Seven Against Thebes. His daughter Antigone was sentenced to be buried alive when she honored the dead body of Polynices against the wishes of the tyrant Creon. Various episodes of the saga formed the subject of the greatest tragedies of Aeschylus and Sophocles.

In Classical times Thebes was the dominant power of the Boeotian League and a bitter enemy of Athens. It sided with the Persians during the Persian invasion, and was an ally of Sparta during the Peloponnesian Wars. In 371BC, Epaminondas of Thebes shattered Spartan hegemony at the Battle of Leuctra, and for a decade afterward his city was the sole master of Greece.

In 338BC it joined forces with Athens to resist Macedonian hegemony, but was defeated at Chaeronia, and was totally destroyed by Alexander the Great when it tried to make a comeback a few years later. In Roman times, according to Strabo, there was hardly even a village of respectable size left at the site. A brief revival as the capital of Othon de la Roche's duchy ended with defeat and destruction by the Catalans at the Battle of Lake Kopais in 1311. The city was rebuilt from scratch after 1830.

The **_Vláhikos gámos_**, a parody of a highland peasant wedding, held on Shrove Monday, attracts enormous crowds. The Vlahs (Vlach, Wallachian) are a Romanian people who settled much of central and NW Greece toward the end of the Middle Ages. Their language is now nearly extinct. The town of Metsovo is considered the center of Vlach culture.

☙ **Dionyssion Melathron** (B) *(Metaxa and Kadmou* ☎ *27.855* Ⅲ*);* **Meletiou** (C) *(Epaminonda 58* ☎ *27.333* Ⅲ*)*.

ENVIRONS

At **Plataea** *(now Platees, 13km/8 miles s of Thebes, then 5km/3 miles w)* the Persians under Mardonius and their Theban allies were defeated by other Greeks in the concluding phase of the Persian wars in 479BC.

Thespiae *(now Thespies, 13km/8 miles w of Thebes, then 7km/4 miles s; minor ruins)* was famed in Antiquity as the only city that had a temple and cult of Eros, god of love. People would go to Thespiae to see the statue of the god that Praxiteles gave as a gift to a "servant of Eros" (some say courtesan) named Glycera. Nero carried the statue off to Rome.

Nearby **Ascra** (Askri) was the birthplace of Hesiod, perhaps the earliest of Greek poets (8th–7thC BC). It was his work that helped popularize a group of local deities called the *Muses*. Calliope, Clio, Erato, Euterpe, Melpomene, Polyhymnia, Terpsichore, Thalia and Urania were originally forest and water spirits who were seen by shepherds to sing and dance to the music of Apollo in a sacred grove deep in a high valley of **Mt. Helicon** (Élikon oros). Later they gained fame as the inspirers of various branches of the arts; to them we owe museums, music and the act of musing.

A few bits of a sanctuary, believed to be of the Nine Sisters, can be seen some distance w of Ascra. Farther up, close to the E summit (1,526m/ 5,006 feet) of the Helicon, the **fountain of Hippocrene**, now called **Krio Pigadi**, was a source of poetic inspiration.

The hill district of s and w Boeotia, including the towns cited here, is inhabited by Arvanites, an Albanian-speaking minority.

TIRYNS (Tiryntha)   See NAFPLIO, page 155.

TRIPOLI
166km (104 miles) sw of Athens. Map 6I5. Population 22,000 ☎ *code: 071.*

The capital of Arcadia is a rather dreary place, but one that you are bound to pass through on a tour of the Peloponnese. Near it are the equally uninteresting ruins of **Tegea** *(5km/3 miles s)* and **Mantinea** *(11km/7 miles N)*, the latter remembered as the site of two famous battles in which the Spartans defeated the Athenians (418BC) and were defeated in turn by the Thebans of Epaminondas (362BC).

✎   **Arcadia** (B) *(* ☎ *22.25.51* ▱ *45 rms* ⊒*); * **Galaxy** (C) *(* ☎ *22.51.95* ▱ *80 rms).*

Reference

Practical information

This chapter is organized into five sections:
- **BEFORE YOU GO**, below
- **GETTING THERE**, page 176
- **GETTING AROUND**, page 177
- **ON-THE-SPOT INFORMATION**, page 181
- **EMERGENCY INFORMATION**, page 186

Each section is organized thematically rather than alphabetically. Summaries of subject headings are printed in CAPITALS at the top of most pages.

Before you go

GREEK TOURIST OFFICES OVERSEAS

The **Greek National Tourist Organization** has representative offices in the following cities:

London   195-197 Regent St., London W1R 8DL ☎(071) 734-5997

New York   645 5th Ave. (Olympic Tower), New York NY 10022 ☎(212) 421-5777

Los Angeles   611 W 6th St., Suite 2198, Los Angeles, CA 90017 ☎(213) 626-6695

Chicago   168 N Michigan Ave., Chicago, IL 60601 ☎(312) 782-1084

Toronto   68 Scollard St., Toronto, Ontario M5R 1G2 ☎(416) 958-2220

DOCUMENTS REQUIRED

EU nationals require a passport or valid identity card to stay for up to three months. **Nationals of all other countries** need a valid passport. For permission to stay more than 3 months, contact the **Aliens Bureau** *(Leoforos Alexandras 173, Athens* ☎*64.45.940)* or the local police.

    Drivers from non-EU countries should have an **international driver's license**, although national licenses from both EU and non-EU countries are generally accepted without fuss. Vehicles need a **valid registration certificate** (logbook) and either the **international green card** or **temporary insurance** obtained at border crossing-points.

HEALTH

Foreigners in Greece cannot obtain free **medical treatment**, and a fee is charged by hospitals for outpatients. The **IAMAT** (International Asso-

172

ciation for Medical Assistance to Travelers) has a list of English-speaking doctors who will call, for a fee. There are member hospitals and clinics throughout Europe, including Athens and other towns in Greece. Membership of IAMAT is free. For information and a free directory of doctors and hospitals, write to **IAMAT** *(417 Center St., Lewiston, NY 14092, USA or 57 Voirets, 1212 Grand-Lancy, Genève, Switzerland).*

UK nationals entitled to full UK health benefits are entitled to the same health cover as Greek citizens upon presentation of form **E111**, which can be obtained at any post office and can be authorized at the counter while you wait. Accompanying the E111 is a leaflet, *Health Care for Visitors to EC Countries,* which gives details on how to claim. Keep the E111 when you return: it has no expiry date. Study also their booklet *The Traveller's Guide to Health,* which gives comprehensive information on vaccinations and diseases and provides useful health checklists. For **private treatment** in Greece, it is important to be insured adequately.

MONEY

The unit of **currency** is the drachma (pl. drachmes). There are coins for 1, 2, 5, 10, 20, 50 and 100dr, and notes for 50, 100, 500, 1,000 and 5,000dr. Any amount of **foreign currency** over US \$500 or the equivalent must by law be declared at the customs entry point, but in practice this requirement is rarely enforced.

Travelers checks issued by all major companies are widely recognized. Major **charge and credit cards** (American Express, Visa and MasterCard/Eurocard/Access; more rarely Diners Club), as well as **Eurocheques**, are accepted in Athens and other common tourist destinations by most shops, travel and car rental agencies, medium-to-better hotels and some restaurants. Bear in mind, however, that some establishments (notably jewelers) will charge a premium of about 7 percent for charge/credit card transactions.

American Express has a **MoneyGram**® money transfer service that makes it possible to wire money worldwide in just minutes, from any American Express Travel Service Office. This service is available to all customers and is not limited to American Express Card members.

The largest American and British banks, including American Express, Barclays, Chase Manhattan, Citibank, Grindlays, Midland and National Westminster, have offices in Athens.

PRICES

These and all prices quoted in this book reflect the conditions in late 1993. The rate of inflation in recent years has averaged 15–20 percent. The rate of exchange at the time of writing was approximately 210 drachmes to one US dollar, or 360 drachmes to one pound sterling.
*   Can of soft drink: 120dr
*   Simple meal at a taverna: 1,800dr
*   Inexpensive pension, for two: 4,000dr
*   Class-A hotel, for two: 15,000dr
*   Museum entrance: 400 or 800dr
*   1 liter super-grade fuel: 200dr

CUSTOMS ALLOWANCES

Any items intended for personal use may be brought into Greece free of charge. Items that may be interpreted as being for commercial use will cause delays and aggravation at Customs. The importation of personal computers (including laptops), video cameras and other electronic equipment, is subject to an astonishing amount of bureaucracy. As a rule, any such items must be registered at the time of entry, in order to avoid problems when you leave the country.

The achievement of the European Single Market in 1993 has in principle freed the movement of goods among EU countries, of which Greece is one. In practice, however, many exceptions and ambiguities remain, and — at least as of late 1993 — Greek Customs officers continue to take a maximalist view of their duties.

Visitors from countries outside the EU are exempt from paying Value-Added Tax (ΦΠΑ in Greek) on purchases in certain shops authorized by Customs to operate a VAT-refund scheme. You must declare your intention to use the scheme at the time of purchase, and will be asked to present your passport and complete a simple form. Ask the retailer to explain how the refund can be made. To validate the refund, you must present the paperwork and goods at a customs checkpoint before going through passport control on leaving the country. Leave enough time to do this. A wise safeguard is to keep a photocopy of the Customs-certified VAT refund document.

WHEN TO GO

The tourist season lasts from April to October, peaking in August. Avoid August if at all possible, as the combination of heat, tourist crowds, shortened tempers and prices inflated by as much as 40 percent can make it a difficult experience. July is noticeably less crowded than August, and June much less so.

April and May have the pleasantest weather; mountains are still snow-capped and greenery and wild flowers carpet the land, although the sea is often chilly. September and October bring bright warm days and warm sea. Winter is a good time to enjoy the countryside, and the absence of tourists makes people remarkably more attentive toward the stray foreigner than they are in summer. Athens, however, is often choked by smog, and most of the islands are depopulated and gloomy.

TIME ZONE

Greek time is seven hours ahead of Eastern Standard Time, two hours ahead of Greenwich Mean Time and an hour ahead of Central European Time. Summer time is observed, along with the rest of continental Europe, from end-March to end-September — almost a month earlier than the UK, the US and Canada. The time difference with these countries is thus one hour greater for some weeks in April and in October.

WHAT TO WEAR

Formal clothing will almost never be needed except when staying at luxury hotels or attending official functions. Topless sunbathing is common at practically all beaches; most tourists never wear more than shorts and T-shirts, although visitors are required to enter churches, monasteries and museums in what are deemed to be "decent" clothes. A light sweater is useful even in summer, as the *meltémi*, the regular N wind of the southern Aegean, can get quite chilly.

What you will *not* normally need is an umbrella. The annual precipitation in Athens is barely 35cm (13.6 inches), and it almost never rains between May and September.

Clothing sizes are infuriatingly different in the US/UK/Europe. If in any doubt, turn to the **clothing sizes chart** near the end of the book.

PREPARATORY READING

Classics: Herodotus' *Histories* is a marvelous compilation of tales, although one is never too sure where history ends and story begins. Thucydides's *The Peloponnesian War,* by contrast, remains a paragon of sober historiography 2,300 years after it was written. Strabo's superbly erudite and readable *Geography* devotes its 8th, 9th and 10th books to Greece. Pausanias's *Guide to Greece* is a Roman-age antiquarian's massively detailed travel guide to Greek monuments.

History and Archeology: John Chadwick, *The Mycenaean World* (1976), is the classic work on the pre-Classical civilization of the Greeks. J. C. Stobart, *The Glory that was Greece* (revised ed. 1985), and M. I. Finlay, *The Ancient Greeks* (1963), present admirably-told accounts of the history, politics, culture and arts of ancient Greece. William Bell Dinsmoor, *The Architecture of Ancient Greece* (1975, 2nd ed. 1985), is a scholarly overview of the subject. Fani-Maria Tsigakou, *The Rediscovery of Ancient Greece* (1981), tells the tale of the heroic age of Hellenic archeology, from the early travelers in the Levant through Schliemann and Evans.

Nicholas Cheetham, *Medieval Greece* (1981), and Steven Runciman, *Mistra* (1980), deal respectively with Byzantine Greece and its fascinating late-medieval swansong in the Peloponnese.

C. M. Woodhouse's works, *The Greek War of Independence* (1952), *The Story of Modern Greece* (1968, 2nd ed. 1977), *The Philhellenes* (1969) and *The Rise and Fall of the Greek Colonels* (1985) present the history of modern Greece from the viewpoint of a historian who played a part in it, as the British mission commander in Athens during the Greek civil war.

Another excellent summary of modern history is given in Richard Clogg, *A Short History of Modern Greece* (1979, 1986).

Literature and travel: Lawrence Durrell's novels and essays (*Prospero's Cell* (1960) is a good example) capture the spirit and colors of Greece better than any other modern English writer. Patrick Leigh Fermor's classic *Mani* (1958, 1984) and *Roumeli* (1964, 1983), are masterpieces of travel prose even if they often blur fact, fancy and prejudice.

Robert Graves' *Greek Myths* (1955) succeeds in breathing life into an oft-retold subject. Marc Dubin, *Greece on Foot* (1986), is an engaging account of a journey in Greece as it is, rather than as it was or should be. Nicholas Gage's novel, *Eleni* (1983), pays homage to the author's mother, a survivor of the Greek civil war.

Getting there

BY AIR

Athens is well served by a wide range of international airlines. TWA and Olympic each have a daily New York–Athens flight throughout the year, and Air Canada and Olympic have twice-weekly flights from Montreal and Toronto. From Britain, British Airways and Olympic each operate two daily London–Athens flights.

Much less expensive are the various charter companies and leftover place brokers ("bucket shops"); they offer a vast array of options in summer but very little off-season. The lowest prices in the summer of 1993 were around US$450 for a New York–Athens round-trip, and £150 for a London–Athens round-trip.

Those flying to Greece on discount tickets should be aware that they may be asked to furnish proof of accommodation. This can be done by purchasing, from a travel agency, **hotel or camping vouchers** sufficient to cover the length of stay in Greece.

BY RAIL

Trans-European trains are infrequent, slow, very crowded in summer, and do not cost any less than charter flights. A **Eurailpass** or other discount scheme might nevertheless make the train journey palatable.

For the quickest route from London, take the evening train from Victoria Station to Cologne, and change for Munich. There, change to the **Attica Express**, which leaves Munich in the evening and arrives in Athens in about 35 hours.

BY BUS

The London–Athens route once popular with shoestring travelers, traversing the former Yugoslavia, is not an option at the time of writing, because of the situation afflicting that region.

Eurolines (UK) (☎ *(071) 730-0202)* currently runs a service from London via Paris, Ancona, Corfu and Patras to Athens. It takes three days and costs about £220 for the round-trip.

BY CAR

Athens is approximately 3,000km (1,875 miles) from London via Calais–Strasbourg–Munich–Belgrade. The drive across former Yugoslavia is affected at present by the difficult conditions prevailing in the region. The Zagreb–Belgrade route is closed to civilian traffic; fuel is scarce and extremely expensive; there are frequent and sometimes hostile security checks in Serbia, and long delays at the Macedonian–Greek border.

Drivers to Greece are therefore recommended to drive down the length of Italy and take the ferry from **Brindisi** to **Igoumenitsa** *(most sailings in the evening, passage 10hrs, around $20/£12.50 for deck seat plus $20/£12.50 for car)* or **Patras** *(passage 18hrs, under $40/£25 for deck seat plus $40/£25 for car)*. Advance reservations are recommended for cars.

BY BOAT
Regular **ferry services** link Venice, Ancona, Bari, Brindisi, Otranto, Rijeka and Dubrovnik to Patras; and Istanbul, Odessa, Haifa, Latakia, Limassol and Alexandria to Piraeus. Fully equipped **yacht marinas** exist at the following locations near Athens:

- **Alimos** ☎98.13.315
- **Glyfada** ☎89.47.979
- **Vouliagmeni** ☎89.60.012
- **Zea** (Piraeus) ☎45.13.944

Getting around

IN ATHENS
Public transport
Work on the long-overdue Athens **metro** started in 1991. As a result, key city-center intersections are paralyzed, and this is expected to continue through 1994 or 1995. A single urban rail line, sometimes called the "**subway**" because it goes underground for a brief stretch in central Athens, runs from **Piraeus** via downtown Athens to the northern suburb of **Kifissia**.

The standard **ticket** for all urban transport (buses, trolleys and rail) is available at urban rail stations and newspaper kiosks, although kiosks in outlying parts of the city may sometimes fail to carry them. Since 1991, Greater Athens has been divided into three transport zones, with a 75dr ticket valid for trips within a zone or two consecutive zones, and a 100dr ticket valid for trips across all three.

Taxis are plentiful and remarkably inexpensive: the fare rarely exceeds 400dr for a trip within central Athens; the airport, however, is subject to a special tariff, and the fare to and from downtown may cost as much as 2000dr. There are numerous phone-a-cab companies, which charge a small extra fee for call-in service.

It is common practice for cab drivers to pick up multiple passengers, in which case each passenger pays fully for his/her part of the trip. Foreigners who balk at this practice are not regarded kindly. Surcharges are paid for each piece of luggage placed in the trunk and for journeys initiated between midnight and 6am. Tips are not expected.

Private transport
Although Greater Athens spreads over a vast area, nearly all points of interest are concentrated in a relatively compact central district, which can easily be explored on foot (see A WALKING TOUR OF ATHENS, pages 41–43). Driving your own car in central Athens is generally both slower and much more exhausting than walking, so avoid it except after midnight, when traffic is less jammed. Parking is difficult, and drivers as a rule display famously short tempers.

To bring air pollution and congestion under control, the access of private cars into central Athens has been restricted to odd- or even-numbered plates between 7am and 8pm on alternating days. This rule, however, does not apply to rented or foreign-registered cars.

Limousine services are available from ☎32.37.942. The limousine terminal is on Voukourestiou, not far from Syntagma Sq. *(map 2 D4).*

OUTSIDE ATHENS
Organized tours
Major tour operators such as **American Express** *(Ermou 2, Syntagma Sq.* ☎*32.44.975* [Fx] *32.27.893, map 2 D4),* **Wagons-Lits/Cook** *(Karageorgi Servias 2, Syntagma Sq.* ☎*32.28.650 and 32.42.281, map 2 D4)* and **Chat Tours** *(Stadiou 4, Syntagma Sq.* ☎*32.22.886, map 2 D4),* as well as numerous smaller enterprises, offer a wide variety of packaged tours out of Athens, utilizing modern, air-conditioned buses and also hydrofoils and cruise boats.

Reservations may be made directly or through the great variety of travel agencies concentrated in the area between Syntagma Sq. and Syngrou Ave. in central Athens, and along the harbor in Piraeus. The following typical tours are intended to give a general idea:

- **Aegina–Poros–Hydra**, 1 day, with lunch, 9,000dr
- **Classical Tour** (Corinth–Epidaurus–Mycenae–Nafplio–Olympia–Delphi), 3 days, with hotel and half-board, 48,000dr
- **Delphi**, 1 day, with lunch, 12,000dr

Driving outside Athens
Roads are generally uncrowded outside Athens, and Greek drivers tend to be sedate by the standards of other Mediterranean countries. Rules and traffic signs involve no surprises — although direction signs can sometimes be maddeningly laconic.

The **National Road** connecting Athens and Thessaloniki is not an expressway (divided highway) in the accepted sense of the term, but a single-lane road with an unusually wide emergency strip. Vehicles customarily drive half-astraddle the strip, allowing faster cars to pass without changing lane. It is a harrowing experience at first, but one gets used to it after a while.

The **Touring and Automobile Club of Greece (ELPA)** claims to provide various services to drivers. Their headquarters are located in the **Tower of Athens** *(Mesogion 2, Athens* ☎ *77.91.615).* The ELPA emergency road assistance service *(* ☎ *104)* is usually avoided by experienced Greek drivers.

More efficient assistance is provided by a new private organization called **Express Service**. In case of a breakdown you call their emergency number ☎**154** from anywhere in Greece, and obtain the name and phone number of the nearest service station.

Lead-free fuel *(amolivdí)* is widely available throughout the country.

CAR RENTAL
Scores of car rental agencies exist along Syngrou Ave. in Athens; many have branches at the harbor of Piraeus and at Elinikon Airport. Rates for weekly rental of a small passenger car, with unlimited mileage, in

high season, inclusive of taxes and legal insurance, vary between 60,000 and 95,000dr. Figures drop drastically, and become surprisingly flexible, in off-season. Note that prices quoted in agency brochures may or may not include taxes and extras.

- **Avis**   Leof. Amalias 48 ☎32.24.951 [Fx]32.20.216, map **1E3**
- **Budget**   Syngrou 8 ☎92.14.771 [Fx]92.24.444, map **1E3**
- **Eurocar**   Syngrou 4 ☎92.15.788, map **1E3**
- **Hertz**   Syngrou 12 ☎99.42.850, map **1E3**
- **Just**   Syngrou 43 ☎90.25.742 [Fx]90.25.572, map **1F3**
- **Payless**   Hatzichristou 20 & Syngrou ☎92.38.842, map **1E3**
- **Staikos**   Syngrou 40–42 ☎92.38.941 [Fx](0754) 51.011, map **1F3**
- **Thrifty**   Syngrou 24 ☎92.21.211 [Fx]92.38.964, map **1E3**

Car rental is also available at other important entry points (Igoumenitsa, Patras) and tourist centers (Delphi, Olympia, Nafplio and others). Agencies generally insist on having the vehicles returned to the point of rental. Cross-border rentals are not available.

RAIL SERVICES

The Greek rail network is rudimentary. Of the two significant railway lines run by the Hellenic Railway Organization (**OSE**), the Northern Line to Thessaloniki *(12 trains daily, 8hrs)* and Alexandroupolis operates from **Stathmos Athinas** (Athens Station, map **1B2**), commonly known as **Larissis** *(☎ 82.13.882, #1 trolley from Syntagma Sq., map 2 D4 or Omonia Sq., map 1 C3).*

The Peloponnese Line to Corinth, Patras, Argos and Kalamata runs from **Stathmos Peloponnisou**, a short distance s of Larissis *(☎ 51.31.601, map 1 B2)*. Return tickets are subject to a 20-percent discount. In addition, there are discounts for persons under the age of 26 and foreign students. Eurail and Interrail passes are valid on Greek trains.

BUS SERVICES

Private bus operators in Greece are organized in co-operative monopolies (**KTEL**) within each province *(nómos)*, and run services among points within the province as well as to and from major centers outside it. In towns served by more than one KTEL, each company may have its terminal in a different part of town, making a multistage bus journey a daunting task indeed.

In Athens, KTEL buses to all points in the Peloponnese, Epirus (NW), Macedonia (N) and Thrace (NE) leave from a joint terminal at **Kifissou 100** *(city bus 051 from Menandrou St., Omonia)*. Buses to Central Greece, including Delphi and all points in Thessaly, leave from the terminal at **Liossion 260** *(city bus 024 from Leof. Amalias and Omonia)*.

The bus system of the Hellenic Railway Organization (OSE) has been phased out.

AIR SERVICES

Olympic Airways, Greece's only domestic airline, runs services between Athens and some 34 points around the country. Fares are heavily subsidized and therefore not expensive; examples are Athens–

Thessaloniki, 13,800dr one-way (less on night flights); Athens–Mykonos, 9,900dr one-way. Advance reservations are essential on flights to most of the Greek islands.

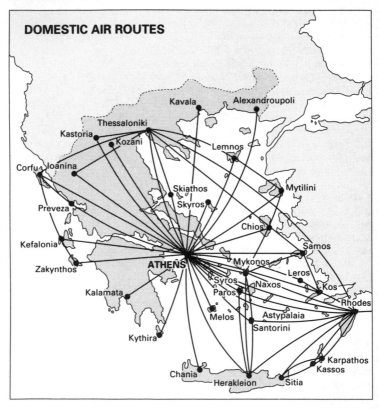

DOMESTIC AIR ROUTES

The Athens town terminal of Olympic Airways is located at **Syngrou 96** (☎ *96.16.6161).* The ticket offices are at **Othonos 6** *(on Syntagma Sq., map* **2***D4* ☎ *92.92.555 for international flights* ☎ *92.92.444 for domestic flights).*

The **Elinikon Airport** is divided into two parts. The west terminal serves Olympic Airways only; the east terminal is reserved for the flights of foreign airlines. There are separate buses for either terminal, both leaving from the corner of Leof. Amalias and Syntagma *(25mins, 160dr).*

A taxi from either terminal to the city center should cost less than 2,000dr. There is a connecting bus service between the two terminals, but it is extremely slow; it is generally best to take a cab.

FERRIES AND CRUISES

For many centuries the sea was the principal medium of travel in Greece, and the unique geographical conditions of the country ensure that boats remain one of the more common means of getting from place to place. All Aegean islands and many points along both E and W coasts of the mainland are served by ship from the harbor of Piraeus.

Local **ferries** run between a large number of ports. Ferry lines are operated by private and rival companies, and as a result the system sometimes displays a spirit of bedlam.

Different schedules apply to each of the seven days of the week. No generalized timetable exists for any port other than Piraeus, let alone for the whole country (☎ *143 for recorded Piraeus timetable, in Greek).* No shipping company or agency will be persuaded to betray so much as an awareness of the services of a rival. As a rule, there is no reliable way of knowing for certain at point A whether and when a boat goes from point B to point C.

The **Flying Dolphin** hydrofoil service operates between Piraeus and Aegina (departures from Piraeus Harbor), Poros, Hydra, Spetses, Ermioni, Porto Heli, Nafplio, Leonidio and Monemvasia (departures from Zea Marina). *(For information in Piraeus ☎42.80.001; in central Athens ☎32.42.281 or call at Karageorgi Servias 2, Syntagma Sq.).*

Aegean cruises ranging from one to 14 days or longer are organized by a variety of companies. A wide array of choices is offered by **Sun Line** *(Iasonos 3, Piraeus ☎45.23.417).* **Viking Tours** *(Filelinon 3, Athens ☎32.29.383)* specialize in smaller boats carrying up to 36 passengers.

Boats can be rented, with or without crew, for sailing alone or as part of a flotilla. Contact the **Hellenic Yachting Association** *(Akti Themistokleous 22, Piraeus ☎45.29.571),* or any travel agency.

On-the-spot information

TOURIST INFORMATION
The **Greek National Tourist Organization** (**GNTO**, sometimes also called **NTOG**; written as **EOT** in Greek) is one of the most efficient governmental bodies of the country. It maintains very helpful information bureaux in Athens and other major tourist centers, operates a chain of hotels located in architectural landmark buildings, and is in charge of the management of most museums and archeological sites.

GNTO Information Bureaux in Athens operate in the following banks:
* **National Bank of Greece**, Karageorgi Servias 2, Syntagma Sq. ☎32.22.545 and 32.34.130, map **2**D4, open daily until 8pm
* **General Bank of Greece**, Ermou 1, Syntagma Sq. ☎32.52.267, map **2**D4, open daily until 6pm

American Express Travel Service is a valuable source of information for any traveler in need of help, advice or emergency services. The Athens office is at Ermou 2, Syntagma Sq. *(☎32.44.975* Fx *32.27.893, map2D4).*

The **tourist police** have the same power as the ordinary police but are also specially briefed to help the visitor. They can be recognized by the shoulder flash *Tourist Police* on their uniforms. Many of them also wear badges indicating the languages they speak. They are often the best source of advice on accommodation — but they are *not* obliged to find you somewhere to stay. For problems and emergencies in Athens call the Tourist Police (☎ *171*).

In case of questions or complaints about hotels anywhere in Greece, call the **Greek Chamber of Hotels** (☎ *32.36.641*) or the **Federation of Hotel Owners** (☎ *32.30.636*) in Athens. These organizations also claim to act as reservation agents for all hotels in Greece, although in practice you will be far better served by contacting the hotels directly.

LANGUAGE

English is well established as the lingua franca of tourism throughout Greece. Most road signs, explanatory placards, tickets etc. are bilingual in Greek and English. Nearly all hotel personnel and most service people who come into routine contact with tourists (waiters, shop-keepers, boatmen, museum guards) have some knowledge of English. In the southwest Peloponnese, for some reason, German seems to be more widely spoken than English.

Speaking a few rudimentary phrases of Greek is of course a sign of goodwill and will be duly appreciated, but bear in mind that an appreciative smile might sometimes be more expressive of your meaning than an *efharistó* (thank you) spoken with an atrocious accent.

PUBLIC HOLIDAYS

Offices, banks and some shops close on the following days:

New Year's Day, January 1; **Epiphany**, January 6; **Shrove Monday**, 41 days before Easter, usually March; **Declaration of Greek Independence** in 1821, March 25; **Easter**, observed Good Friday through Easter Monday; **Labor Day**, May 1; **Whit Monday**, 50 days after Easter; **Dormition of the Virgin**, August 15; **Óhi Day**, rejection of the Italian ultimatum in 1940, October 28; **Christmas**, December 25–26.

Note that the Greek Orthodox Easter is celebrated according to the Julian calendar, and usually falls on a date from one to four weeks later than it does in Western Christian observance.

SHOPPING AND BUSINESS HOURS

Shopping hours are a science unto themselves, as there are different legally stipulated hours for each type of establishment, each day of the week and each season of the year, and these change frequently, too.

Most (but by no means all) shops are expected to open 8.30am–3pm on Monday, Wednesday and Saturday; whereas on Tuesday, Thursday and Friday they work two shifts separated by a siesta, usually 8.30am–2pm and 5pm–8pm. Food and grocery stores are generally open 8am–8pm Monday–Friday, 8am–3pm Saturday, and for a few hours on Sunday.

With regard to banks, offices, museums and archeological sites it is safest to assume than *nothing* will be open after 3pm on any day, and to count yourself lucky if something is. In high-tourist zones such as the Athenian Plaka, some shops will stay open routinely until past 9pm, sometimes until midnight, including Sundays.

CURRENCY EXCHANGE

Most hotels, tourist stores, travel agencies and many individuals are happy to exchange major Western currencies, but will inevitably charge a slight commission on top of the bank rate. Better exchange rates for money and travelers checks are obtained at banks, which are usually open from Monday to Thursday 8am–2pm, Friday 8am–1.30pm. On Sunday and holidays some banks are open at airports, ports and border crossings.

In Athens, the **National Bank of Greece**, at the corner of Stadiou and Syntagma Sq. *(map 2D4)*, remains open for money exchange from Monday to Friday until 9pm, on Saturday and Sunday until 8pm. **Post offices** also exchange money, and may offer better rates than banks.

MUSEUMS AND SIGHTS

The standard **opening hours** for all museums and archeological and historical sights managed by GNTO are Tuesday–Sunday 8.30am–3pm, closed Monday. This general rule is subject to a bewildering array of variations. The most popular tourist sights are usually open in season until 5 or 6pm, and either do not close at all on Monday or do so only until noon. Some museums proudly display a shield listing different opening and closing hours for every day of the week, not counting holidays and special occasions.

Standard **entry charges** are currently about 400dr for run-of-the-mill sights, about 1,000dr for major sights such as Delphi and Olympia, and about 1,500dr for the Acropolis and the National Archeological Museum in Athens. Entry to most museums is free of charge on Sundays, at least for Greeks and those who can pass themselves off as one.

Visitors are required to pay an extra fee for the use of video cameras (usually about 1000dr) and photographic flash equipment (about 600dr). The use of tripods and professional camera equipment generally requires permission.

DISABLED TRAVELERS

Disabled visitors to Greece should not expect the specially adapted facilities that are now common in other Western countries. GNTO has a list of tour operators that may be able to assist with arrangements.

MAIL AND TELEPHONE SERVICES

The post office (**ELTA**) and the telephone system (**OTE**) are independent of each other.

Post offices *(tahidromío)* are in principle open Monday–Friday 8am–1pm, 3–7pm. The office at Syntagma Sq. in Athens is open Monday–Saturday 7.30am–1.30pm, Sunday 7.30am–1.30pm. Letters can be posted in yellow mail boxes, which sometimes have two compartments marked *Esoterikoú* (domestic) and *Exoterikoú* (foreign).

Stamps can also be bought in kiosks. There is a single rate for postcards and letters (120dr to the US, 90dr to Europe).

General delivery (poste restante) in Athens should be addressed to the main post office at Eolou 100 *(Omonia Sq.)*.

183

The **phone system** is now undergoing long-overdue modernization and soon may cease to be the worst in non-ex-socialist Europe. **Public phones**, where they exist — and work — operate on 10dr coins and usually permit local calls only.

Card phones allowing long-distance as well as local calls are becoming increasingly common, but the cards themselves are often difficult to come by.

Long-distance calls can otherwise be made from an OTE office in towns or a post office in villages: in both cases you make your call from a booth and then pay for it at the counter. In addition, many kiosks and cafés offer a public telephone service.

For **international calls**, look in the telephone directory for the direct dialing code for your country.

- **00** gives an international connection, then wait for another tone.
- Dial a **1** for the United States or Canada, **44** for the United Kingdom, **353** for Ireland.
- Then dial the area code (leaving off any initial 0) and the number.

For **long-distance calls in Greece**, dial the local code (always with 0) and number. In Athens ☎**134** for general telephone information (in Greek) ☎**131** for numbers in Athens and Attica ☎**132** for numbers elsewhere in Greece. Be patient!

TIPPING

Restaurant and hotel bills include a 15-percent service charge, so no additional tip is expected. **Waiters**, however, will often be subsisting on your charity, so you may wish to leave them about 10 percent. In smaller, family-run places it is customary to leave the small change. In upper-category hotels, a small tip may be appropriate for **porters**, **attendants**, etc. **Taxi drivers** do not expect a tip unless they have performed some extra service.

Cabin and **dining-room stewards** on **cruise ships** should be tipped according to length of cruise and quality of service. On **night trains**, 500dr slipped to the sleeping-car attendant will do wonders.

Public bathrooms usually employ an old lady who supplies toilet paper and eau de cologne for a few coins; this must be recognized as a form of public charity. **Cinema and theater ushers** and **cloakroom attendants** fall into the same category, although usually with much less charm.

ELECTRIC CURRENT

The standard throughout Greece is 220V AC (50Hz), which means that appliances bought in North America will require a converter, and British appliances a simple adaptor. Neither is readily available within Greece, so bring one with you. In some very remote places, especially the islands, you may find 110V AC, so ask before you plug in.

ENGLISH PUBLICATIONS AND BROADCASTS

The English-language daily *Athens News* reports on local news and events, consistent with the unfortunate standards of Greek journalism.

The weekly *Greek News* is published on Fridays. *The Athenian*, a monthly journal, has up-to-date entertainment and restaurant reviews. In addition, several English-language program magazines are available from kiosks. The GNTO publishes leaflets in English on different topics.

The recent liberalization of airwaves has spawned an extraordinary (not to say anarchic) variety of TV and radio stations, several of which broadcast at least partly in English. TV movies are as a rule shown in the original language (usually English) with Greek subtitles.

Global satellite channels such as **CNN**, **BBC**, **Euronews** and **MTV** are widely available. The **Galaxy** (92FM) and **Olympic Action** (102.1FM) radio stations broadcast partly in English. The **US Armed Forces Radio** operates on 1484 and 1594 KHz AM, with news every hour on the hour.

CONSULATES IN ATHENS

- **Australia**   Dim. Soutsou 37 ☎64.47.303
- **Canada**   Ioan. Genadiou 4 ☎72.39.511, map **2D5**
- **Ireland**   Vass. Konstantinou 7 ☎72.32.771, map **2E5**
- **New Zealand**   An. Tsoha 15–17 ☎64.10.311, off map **2D6**
- **United Kingdom**   Ploutarchou 1 ☎72.36.211, map **2D5**
- **United States**   Vass. Sofias 91 ☎72.12.951, map **2D5**

PLACES OF WORSHIP

- **Beth Shalom Synagogue**   Melidoni 5 ☎32.52.823, map **1D2**
- **St Andrew's International/Protestant Church**   Sina 66 ☎27.70.964, map **2C4**
- **St Denis Roman Catholic Cathedral**   Panepistimiou (Venizelou) 24 ☎36.23.603, map **2D4**
- **St Paul's English Church**   Filelinon 29 ☎72.14.906, map **2E4**
- **Trinity Baptist Church**   Vouliagmenis 58, Ano Elinikon, ☎96.49.489, off map **1aF4**

There are also churches in Athens for the observances of 7th Day Adventists, Christian Scientists and Jehovah's Witnesses. Other Protestant churches exist in Thessaloniki and Patras. There are 21 Roman Catholic churches in Greece, mostly in the islands but also in Thessaloniki, Patras, Kalamata and Nafplio. The only other synagogue is in Thessaloniki.

USEFUL ADDRESSES

- **American-Hellenic Chamber of Commerce**   Valaoritou 17 ☎36.18.385, map **2D4**
- **American Library (Hellenic–American Union)**   Massalias 22, 4th floor ☎36.37.740. Open Monday 11.30am–6.30pm; Tuesday, Wednesday, Friday 9.30am–2.30pm; Thursday 11.30am–4.30pm
- **American School of Classical Studies (Gennadius Library)**   Souidias 61 ☎72.10.536, map **2D5**. Open Monday, Wednesday, Friday 9am–5pm; Tuesday, Thursday 9am–8pm; Saturday 9am–2pm
- **American Women's Organization** ☎60.09.800 ext. 345, Monday, Wednesday, Friday 11am–1pm

- **British Council** Kolonaki Sq. 17 ☎36.33.211, map **2**D4. Library open Monday–Thursday 9.30am–1.30pm and 5.30pm–8pm; Friday 9.30am–1.30pm
- **English-Speaking Society** meets every Wednesday 8–10pm at the Athenian Pastry Shop, Kifissias 320, Psyhiko ☎67.25.485
- **Goethe-Institut** Omirou 14–16 ☎36.08.111, map **2**D4
- **Institut Français** Sina 31 ☎36.24.301, map **2**D4
- **National Library of Greece** Panepistimiou ☎36.14.413, map **2**C4. Open Monday–Thursday 9am–8pm; Friday–Saturday 9am–2pm
- **YMCA** and **YWCA** Amerikis 11 ☎36.24.291, map **2**D4.

Emergency information

The most readily available source of assistance in an emergency is the reception desk of your hotel.

The following emergency telephone numbers operate throughout the country, unless otherwise indicated:

- **Police** (cities) ☎100
- **Gendarmerie** (countryside) ☎109
- **Tourist Police** ☎171
- **Emergency road service** (ELPA) ☎104; Express Service ☎154
- **Lost and found** ☎(01) 77.05.771
- **Lost and found (buses and taxis)** ☎(01) 52.30.111
- **US citizens emergency aid** ☎(01) 98.12.740

MEDICAL EMERGENCIES IN ATHENS

- **Doctors** 2–7am ☎105
- **First aid and ambulance** ☎166
- **Emergency dental treatment** The **ELPIS dental hospital** (☎64.34.001) answers emergency calls in Athens between 10pm and 6am.
- **All-night pharmacies (farmákio)** In Athens ☎107 for a list, or look in the *Athens News*. In other areas, a list of late-night pharmacies is displayed in all pharmacists' windows.

Clothing sizes chart

LADIES
Suits and dresses

Australia	8	10	12	14	16	18	
France	34	36	38	40	42	44	
Germany	32	34	36	38	40	42	
Italy	38	40	42	44	46		
Japan	7	9	11	13			
UK	6	8	10	12	14	16	18
USA	4	6	8	10	12	14	16

Shoes

USA	6	$6\frac{1}{2}$	7	$7\frac{1}{2}$	8	$8\frac{1}{2}$
UK	$4\frac{1}{2}$	5	$5\frac{1}{2}$	6	$6\frac{1}{2}$	7
Europe	38	38	39	39	40	41

MEN
Shirts

USA, UK Europe, Japan	14	$14\frac{1}{2}$	15	$15\frac{1}{2}$	16	$16\frac{1}{2}$	17
Australia	36	37	38	39.5	41	42	43

Sweaters/T-shirts

Australia, USA, Germany	S	M	L	XL
UK	34	36-38	40	42-44
Italy	44	46-48	50	52
France	1	2-3	4	5
Japan		S-M	L	XL

Suits/Coats

UK, USA	36	38	40	42	44
Australia, Italy, France, Germany	46	48	50	52	54
Japan	S	M	L	XL	

Shoes

UK	7	$7\frac{1}{2}$	$8\frac{1}{2}$	$9\frac{1}{2}$	$10\frac{1}{2}$	11
USA	8	$8\frac{1}{2}$	$9\frac{1}{2}$	$10\frac{1}{2}$	$11\frac{1}{2}$	12
Europe	41	42	43	44	45	46

CHILDREN
Clothing

UK

Height (ins)	43	48	55	60	62	
Age	4-5	6-7	9-10	11	12	13

USA

Age	4	6	8	10	12	14

Europe

Height (cms)	125	135	150	155	160	165
Age	7	9	12	13	14	15

CONVERSION FORMULAE

To convert	Multiply by
Inches to Centimeters	2.540
Centimeters to Inches	0.39370
Feet to Meters	0.3048
Meters to feet	3.2808
Yards to Meters	0.9144
Meters to Yards	1.09361
Miles to Kilometers	1.60934
Kilometers to Miles	0.621371
Sq Meters to Sq Feet	10.7638
Sq Feet to Sq Meters	0.092903
Sq Yards to Sq Meters	0.83612
Sq Meters to Sq Yards	1.19599
Sq Miles to Sq Kilometers	2.5899
Sq Kilometers to Sq Miles	0.386103
Acres to Hectares	0.40468
Hectares to Acres	2.47105
Gallons to Liters	4.545
Liters to Gallons	0.22
Ounces to Grams	28.3495
Grams to Ounces	0.03528
Pounds to Grams	453.592
Grams to Pounds	0.00220
Pounds to Kilograms	0.4536
Kilograms to Pounds	2.2046
Tons (UK) to Kilograms	1016.05
Kilograms to Tons (UK)	0.0009842
Tons (US) to Kilograms	746.483
Kilograms to Tons (US)	0.0013396

Quick conversions

Kilometers to Miles	Divide by 8, multiply by 5
Miles to Kilometers	Divide by 5, multiply by 8
1 meter =	Approximately 3 feet 3 inches
2 centimeters =	Approximately 1 inch
1 pound (weight) =	475 grams (nearly $\frac{1}{2}$ kilogram)
Celsius to Fahrenheit	Divide by 5, multiply by 9, add 32
Fahrenheit to Celsius	Subtract 32, divide by 9, multiply by 5

Greek in a nutshell

THE GREEK ALPHABET

Letter		Name ancient/ modern	Romanized form
A	α	alpha	a
B	β	beta/vita	v
Γ	γ	gamma	g
Δ	δ	delta	d
E	ε	epsilon	e
Z	ζ	zeta/zita	z
H	η	eta/ita	i
Θ	θ	theta	th
I	ι	iota	i
K	κ	kappa	k
Λ	λ	lambda	l
M	μ	mu/mi	m
N	ν	nu/ni	n
Ξ	ξ	xi	x
O	o	omicron	o
Π	π	pi	p
P	ρ	rho/ro	r
Σ	σ, ς	sigma	s
T	τ	tau/taf	t
Y	υ	upsilon/ipsilon	y or i
Φ	φ	phi	ph or f
X	χ	chi/hi	ch or h
Ψ	ψ	psi	ps
Ω	ω	omega	o

PRONUNCIATION

Vowels

A, E, I present no problem. O and Ω are both pronounced *o*. H and Y, which used to be long *e* and *y* in Classical Greek, are now both pronounced *i* as in *pizza*.

Diphthongs

AI – *e* as in *bed*
AY – *av* or *af*
E I – *i* as in *pizza*
EY – *ev* or *ef*
O I – *i* as in *pizza*
OY – *u*

Double dots on a vowel indicate that it is not part of a diphthong, and is voiced separately. Thus, Karaïskaki (Sq.) is pronounced kara-iskaki, not kareskaki.

Consonants

Z, K, Λ, M, N, Ξ, Π, P, Σ, T, Φ, Ψ present no problems.
B, which used to be *b* in Classical Greek, is now *v*.
Δ is a soft *th* as in *this*.
Θ is a hard *th* as in *thing*.

189

Γ is tricky. Before E or I, it is pronounced *y* as in *yet.* Elsewhere it is never a hard *g* as in *go,* but halfway between *g* and *h.*
X is a hard *h,* but not quite a *kh.*

Double consonants

N T – *d* or *nd*   M Π – *b* or *mb*
Γ K – *g* as in *go*
The *d, b, g* sounds only occur in borrowed foreign words.
Γ Γ – *ng*   Γ Ξ – *nx*

GRAMMAR
Nouns

Greek nouns are masculine, feminine or neuter in gender. Typically, but not always, **masculine** nouns end in -os, **feminine** nouns end in -i or -a, and **neuter** nouns end in -o.

Depending on their position in the sentence, nouns can be in one of three cases: **nominative** (subject of the action), **accusative** (object of the action, or any word following a preposition), or **genitive** (possessor of another noun). In the sentence, "John took Jack's wife to the movies," John is nominative, Jack is genitive, wife and the movies are accusative.

Adjectives agree in gender and case with the nouns they modify.

	masculine (man)	**feminine** (day)	**neuter** (water)
Nom. singular	o andros	i mera	to nero
Acc. singular	to andro	ti mera	to nero
Gen. singular	tou androu	tis mera	tou nerou
Nom. plural	i andri	i meres	ta nera
Acc. plural	tous androus	tis meres	ta nera
Gen. plural	ton andron	ton meron	ton neron

Verbs

Greek verbs have suffixes indicating person and tense. Here are the present tenses of the verbs *to be* (I am, you are, he is, etc.), *to want* (I want, etc.) and *to go.*

		be	**want**	**go**
I	ego	ime	thelo	pao
you (sing.)	esi	ise	thelis	pas
he, she, it	aftos, afti, afto	ine	theli	pai
we	emis	imaste	theloume	pame
you (plur.)	esis	isthe	thelete	pate
they	afti, afti, afta	ine	theloun	paoun

REFERENCE WORDS

Monday	*Deftéra*
Tuesday	*Tríti*
Wednesday	*Tetárti*
Thursday	*Pémpti*
Friday	*Paraskeví*
Saturday	*Sávvato*
Sunday	*Kyriakí*

January	*Ianouários*	July	*Ioúlios*
February	*Fevrouários*	August	*Ávgoustos*
March	*Mártios*	September	*Septémvrios*
April	*Aprílios*	October	*Októvrios*
May	*Máios*	November	*Noémvrios*
June	*Ioúnios*	December	*Dekémvrios*

1	éna	11	éndeka	21	ikossiéna
2	dyo	12	dódeka	22	ikossidío
3	tría	13	dékatria	30	triánda
4	téssera	14	dékatéssera	40	saránda
5	pénde	15	dékapénde	50	penínda
6	éxi	16	dékaéxi	60	exínda
7	eptá	17	dékaeptá	70	evdomínda
8	októ	18	dékaoktó	80	ogdónda
9	ennéa	19	dékaennéa	90	enenínda
10	déka	20	íkossi	100	ekató

First	*prótos*	Third	*trítos*
Second	*défteros*	Fourth	*tétartos*

Quarter past	. . . . *ke tétarto*	Quarter to six	. . . . *éxi*
Half past	. . . . *ke missí*	*pará tétarto*	
Quarter to	*pará tétarto*		

Mr	*kyrios*	Ladies	*ginekón*
Mrs	*kyría*	Gents	*andrón*

Red	*kókkino*	Blue	*blé*
Yellow	*kítrino*	Black	*mávro*
Green	*prássino*	White	*áspro*

BASIC COMMUNICATION

Yes	*ne*	Next week	*tin álli evdomáda*
No	*óhi*	Last week	*tin perasméni*
Please	*parakaló*		*evdomáda*
Thank you	*efharistó*	. . . . days ago	*prin apó . . . .*
I'm very sorry	*lipáme*		*méres*
	polí	Month	*mínas*
Excuse me	*signómi*	Year	*hrónos*
Not at all/you're welcome		Here	*edó*
	parakaló	There	*ekí*
Hello	*yiá sou*	Big	*megálo*
Good morning	*kaliméra*	Small	*mikró*
Good afternoon	*kalispéra*	Hot	*zestó*
Good night	*kaliníhta*	Cold	*kryo*
Goodbye	*adío*	Good	*kaló*
Morning	*proí*	Bad	*kakó*
Afternoon	*apógevma*	Beautiful	*oréo*
Evening	*vrádi*	With	*me*
Night	*níhta*	And	*ke*
Yesterday	*htés*	But	*allá*
Today	*símera*	Open	*aniktó*
Tomorrow	*ávrio*	Closed	*klistó*

191

Entrance   *íssodos*
Exit   *éxodos*
Free   *tzámpa*
Left   *aristerá*
Right   *dexiá*
Straight ahead   *issia embrós*
Near   *kontá*
Far   *makriá*
Above   *apó páno*
Below   *apó káto*
Front   *embrós*
Behind   *písso*
Early   *norís*
Late   *argá*
Pleased to meet you.   *Hárika pou sas gnórissa/héro poly.*
How are you?   *Pos iste?*
Very well, thank you.   *Polí kalá, efharistó.*
Do you speak English?   *Miláte Angliká?*
I don't understand.   *Den katalavéno.*
Please explain.   *Parakaló exigíste.*

Please speak more slowly.   *Parakaló milíste pió argá.*
My name is . . . .   *To onomá mou íne . . . .*
I am American/English.   *Íme Amerikanós/Ánglos.*
Where is/are . . . ?   *Poú íne . . . ?*
Is there a . . . ?   *Ypárkhi éna . . . ?*
What?   *Tí?*
When?   *Póte?*
How much?   *Pósso?*
That's too much.   *Íne pára pollá.*
Expensive   *akrivó*
Inexpensive   *fthinó*
I would like . . . .   *Tha íthela . . . .*
Do you have . . . ?   *Éhete . . . ?*
Where is the toilet?   *Poú íne i toualéta.*
Where is the telephone?   *Poú íne to tiléfono?*
That's fine/OK.   *Poly oréa/O.K.*
I don't know.   *Den xéro.*
What time is it?   *Ti óra íne?*
I feel ill.   *Den esthánome kalá.*

SHOPPING

Where is the nearest/a good . . . ?   *Poú íne to plisiéstero/éna kaló . . . ?*
Can you help me/show me some . . . ?   *Boríte na me voithíssete/na mou díxete meriká . . . ?*
I'm just looking.   *Aplós kyttázo.*
Do you accept credit cards . . . . travelers checks?   *Pérnete credit cards . . . . travelers checks?*
Can you deliver to . . . ?   *Boríte na to meteférete sto . . . ?*
I'll take it.   *Tha to páro.*
I'll leave it.   *Tha to afísso.*
Can I have it tax-free for export?   *Boró na to páro aforológito gía exagoghi?*
This is faulty. Can I have a replacement/refund?   *Aftó éhi elátoma. Boró na to alláxo/na páro tá leftá písso?*
I don't want to spend more than . . . .   *Den thélo na xodépso perissótera apó . . . .*
I'll give you . . . . for it.   *Tha sas dósso . . . . gi'aftó.*
Can I have a stamp for . . . ?   *Boró naého éna gramatóssimo giá . . . ?*
Sale   *ekptósis*

Shops

Antique store   *antíkes*
Art gallery   *gallerí érgon téhnis*
Baker   *foúrnos*
Bank   *trápeza*

Beauty parlor   *institoúto kallonís*
Bookstore   *vivliopolío*
Butcher (and variants)   *kreopolío*
Cake shop   *zaharoplastío*

Clothes store   *katástima idón rouhismoú*
Department store   *megálo katástima*
Fish store   *psarádiko*
Greengrocer   *manáviko*
Grocer   *bakáliko*
Hairdresser   *kommotírio*
Jeweler   *kosmimatopolío*
Market   *agorá*
Newsstand   *efimeridopólis*
Optician   *optikós*

Pharmacy/chemist   *farmakío*
Photographic store   *fotografío*
Post office   *tahidromío*
Shoe store   *katástima ypodimáton*
Supermarket   *super market*
Tailor   *rafío*
Tobacconist   *kapnopolío*
Tourist office   *touristikó grafío*
Toy store   *katástima pehnidion*
Travel agent   *touristikos práktor*

From the pharmacy

Antiseptic cream   *antisiptikí kréma*
Aspirin   *aspirínes*
Bandages   *epídesmi*
Band-Aid/sticking plaster   *lefkoplástis*
Diarrhea/upset stomach pills   *diárria/hápia giá stomahikí diatarahí*
Indigestion tablets   *hápia gia dyspepsia*
Insect repellant   *ygró giá éntoma*
Sanitary napkins   *serviétes ygías*

Shampoo   *sampouán*
Soap   *sapoúni*
Sunburn cream   *kréma giá engávmata apó ton ílio*
Sunglasses   *gialiá ilíou*
Suntan cream/oil   *kréma/ládi mavrísmatos*
Tampons   *tampón*
Tissues   *hartomándila*
Toothbrush   *odontóvourtsa*
Toothpaste   *odontókrema*
Travel sickness pills   *hápia giá naftía*

Clothing

Bathing suit   *mayó*
Bra   *soutién*
Dress   *fórema*
Jacket   *sakkáki*
Pullover   *poulóver*
Shirt   *poukámiso*

Shoes   *papoútsia*
Skirt   *foústa*
Socks   *káltses*
Stockings/pantihose/tights   *káltses nylon/kalson*
Trousers   *pantelóni*

Miscellaneous

Film   *film*
Letter   *grámma*
Money order   *émvasma*

Postcard   *kart postál*
Stamp   *grammatósimo*
Telegram   *tilegráfima*

DRIVING

Gas/service station   *stathmós venzínis*
Unleaded   *amolivdi*
Fill it up.   *Gemíste to.*
Give me . . . . drachmes worth.   *Válte moú venzíni . . . . drahmón.*
I would like . . . . liters of gas/petrol.   *Tha íthela . . . . lítra venzíni.*
Can you check the . . . ?   *Boríte na kittaxete to . . . ?*
There is something wrong with the . . . .   *Káti den pái kalá me to . . . .*

Battery   *bataría*
Brakes   *fréna*
Engine   *mihaní*
Exhaust   *exátmissi*
Lights   *fóta*

Oil   *ládia*
Tires   *lástiha*
Water   *neró*
Windshield   *parbríz*

193

My car won't start   *To aftokínito dén xekinái.*
My car has had a flat tire.   *Émina apó lástiho.*
How long will it take to repair?   *Se pósso keró tha íne étimo?*

Other methods of transport

Aircraft *aeropláno*	Ticket *issitírio*
Airport *aerodrómio*	Ticket office *grafío*
Bus *leoforío*	*isstiríon*
Bus stop *stássi leoforíou*	One-way/single *monó*
Coach *poúlman*	Round trip/return *met' epistrofís*
Ferry/boat *ferry/plío*	Half fare *missó issitírio*
Ferry port *limáni ferry boat*	First/second/economy *próti/*
Hydrofoil *yptámeno delfíni*	*défteri/tríti*
Station *stathmós*	Sleeper/couchette *me krevváti/*
Train *tréno*	*kousétta*

FOOD AND DRINK

Have you a table for . . . ?   *Éhete éna trapézi giá . . . ?*
I want to reserve a table for . . . . at . . . .   *Thélo na klísso éna trapézi*
    giá . . . . stis . . . .
A quiet table.   *Éna íssiho trapézi.*
A table near the window.   *Ena trapézi kondá sto paráthiro.*
Could we have another table?   *Boroúme na éhoume állo trapézi?*
I only want a snack.   *Thélo káti elafró.*
The menu, please.   *Ton katálogo parakaló.*
I'll have . . . .   *Tha páro . . . .*
Can I see the wine list?   *Tón katálogo tón krassión parakaló?*
I would like . . . .   *Thélo . . . .*
What do you recommend?   *Tí moú synistáte ná páro?*
What do you want to drink?   *Tí thá piíte?*
I did not order this.   *Den to parángila aftó.*
This is bad.   *Avtó íne halasméno.*
Can this be changed?   *Borité ná tó alláxete?*
Lunch/dinner   *gévma/dípno*
Bring me another.   *Férte moú állo éna.*
The bill, please.   *Tón logariasmó parakaló.*
Is service included?   *To servís perilamvánete?*

Some essential words

Restaurant *estiatório*	Mineral water *emfialoméno neró*
Taverna *tavérna*	Carbonated/noncarbonated *me*
Hot *zestó*	*anthrakikó/horís anthrakikó*
Cold *kryo*	Flask/carafe *karáfa*
Glass *potíri*	Red wine *kókkino krassí*
Bottle *boukáli*	White wine *áspro krassí*
Half-bottle *missó boukáli*	Rosé wine *kokkinéli*
Beer/lager *bíra/láger*	*krassí*
Orangeade/lemonade *mía porto*	Cheers! *Stín ygiá sas!*
kaláda/lemonáda	Sweet *glykó*
Water *neró*	Salt *aláti*
Iced . . . . *pagoméno*	Pepper *pipéri*

Oil   *ládi*
Vinegar   *xídi*
Bread   *psomí* (*ártos* when written)
Butter   *voútyro*
Cheese   *tyrí*
Egg   *avgó*
Milk   *gála*
Pastry store   *zaharoplastío*
Coffee house   *kafenío*
Coffee   *kafé*

Greek/Turkish coffee   *ellinikó kafé*
   without sugar   *skéto*
Ice cream   *pagotá*
Chocolate   *sokoláta*
Honey   *méli*
Sugar   *záhari*
Tea   *tsái*
Steak   *fileto*
   well done   *kalopsiméno*
   medium   *métrio*
   rare   *senián*

Menu guide

Kouvér   cover charge
Orektiká   appetizer
Psária   fish
Kymádes   minced meat
Salátes   salad
Psomí   bread

Tyriá   cheese
Froúta   fruit
Glyká   dessert
Potá   drink
Byres   beer
Anapsyktiká   soft drink

Arní   lamb
Avgolémono   chicken broth with rice, lemon and egg
Bakaliáros   fried salt cod, usually served with *skordaliá*
Baklavá   thin pastry layers stuffed with nuts and spices, doused in syrup
Bourekákia   tiny stuffed flaky pastry pasties
Dolmádes/dolmadákia   stuffed vine or cabbage leaves
Fasólia   beans
Gemísta   tomatoes or green peppers stuffed with mincemeat
Giouvarlákia   boiled meatballs in sour sauce
Giouvétsi   casserole, usually shrimp
Hiríno   pork
Keftédes   fried meatballs
Kokorétsi   liver and kidneys on skewer
Kotópoulo   chicken
Kreatópitta   triangular flaky pastry containing minced meat
Loukoumádes   fritters in syrup

Melitzánes   eggplant/aubergines
Melitzanosaláta   mashed eggplant/aubergine salad
Mezé (pl. mezédes)   appetizer(s)
Moskhári   veal
Moussaká   mince and eggplant/ aubergine layers topped with béchamel and cheese sauce
Pagotá   ice cream
Pastítsio   baked macaroni with bechamel sauce
Pikilía   mixed plate of appetizers
Saganáki   fried cheese with lemon
Spanakópita   flaky pastry with spinach filling
Souvláki   pieces of meat grilled on skewer
Stifádo   meat chunks and onions in broth
Taramasaláta   cod's roe purée
Tyrópitta   flaky pastry cheese pasties
Tzatzíki   yogurt dip with garlic and cucumber
Yaoúrti   yogurt

Fish and seafood

Astako   lobster
Barboúnia   red mullet
Garídes   shrimps
Kalamáres   squid
Ksifias   swordfish

Lithrínia   sea bass
Marídes   whitebait
Mydia   mussels
Ohtopódi   octopus
Strídia   oyster

Index

- Page numbers in **bold** type indicate main entries.
- *Italic* page numbers indicate illustrations, plans and maps.
- See also the LIST OF STREET NAMES on pages 295–6.

List of street names

- Listed below are all streets mentioned in the text that fall within the area covered by our color maps **1** and **2**.
- Map numbers are printed in bold type. Some smaller streets are not named on the maps, but the map reference given below will help you locate the correct neighborhood.

KEY TO MAP PAGES

1–2 CENTRAL ATHENS
3–4 CENTRAL GREECE
5–6 THE PELOPONNESE
7 ATTICA

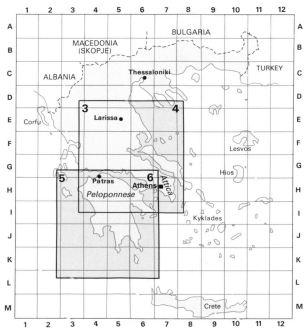

KEY TO MAP SYMBOLS

Area Maps

=O=	Highway (with access point)
▬	Main Road
▬	Secondary Road
▬	Minor Road
▬	Scenic Route
---	Ferry
▬	Railway
✈	Airport
✈	Airfield
⛪	Monastery
∴	Ancient Site, Ruin
♜	Castle
⊗	Good Beach
4	Adjoining Page No.

City Maps

▓	Major Place of Interest
░	Other Important Building
☐	Built-up Area
▒	Park
† †	Cemetery
✝ †	Church
☾	Mosque
✡	Synagogue
⊞	Hospital
i	Information Office
⊠	Post Office
✋	Tourist Police
☛	Parking Lot
—S—	Subway
+++++	Funicular Railway
→	One-way Street

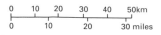

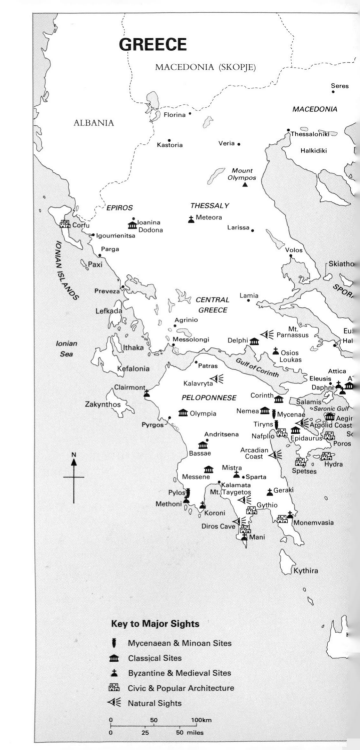

GREECE

MACEDONIA (SKOPJE)

ALBANIA

MACEDONIA

Seres

Florina

Kastoria

Veria

Thessaloniki

Halkidiki

Mount Olympos

EPIROS

THESSALY

Meteora

Corfu

Ioanina
Dodona

Igoumenitsa

Larissa

Parga

Volos

Skiatho

Paxi

IONIAN ISLANDS

Preveza

CENTRAL GREECE

Lamia

SPOR

Lefkada

Agrinio

Ionian Sea

Messolongi

Delphi

Mt. Parnassus

Eu

Hal

Ithaka

Osios Loukas

Kefalonia

Patras

Gulf of Corinth

Attica

Eleusis

A

Clairmont

Kalavryta

Daphni

Zakynthos

PELOPONNESE

Corinth

Salamis

Saronic Gulf

Olympia

Nemea

Mycenae

Aegin

Pyrgos

Tiryns

Argolid Coast

Andritsena

Nafplio

Epidaurus

So

Poros

Bassae

Arcadian Coast

Mistra

Hydra

Messene

Sparta

Spetses

Pylos

Kalamata
Mt. Taygetos

Geraki

Methoni

Gythio

Koroni

Diros Cave

Monemvasia

Mani

Kythira

N

Key to Major Sights

Mycenaean & Minoan Sites

Classical Sites

Byzantine & Medieval Sites

Civic & Popular Architecture

Natural Sights

0   50   100km

0   25   50 miles

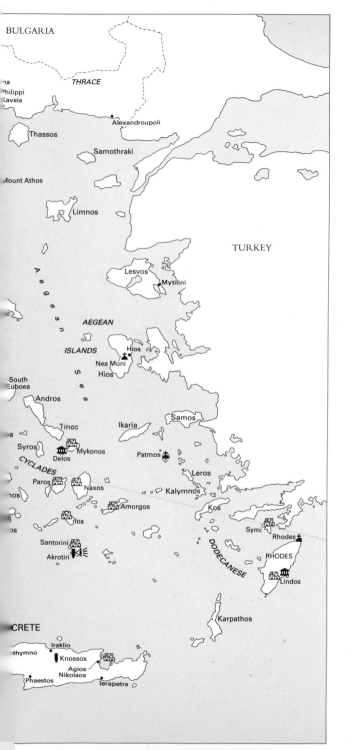

BULGARIA

THRACE

na
Philippi
Kavala

• Alexandroupoli

Thassos

Samothraki

Mount Athos

Limnos

TURKEY

Aegean

AEGEAN

Lesvos
• Mytilini

ISLANDS

Hios
Nea Moni
Hios

South
Euboea

Andros

Sea

Samos

Tinos

Ikaria

ea

Syros
Delos

Mykonos

Patmos

CYCLADES

Leros

Paros

Naxos

Kalymnos

nos

Amorgos

Kos

Ios

Symi

Rhodes

os

Santorini

RHODES

Akrotiri

DODECANESE

Lindos

Karpathos

CRETE

Iraklio

thymno

Knossos

Agios
Nikolaos

Phaestos

Ierapetra

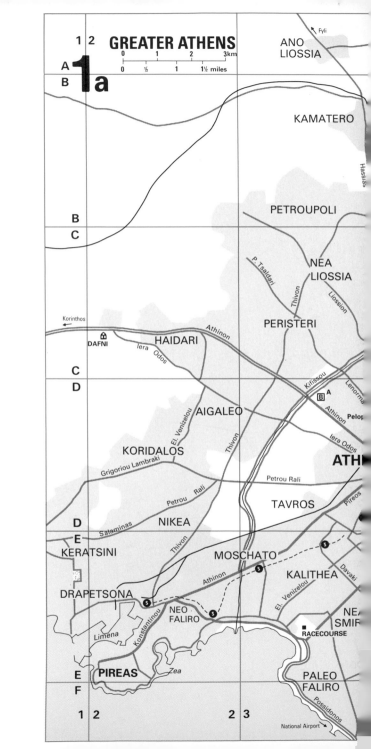

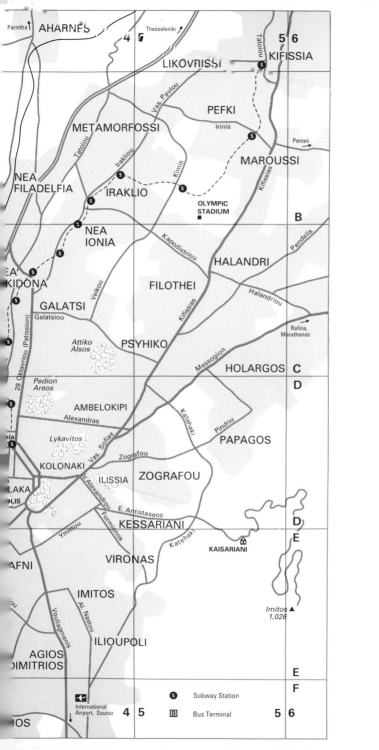

Parnitha ↑ AHARNES

Thessaloniki ↑

Tatoiou

5 6

KIFISSIA

LIKOVRISSI

Vas. Pavlou

PEFKI

Irinis

Penteli →

METAMORFOSSI

Tatoiou

Irakliou

MAROUSSI

NEA
FILADELFIA

Kimis

IRAKLIO

Kifissias

OLYMPIC
STADIUM
■

B

NEA
IONIA

Kapodistriou

HALANDRI

Pendelis

Veikou

FILOTHEI

EA
KIDONA

GALATSI

Galatsiou

Kifissias

Halandriou

Halandriou

Attiko
Alsos

PSYHIKO

Rafina,
Marathonas →

28 Oktovriou (Patission)

Messogion

HOLARGOS C

D

Pedion
Areos

AMBELOKIPI

Alexandras

Katehaki

Pindou

PAPAGOS

Lykavitos

Vas. Sofias

Zografou

ia

KOLONAKI

ILISSIA

ZOGRAFOU

V. Alexandrou

LAKA
LIS

E. Antistaseos

D

Ymittou

Formionos

KESSARIANI

E

Katehaki

KAISARIANI ♟

AFNI

VIRONAS

IMITOS

Al. Nastou

Imitos ▲
1,026

ou

Vouliagmenis

ILIOUPOLI

AGIOS
DIMITRIOS

E

F

✈

International
Airport, Sounio 4 5

Ⓢ Subway Station

Ⓑ Bus Terminal 5 6

OS ↓

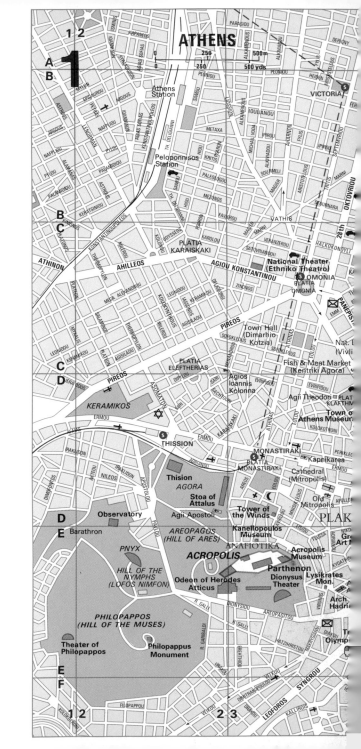

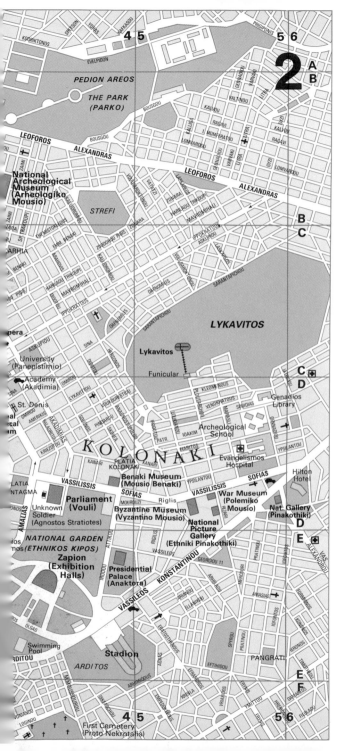

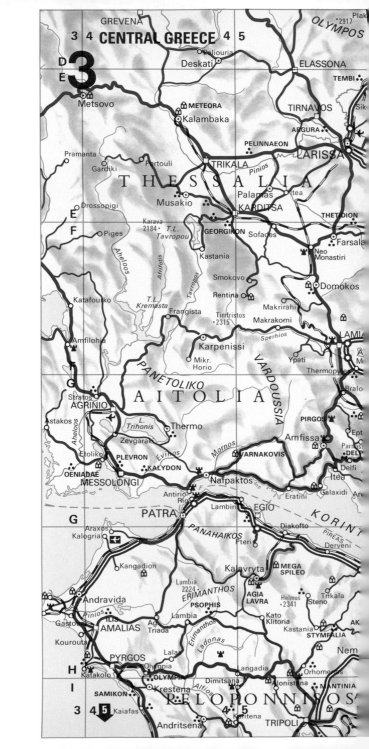

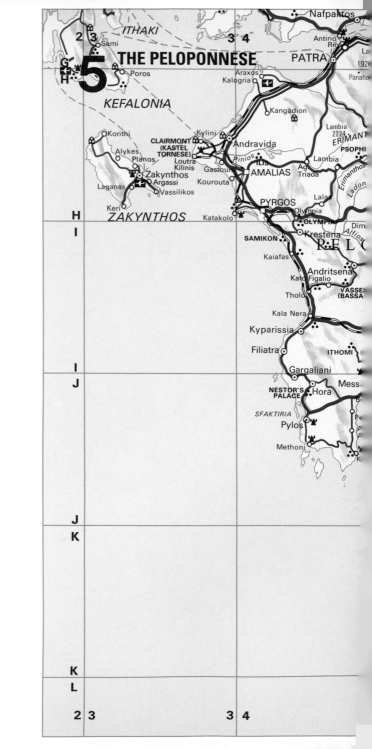

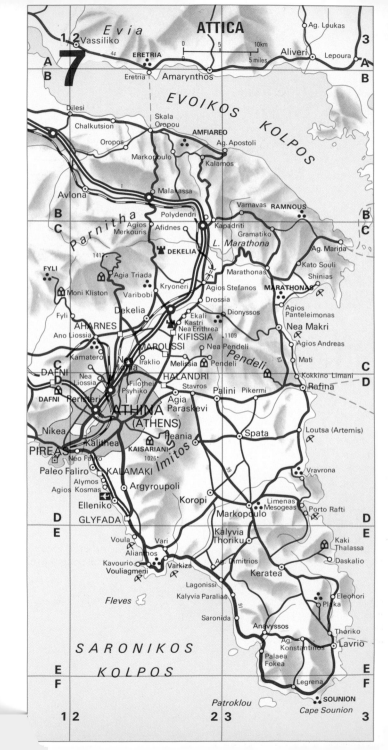

What the papers say:

• "The expertly edited American Express series has the knack of pinpointing precisely the details you need to know, and doing it concisely and intelligently." (**The Washington Post**)

• "(Venice) . . . the best guide book I have ever used." (**The Standard — London**)

• "Amid the welter of guides to individual countries, American Express stands out . . . . " (**Time**)

• "Possibly the best . . . guides on the market, they come close to the oft-claimed 'all you need to know' comprehensiveness, with much original experience, research and opinions." (**Sunday Telegraph — London**)

• "The most useful general guide was *American Express New York* by Herbert Bailey Livesey. It also has the best street and subway maps." (**Daily Telegraph — London**)

• " . . . in the flood of travel guides, the *American Express* guides come closest to the needs of traveling managers with little time." (**Die Zeit — Germany**)

What the experts say:

• "We only used one guide book, Sheila Hale's *AmEx Venice,* for which she and the editors deserve a Nobel Prize." (**travel writer Eric Newby, London**)

• "Congratulations to you and your staff for putting out the best guide book of *any* size *(Barcelona & Madrid).* I'm recommending it to everyone." (**travel writer Barnaby Conrad, Santa Barbara, California**)

• "If you're only buying one guide book, we recommend American Express . . . . " (**Which? — Britain's leading consumer magazine**)

• "The judges selected *American Express London* as the best guide book of the past decade — it won the competition in 1983. [The guide] was praised for being 'concise, well presented, up-to-date, with unusual information.' " (**News release from the London Tourist Board and Convention Bureau**)

What readers from all over the world say:

• "We could never have had the wonderful time that we did without your guide to *Paris*. The compactness was very convenient, your maps were all we needed, but it was your restaurant guide that truly made our stay special . . . . We have learned first-hand: *American Express — don't leave home without it.*" (A. R., Virginia Beach, Va., USA)

• Of Sheila Hale's *Florence and Tuscany:* "I hope you don't mind my calling you by your first name, but during our recent trip to Florence and Siena [we] said on innumerable occasions, 'What does Sheila say about that?' " (H.G., Buckhurst Hill, Essex, England)

• "I have visited Mexico most years since 1979 . . . Of the many guides I have consulted during this time, by far the best has been James Tickell's *Mexico,* of which I've bought each edition." (J.H., Mexico City)

• "We have heartily recommended these books to all our friends who have plans to travel abroad." (A.S. and J.C., New York, USA)

• "Much of our enjoyment came from the way your book *(Venice)* sent us off scurrying around the interesting streets and off to the right places at the right times". (Lord H., London, England)

• "It *(Paris)* was my constant companion and totally dependable . . . . " (V. N., Johannesburg, South Africa)

• "We found *Amsterdam, Rotterdam & The Hague* invaluable . . . probably the best of its kind we have ever used. It transformed our stay from an ordinary one into something really memorable . . . . " (S.W., Canterbury, England)

• "Despite many previous visits to Italy, I wish I had had your guide *(Florence and Tuscany)* ages ago. I love the author's crisp, literate writing and her devotion to her subject." (M. B-K., Denver, Colorado, USA)

• "We became almost a club as we found people sitting at tables all around, consulting their little blue books!" (F.C., Glasgow, Scotland)

• "I have just concluded a tour . . . using your comprehensive *Cities of Australia* as my personal guide. Thank you for your magnificent, clear and precise book." (Dr. S.G., Singapore)

• "We never made a restaurant reservation without checking your book *(Venice)*. The recommendations were excellent, and the historical and artistic text got us through the sights beautifully." (L.S., Boston, Ma., USA)

• "The book *(Hong Kong, Singapore & Bangkok)* was written in such a personal way that I feel as if you were actually writing this book for me." (L.Z., Orange, Conn., USA)

• "I feel as if you have been a silent friend shadowing my time in Tuscany." (T.G., Washington, DC, USA)

American Express Travel Guides

spanning the globe....

EUROPE
Amsterdam, Rotterdam
  & The Hague
Athens and the
  Classical Sites
Barcelona, Madrid &
  Seville
Berlin, Potsdam &
  Dresden
Brussels
Dublin
Florence and Tuscany
London
Paris
Prague
Provence and the
  Côte d'Azur
Rome
Venice
Vienna & Budapest

NORTH AMERICA
Boston and New
  England
Los Angeles & San
  Diego
Mexico
New York
San Francisco and
  the Wine Regions
Toronto, Montréal &
  Québec City
Washington, DC

THE PACIFIC
Cities of
  Australia
Hong Kong & Taiwan
Singapore &
  Bangkok
Tokyo

*Clarity and quality of information, combined
with outstanding maps — the ultimate in
travelers' guides*

Buying an AmEx guide has never been easier....

The *American Express Travel Guides* are now available by mail order direct from the publisher, for customers resident in the UK and Eire. Payment can be made by credit card or cheque/P.O. Simply phone through your credit card order on **0933 410511** (office hours Mon–Fri 9am–5pm), or complete the form below (it can be photocopied), and send it, together with your remittance.

☐ Amsterdam, Rotterdam & The Hague
1 85732 918 X £8.99

☐ Athens and the Classical Sites
1 85732 308 4 £8.99

☐ Barcelona, Madrid & Seville
1 85732 160 X £8.99

☐ Berlin, Potsdam & Dresden
1 85732 309 2 £8.99

☐ Boston and New England
1 85732 310 6 £8.99

☐ Brussels
1 85732 966 X £8.99

☐ Cities of Australia
1 85732 921 X £9.99

☐ Dublin
1 85732 967 8 £7.99

☐ Florence and Tuscany
1 85732 922 8 £8.99

☐ Hong Kong & Taiwan
0 85533 955 1 £9.99

☐ London
1 85732 968 6 £7.99

☐ Los Angeles & San Diego
1 85732 919 8 £8.99

☐ Mexico
1 85732 159 6 £9.99

☐ New York
1 85732 971 6 £8.99

☐ Paris
1 85732 969 4 £7.99

☐ Prague
1 85732 156 1 £9.99

☐ Provence and the Côte d'Azur
1 85732 312 2 £9.99

☐ Rome
1 85732 923 6 £8.99

☐ San Francisco and the Wine Regions
1 85732 920 1 £8.99

☐ Singapore & Bangkok
1 85732 311 4 £9.99

☐ Tokyo
1 85732 970 8 £9.99

☐ Toronto, Montréal & Québec City
1 85732 157 X £8.99

☐ Venice
1 85732 158 8 £9.99

☐ Vienna & Budapest
1 85732 962 7 £9.99

☐ Washington, DC
1 85732 924 4 £8.99

While every effort is made to keep prices low, it is sometimes necessary to increase them at short notice. *American Express Travel Guides* reserve the right to amend prices from those previously advertised.

Please send the titles ticked above.   **ATH**

Number of titles @ £7.99   Value: £

Number of titles @ £8.99   Value: £

Number of titles @ £9.99   Value: £

Add £1.50 for postage and packing   £___1.50

Total value of order: £_____

I enclose a cheque or postal order ☐ payable to Reed Book Services Ltd, or please charge my credit card account:

☐ Barclaycard/Visa   ☐ Access/MasterCard   ☐ American Express

Card number ☐☐☐☐☐☐☐☐☐☐☐☐☐☐☐☐☐☐

Signature_____ Expiry date _____

Name _____

Address _____

_____ Postcode _____

Send this order to American Express Travel Guides, Cash Sales Dept, Reed Book Services Ltd, PO Box 5, Rushden, Northants NN10 6YX ☎(0933) 410511.